"A digital bank should aspire to be like their BigTech peers, as Chris argues in this book. Highly elastic IT infrastructures, relentless focus on client-centric product design that leverages Big Data perspectives, and intensive investment in engineering and tech talents are all essential ingredients for the success of modern digital businesses. They serve as some of the most important guiding principles on our path to become one of the world's leading digital banks. This book is a must-read for bank leaders, especially those about to embark on their own digital transformation journeys."

—Henry Ma
VP and CIO, WeBank (a division of Tencent)

"Chris Skinner has been at the forefront of analyzing the intersection—collision, some might say—of technology and banking. In his daily blog, his lectures, his consulting practice, and his books, Chris sees things that others miss and helps the reader understand their significance. His latest book *Doing Digital* offers concrete, tactical lessons learned from CEOs and other top leaders who were among the first to grasp the full implications of the digital revolution and are transforming their banks accordingly. Told with Chris's trademark wit, *Doing Digital* is at heart a story of successful management of profound change and the visionary leadership that journey requires. Highly recommended."

—Tillman Bruett
Global Practice Lead, Financial Services and Investment, DAI,
and Former Director, United Nations Secretary-General's Task Force
on Digital Financing of the Sustainable Development Goals

"Chris Skinner's work resists the twin temptations to romanticize technology and to dismiss bankers as dinosaurs lumbering towards the tar pits. Chris has the historical grounding to understand the indispensable role that banking plays in advancing prosperity. He also has the imagination to see what a truly digital bank could be, and a clear-eyed understanding of what it takes to get there. *Doing Digital* is a valuable resource not just for bankers but for anyone interested in change management, especially when the stakes are high."

—M. Mudassar Aqil
Chief Executive Officer, Telenor Bank (Pakistan)

"Deeply insightful, highlighting the challenges and more importantly the opportunities our industry faces."

—Nick Ogden
Serial entrepreneur, Founder of WorldPay and
Executive Chairman of ClearBank

"In the sea of proclamations from pundits that banks must become digital, *Doing Digital* stands out for its ability to prescribe specific actions banks must take, and describe what banks who are doing digital transformation well are actually doing. It's refreshing to see a book that helps instead of hypes."

—Ron Shevlin
Author of *Smarter Bank* and The Fintech Snark Tank on Forbes

"For the past ten years my role at Silicon Valley Bank has provided me a front row seat to the banking changes that Chris Skinner has chosen to chronicle and debate. His resume, endless travel and curiosity give him a unique perspective from which to opine and predict. He has used this vantage point and his wit to push banks to become more self-aware, introduce technologists into their leadership ranks, and understand that all is not lost. But that time is truly running out. The company I work for banks, invests in and competes with the world of FinTech that Chris follows. We see first-hand, on a daily basis, the world that he describes and the change companies like Stripe, Amazon, Brex and JPMC are making to reframe the competitive landscape. It's here. This new landscape has pushed many banks and SVB to change.

"Chris's new book is a great read that highlights the banks that are in the midst of making these changes and a walk through the "how" with their leaders. No pontification re his thoughts on the topic but real-time insights into what other banks are doing and their thinking behind their transition to stay competitive. If you don't follow his daily blog, start. If you want more detailed insights from your peer banks you soon may be lapped by—read his books. I'd suggest starting with *Doing Digital*."

—Mark Sievert
Managing Director, Global Payments & Merchant Service Solutions,
Silicon Valley Bank

"Transforming an incumbent financial institution's processes and systems to be fit for purpose in the digital age is no small matter. But Chris Skinner argues convincingly that the real transformation challenge is ultimately cultural. From having technologists as well as bankers in the C-suite, to forming effective partnerships with FinTechs, to expanding the mindsets among staff, and above all to serving as trusted stewards of the 'new oil' of customer data, the digital bank represents a significant break from the past. As Chris's work demonstrates, the narrative for financial services is becoming much more future-oriented and strategic, less inward-focused and more receptive to collaborations and partnerships. *Doing Digital* is a vital contribution to that narrative."

—Matthew Blake
Head of Financial & Monetary System Initiatives,
Member of the Executive Committee, World Economic Forum

"Chris understands that successful financial institutions integrate digital into their core, rather than approach it as a project. *Doing Digital* spotlights leaders who not only understand this but have rewired their organization around this thinking."

—Mike Heffner
Vice President, Global Industry Leads, Appian

"FinTech is about improving rather than replacing the traditional financial sector. Chris Skinner shows how fintech is helping to lower investment barriers, make the banking industry more transparent, and promote financial inclusion."

—Professor Ba Shusong
Chief Economist, China Banking Association and
Chief China Economist, HKEX

DOING
DIGITAL

DOING DIGITAL

DIGITAL

LESSONS FROM LEADERS

CHRIS SKINNER

mc Marshall Cavendish
Business

Published in 2020 by Marshall Cavendish Business
An imprint of Marshall Cavendish International

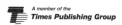
A member of the
Times Publishing Group

Other Marshall Cavendish Offices:
Marshall Cavendish Corporation, 99 White Plains Road, Tarrytown NY 10591-9001, USA • Marshall Cavendish International (Thailand) Co Ltd, 253 Asoke, 12th Flr, Sukhumvit 21 Road, Klongtoey Nua, Wattana, Bangkok 10110, Thailand • Marshall Cavendish (Malaysia) Sdn Bhd, Times Subang, Lot 46, Subang Hi-Tech Industrial Park, Batu Tiga, 40000 Shah Alam, Selangor Darul Ehsan, Malaysia.

Marshall Cavendish is a registered trademark of Times Publishing Limited

National Library Board Singapore Cataloguing-in-Publication Data

Name: Skinner, Chris.
Title: Doing digital : lessons from leaders / Chris Skinner.
Description: Singapore : Marshall Cavendish Business, [2020]
Identifier(s): OCN 1133229642 | ISBN 978-981-4841-43-6 (hardcover)
Subject(s): LCSH: Banks and banking—Automation. | Banks and banking—Data processing. | Banks and banking—Technological innovations.
Classification: DDC 332.10285—dc23

Printed in Singapore

*For my family—my beautiful wife Kamila,
my sweet little boys Eddie and Freddie,
and my dearest mother Gladys.
Without them, I am nothing.*

" For businesses that aren't born digital, traditional mindsets and ways of working will always run counter to those needed for today's world. "

Chris Skinner

" We have positioned ourselves as a FinTech bank. FinTech is not only the application of technology for the bank, but also the comprehensive transformation of the business model, organisation, mechanisms and process, by utilising the concepts and methods of FinTech. This means that we have to change our mentality and organisation structure to fit the new business model. "

Min Hua, *Head of Strategy, CMB*

" If we don't transform, we die "

The common refrain of all banks studied for this book

ACKNOWLEDGEMENTS

In developing the idea for this book, I noticed that more and more banks were starting to transform. This specifically struck me through the work of challenger consulting firm 11:FS, which I helped establish. The work of the team there, their rapid growth and the big banks they were working with to deliver digital banking services made me want to get some real hands-on input from banks that are digitally transforming. As a result, I wrote a list of the big banks I thought were dealing with digital transformation well and feel privileged that BBVA (Spain), CMB (China), DBS (Singapore), ING (the Netherlands) and JPMorgan Chase (USA) all accepted my invitation to participate. To all of the people I met and interviewed in the process of producing this book, thank you for your time and help.

In particular, there are a few individuals who deserve specific recognition for their assistance in making this happen. In BBVA, thanks to Chris Semple; in CMB, thank you to Gwen Gao; in DBS, thank you to all of the people I met there, but specific thanks to Sandy Tan and Edna Koh for organising everything; in ING, thanks to Marc Smulders; and, finally, thanks to Pablo Rodriguez, Paul Lussier and Emily Schaefer for all of their help at JPMorgan Chase.

CONTENTS

FOREWORD

BY **DAVID M. BREAR**, GROUP CEO AT 11:FS

It's about time someone wrote this book.

Not the carefully worded white papers, the generic press releases or the polished conference keynotes. But an in-depth look at why banks are transforming and how they are setting about actually doing it.

Large banks are shovelling billions into "digital" projects: new apps, chatbots and APIs. They will confidently tell you that they are "digital" and they will survive the technological and cultural shifts that are changing consumer expectations, business models and entire industries before our eyes.

Meanwhile, they're dealing with ever-increasing operating costs through legacy technology, resources and real estate. Their innovation spend is just layering more and more cost into operational spend without decommissioning the spaghetti that keeps the show on the road.

This was an acceptable outcome when "winning" was purely about size of customer base and everyone in financial services was treading water at the same pace. Threats were slow to appear. As a result, banking experiences were isolated and isolating. Banks delivered their own products within the walled garden of their own branches, websites and phone lines.

The world has changed, and banks are now busy trying to readjust to the new realities of digitally native, intelligent services that upend all of that.

End-to-end experiences through powerful APIs, curated marketplaces where the best services offer their wares, and integrated platforms where products and services solve a group of interrelated problems. The offerings are contextual, personal and should feel like they are "yours" as an individual not as just another customer.

This book looks to unpack how some banks, carefully selected by Chris, set about tackling that fundamental shift. They are changing how they do change and that is the real and lasting value it delivers. It isn't the specific models the banks chose, although there are interesting lessons in that. The following pages offer valuable insight around what you absolutely cannot do.

You cannot underestimate the scale of the task. You cannot underestimate the time and effort that's required to achieve this transformation, mistaking activity for meaningful progress. If you mistake digitalising existing products and services for creating truly digital services, you're in trouble.

You cannot assume that because you're a market leader today, you will be tomorrow. While so much of this seems within touching distance, banks need to act fast. Having scale and ambition is nothing without meaningful execution.

New entrants don't need to write a five-year business case, they have no "digital" strategy, they were born and raised digital. They don't need to get fourteen committees to approve. They have agility—and I don't mean a delivery methodology—to move from idea to it being safely and securely executed in a fraction of the time it currently takes incumbent banks.

It means having small, autonomous, multi-disciplinary teams that can take an idea to execution, not pass it from one team to another. Give the right remit to a small team of highly skilled talent, laser-focused on solving real customer problems, and they can achieve great things.

Firms with this attitude and ability to get great services into the hands of customers, iterate them and continually push new ideas will continue to accelerate away from the chasing pack.

We've seen it happen already in other industries where incumbents fell into the trap of digitisting what came before, rather than truly digital services. Newspapers were an analogue product. Vast editorial, advertising, printing and supply chain operations, delivering news and views to your door every morning. Many newspapers have "digitised", publishing identical versions of their physical products onto tablets and phones. It has taken new players with new approaches and business models to move towards truly digital services. Twitter and YouTube being great examples of this.

Digitisation looks good for large incumbents, financial service players—cost-cutting, good headlines and relatively happy customers. All is looking good until—boom—truly digital services start to appear in our industry.

That is where we are right now today.

Understanding the virtues of being digital is the pathway to delivering truly differentiated digital banking services. The characteristics of the new technologies are how they support building real-time, intelligent, contextual services that are human and extendable.

What is fascinating, as you'll find as you read through the various chapters, is none of the banks featured consider their work to be "done". They appreciate that this is a continuous work in progress. And that's because digital banking is only 1 per cent finished.

It's time to get back to work. Let's get to doing digital.

INTRODUCTION

I have been writing a daily blog for over a decade. During that time, the dialogue has moved from the challenge of regulatory change to the impact of the global financial crisis to the rise of digital change to financial inclusion and more. While all of these themes have been discussed in my previous books, one of the most recurring themes has been how banks are stumbling along, trying to keep up. Some commentators go to extremes and say banks are dumb and are going to be destroyed. I am not one of those commentators. Banks are not dumb, just challenged.

The main challenge banks face is that they were created during the Industrial Revolution and have a business model built for the physical distribution of paper through localised networks of buildings and humans. The business model was based on transactions using cash, cheques, passbooks, ledgers, letters of credit, bills of lading, contracts and such like.

When technology arrived in the 1960s, banks were early in the game of adopting such technologies to cement their structures in place. The IBM mainframe developed systems in COBOL (common business-oriented language) and other programming languages to automate the ledgers of the bank branch network; the ATM was added to give external access to cash when branches were closed, typically from 3:30 in the afternoon to 9:30 the next morning; call centres developed further remote access to the branch ledger, enabling you to check balances and transactions out of hours; online banking allowed you to access the branch ledger yourself from a home computer; and mobile apps now do the same.

However, the core back-end system is still the same: a branch ledger debit and credit system of transactions on an account. This is the fundamental challenge for large incumbent banks because, today, they have to reinvent their business model around the digital distribution of data in a globalised network focused on software and servers. This is the issue. How does a large bank with billions of capital, millions of customers and centuries of history reinvent its business model from being a processor of paper to being a manager of data?

This has been touched upon in all three of my previous books. *Digital Bank* specifically offered advice on how to meet this challenge; *ValueWeb* offered insights into how blockchain and the mobile network were flattening fees to offer cheap, real-time value exchange; and *Digital Human* described the new digital bank business model, as well as discussed financial inclusion in depth.

I then reflected on the fact that so many people were saying that banks were dumb, lacking understanding of how to implement digital change and viewing digital as just another channel to add to mobile and the call centre, rather than realising that it is a transformational challenge.

Now, I have worked with banks all of my professional life and know that they are not dumb. They are fairly intelligent but lack the right leadership to implement digital transformation in many cases. Many banks I meet have good middle management and a good line of business owners, but they are not structured correctly for the digital age. They have too many silos, too many business owners, too much politics and too little ability to reinvent those old branch core systems and build a digital bank business model. That challenge is not easy.

This is why most banks are adding digital as a function, a project and a channel to their existing structures, rather than reinventing their business model. These banks are doomed. This book makes that clear. There are too many start-ups and large technology firms facing regulatory changes, technology opportunities and big bank budgets to survive in the digital age without reinventing your business model.

Any bank that has not embraced digital as a transformational process, but just as an evolutionary process, will sleepwalk into history. This has been the theme of all of my writing for the past ten years. Banks need to reinvent themselves for the digital age, not just add digital as an extra layer. The latter is just lipstick on a pig, as they say. The thing is that I equally meet many banks that say they know they need to change. They just do not know what they need to change, or how. This is where the real heart of this book hits.

Further to recognising that digital is transformation that requires strong leadership, I sat down three years ago and started to make a list of the banks that I thought were making this change effectively. I purposefully did not list small, domestic banks, as many of them are already making effective digital change, but instead targeted larger banks that have embraced digital transformation well.

My list was small. A mere nine large banks worldwide that I thought were making digital transformation happen. What were these nine banks doing that the rest of the world's banks were not? Now that is a very good question.

I approached these banks and five of them agreed to participate in my new project, *Doing Digital: Lessons from Leaders*. The selected banks were of substantial size and variety, and I was hugely gratified to have the co-operation of BBVA, ING, JPMorgan Chase, DBS and China Merchants Bank (CMB). What did these banks do? How did they make digital transformation happen? What can we learn from them?

The project took me from Madrid to Amsterdam to New York to Singapore to Shanghai. Each bank opened its doors to my inquisitive mind, and shared with me its process of digital transformation so far. Such a process is continuous. The transformation is never finished. However, they are all some way down the line of implementing change.

CMB started with a digital model, BBVA has been changing its model for almost two decades while the remainder are late to the game but catching up fast. Let's look for a moment at a bank that did not take part in my research. Interestingly, Barclays Bank has seen the most dramatic changes in the past few years. In 2016, the bank had 130,000 employees and a market valuation of $30 billion[1]; in 2018, the bank had 83,500 employees and a valuation of $40 billion. How did a bank lose a third of its staff but increase its value by a third?

That is the sort of question that I have asked and tried to answer in *Doing Digital*. In the process, I have met many members of executive leadership teams (CxOs) and their direct reports, and discovered around thirty lessons of change that are common to the selected five major banks from around the world. These thirty lessons come from leaders who are implementing digital transformation, thus providing the answer to that fundamental issue: we know we need to change, we just do not know what or how.

This book gives you the what and how to change in the process of digital transformation. I am not sure that it will work for everyone, but it has worked for these five major banks and, as I can see through external observation, seems to be working for many others.

In fact, as I reached the end of the process of producing *Doing Digital*, I realised that this is not really a technology book or a book about banking. It is a book about change. How to make dramatic change happen, to be precise. How to turn an age-old institution into one that is nimble and refreshed for the digital age. Or how to make the elephant dance, as the old adage goes.

The lessons here could equally apply to a retail firm, an airline or any organisation struggling with what digital means and how to embrace it. The lessons learnt build on thirty years of my experience of dealing with business transformation projects, and tease out specific nuances of how digital transformation can be implemented successfully.

One of the surprises for me, for example, during this process was to hear some of the CEOs and chairs of these banks talk about how they

---

1   Unless otherwise stated, the currency used throughout this book is the US dollar (US$).

needed room to breathe. The focus on quarterly shareholder returns and investor relations places inordinate pressure on most executives to purely manage numbers and ensure that financial objectives are met. This does not cut the ice when you are in a transformation process. During a transformational process, the focus has to be on the change, not the short-term results. Therefore, one key lesson is that the banks making transformational change happen to have a board that manages the returns and relations with the investment community while protecting the leadership of the bank from worrying about those financials and giving them the mandate to focus on the change. That is a fundamental.

There are many more insights as you read this book. I trust you will find it useful, and would love your feedback.

Chris Skinner
Spring 2020

WHY BANKS HAVE TO DIGITALLY TRANSFORM

I am a technologist and have spent all of my career looking at how technology might change the future of finance and financial services. When looking to the future, it is determined by four forces of change: political, economic, social and technological.

For me, technology is the core driver change, but this does not belittle the others. All of them impact financial markets and businesses equally and I am sure you would agree that these changes have become particularly frenetic in the last decade. This is partly inspired by the global financial crisis, but equally enabled by the technology structures that we have today.

Take Cloud Computing, artificial intelligence (AI), the mobile phone network and Open Banking, which incorporates application program interfaces (APIs), which, in turn, provide plug-and-play code that can be taken and dropped from any provider to any other service that you want to use. These technologies have transformed the landscape of the world in the last decade, and are now greatly changing banking as finance and technology become integrated. Today, we call this FinTech. FinTech has grown from nothing to a market that received $111.8 billion of investment in start-up firms in 2018.

The first time that I encountered FinTech was over a decade ago at a meeting in London, during which someone had the idea of launching a business that they called "an eBay for money". Their idea was that you could have people who have money connected to people that need money through a platform and an algorithm. That company was Zopa.

Over the past fifteen years, Zopa has done pretty well in the United Kingdom, as have many other peer-to-peer lenders and FinTech start-ups. For example, 36 per cent of all new personal loans were originated by FinTech companies in the United States in 2017, according to Bloomberg, compared to just 1 per cent in 2010. That is the reason why the integration of finance and technology is such a hot market space.

According to KPMG, $111.8 billion was invested in FinTech companies globally in 2018, which is more than double the amount of the year before. That covers peer-to-peer payments and lending, as well as everything to do with roboadvice through to AI through to cryptocurrencies through to blockchain distributed ledger technology. There are thousands of things happening in each of these areas. Faced with these changes, I claim that the business model of the banking industry is completely broken.

The business model of banking was designed for the physical distribution of paper in a localised network through buildings and humans. Technology was then implemented to cement that structure in place. Now, we need to rip that structure apart because what we are dealing with today is the digital distribution of data through software and servers on a global network. The latter is a radically different business model for any business, but is now particularly relevant for financial services due to the rise of Open Banking.

The financial services industry has not been impacted much by this change so far, when compared with the changes we have seen in entertainment, consumption, media, books and other markets. This is purely because it has taken a long time to get to where we are. In fact, it is only in the last decade that it has really started to hit the road. You can see it hit the road in the valuations, vision and rapid expansion of new start-up companies like PayPal, which is one of the oldest FinTech firms around. Much like Ant Financial, which makes up a case study in the last third of *Digital Human*.

If I had to pick one standout start-up, it would be Stripe. Stripe is my favourite FinTech start-up and is also one of the biggest FinTech unicorns[2] out there. If you don't know what Stripe does, it was launched in 2011 with seven lines of code that enable a merchant to set up checkout online fast and easy. It's plug-and-play code. An API. That is why the Ubers, Airbnbs and Indiegogos of this world are all using Stripe—because it is incredibly easy to just drop that code in and then you can take and make payments. It is so simple that after five years, in October 2016, the firm had a $9.2 billion valuation, with just 400 members of staff.

Another reason why it is one of my favourite FinTech start-ups is that it was started by Patrick and John Collison, two brothers from Ireland. When they launched the idea for this business back in 2010, they were just nineteen and twenty-one years old. And here is a key point about how the world has changed with digitalisation: FinTech has created an equal relationship where almost anyone of any age can launch a financial service system.

For example, Vitalik Buterin, the developer who founded Ethereum, was nineteen years old when he started that idea. Ethereum provides distributed ledger services, also called "smart contracts on blockchains". The vision behind Ethereum was discussed in depth in *ValueWeb*, and offers the potential to become the backbone of how corporations, governments and businesses run their next-generation infrastructures. In other words, Buterin's code might become the backbone of our world tomorrow and be as fundamental as the creation of the internet itself.

That is how fundamental this is. Kids who can code are dramatically changing the financial markets but they don't understand the financial markets. They don't understand why banks are regulated the way they are. They don't understand how banks got to where they are. This is why I see FinTech as a parent–child relationship. The Fin needs to act as the parent, mentoring and nurturing the child, which is the Tech. That is exactly what is happening today. A lot of banks are starting to collaborate and work with the FinTech start-up community, including the Stripes of this world.

---

2   Technology start-up firms founded after 2000 that have achieved pre-initial public offering (IPO) valuations of $1 billion or above

However, the most telling figures here are when you analyse the changes in the big banks. For example, I often quote Stripe's $9.2 billion valuation from October 2016 to show how new firms providing platforms for digital connectivity are smashing old firms providing finance through physical connectivity.

Figure 1.1 Market capitalisation from October 2016

FIRM	ESTABLISHED	EMPLOYEES	MKT CAP
JPMorgan Chase	1799	235,000	$245B
PayPal	1999	13,000	$48B
Deutsche Bank	1870	101,000	$17B
Ant Financial	2015	5,000	$60B
Stripe	2011	400	$9.2B
Barclays	1692	130,000	$30B

Comparing Stripe and Barclays Bank, you can see that the average Stripe employee generated a hundred times more value, by market capitalisation, than a Barclays employee.

Two years later, Stripe's valuation was at $20 billion. That is a doubling of value in two years. Barclays is more interesting, however. The figures went from 130,000 people generating $240,000 of value per person to 83,500 employees generating $480,000 of value per person.

Figure 1.2 Market capitalisation from October 2018

FIRM	ESTABLISHED	EMPLOYEES	MKT CAP
JPMorgan Chase	1799	256,000	$385B
PayPal	1999	18,700	$105B
Deutsche Bank	1870	97,500	$21B
Ant Financial	2015	7,000	$150B
Stripe	2011	1,000	$20B
Barclays	1692	83,500	$40B

When comparing the numbers, Stripe had gone from generating one hundred times more value per person in October 2016 to just over twenty times more value per person two years later. Stripe had not changed. Barclays Bank had. In fact, just in case you missed it, Barclays Bank shed over a third of its workforce and increased its valuation by a third in just two years.

That turnaround is down to some drastic action, not an evolution. It is why we are living in such interesting times, because we are living in a world where FinTech is making banks do what they have always done, but cheaper, faster and better with technology. If banks understand that, then they will collaborate with, partner, invest in and mentor these thousands of new companies. This is why these start-up firms are getting billions of dollars in investment from such banks so that they can be part of their marketplace, part of their community. In turn, it enables the banks to bring the capabilities of those start-up firms to their customers. This is a digital revolution of planet earth, and goes much further than just changing banking, however. In fact, there are seven new ways in which finance delivered by technology is changing the game.

The first way in which we find finance delivered by technology different is that it is **real time**. We are able to fund, save, spend, invest, transact, trade, borrow and more in time windows identified as relevant to us, not in annualised products offered by institutions. The only reason why products were annual was because it was too difficult to service them more regularly in a physical distribution model with buildings and humans. In a digital distribution model, software, servers and algorithms can offer everything immediately and for as long as you want. Forget a yearly service, let's just borrow for the next few hours.

The second way in which we find finance delivered by technology different is that it is all the time and **everywhere**. The idea of any downtime anytime is unacceptable. If I want it, I want it now, so let me get it now. Whether I am in the Himalayan mountains or in Timbuktu, I want it and I want it now. Any barriers to access will be seen as a reason to switch to another provider.

The third way in which we find finance delivered by technology different is that it is **seamless**. I don't want to think about money and banking, but want it to be stitched into the fabric of my lifestyle, and supportive of the way I live. Banking should be invisible, frictionless and seamless. If I need to think about my money, it is purely because my devices are telling me that there is something important to think about. Otherwise, I don't want to know.

The fourth way in which we find finance delivered by technology different is that it is **personalised**. If things are happening in my financial world that I should know about, then tell me to my face or, rather, my device. I shouldn't have to be concerned about covering my next mortgage payment by moving funds from my savings unless my savings account is empty. If it is empty, don't tell me "Your savings account is empty". Instead, tell me "Chris, you have funds arriving next week but your mortgage payment goes out today. Don't worry about it. I've taken care of it by using a 12-hour loan facility at a cost of $5. If you want to change this, swipe here."

The fifth way in which we find finance delivered by technology different is that it is not only personalised but **predictive**. That's kind of illustrated by the point above, but it goes further and deeper than this. With the deep mining of my financial lifestyle data, the bank should be able to predict my financial lifestyle needs. My favourite example of this today is the bank that works out I catch the underground every day but always pay day by day rather than buy a season ticket. That is because I do not have the funds for a season ticket. In this instance, the bank texts "Hey Chris, you could save £1,000 a quarter with a season ticket for £2,500. Swipe here if you want one." Okay, so the bank is wrapping up a personalised offer in a loan but at least it has mined my data, worked out why I cannot buy a season ticket and offered me one based on predictive and personalised contextual information.

The sixth way in which we find finance delivered by technology different is that it is **for everyone**. Why should anyone be unable to move money between friends and family? Why should banking only be for the rich? Everyone should have the basic human right to send money freely, cheaply and easily to anyone else. This is being delivered by technology services for the unbanked, underbanked and underserved. In fact, the biggest change in our world in the last decade is that digital services can reach the unreachable. It is a major transformation to everything in life.

The seventh way in which we find finance delivered by technology different is that it **reaches the unreachable**. Building on the last point, the new world of finance can reach the long tail of customers previously overlooked, and start doing new things for them. The long tail are kids uneducated in money who now get financial literacy through apps. The long tail are the elderly who are scammed and conned because they are financially vulnerable; they are now protected through connectivity to those who care about them. The long tail are the addicts, the depressed, the gamblers and the mentally ill, all of whom need help with their financial accounts so that they do not drain them of funds on activities that they are trying to get away from. All of these people are now reachable and capable of being supported rather than overlooked.

This is why we have seen radical change to our world in the last decade and there are many developments of non-traditional finance that are creating inclusive societies and new models of finance. In fact, I would cite five areas of change.

First, there is **financial inclusion**. The fact that anyone who can get access to a mobile telephone can now get access to finance is why so many people are getting engaged in trading and transacting. According to the World Bank, 69 per cent of adults—3.8 billion people—now have an account at a bank or mobile money provider, a substantial rise from the mere 51 per cent in 2011, all thanks to the mobile phone and the internet. That is financial inclusion for you. Get a phone, get a credit history, get a bank account. It is more than that though. It is more to do with the fact that the internet and mobile telephone is a cheap way of supporting anyone with a bank account, whether that person has a few cents or a few million. Digital is cheap.

Second, there is **financial literacy**. Considering finance is the major factor in our lives for comfort and wealth, it is also one of the areas most overlooked in our school years. There are now many firms focused on providing financial literacy for children, using gamification technologies to make it fun and easy.

Third, there is **financial capability for the financially less abled**. This builds on financial literacy but is focused specifically on the most vulnerable financial users, such as financial management for the elderly. If a parent gets dementia, Alzheimer's, Parkinson's or another disease that means they can no longer cope, these apps help their children—if they have them—to look after their finances or, at least, help them to avoid being ripped off by scammers and criminals.

Fourth is **financial wellness** overall. Psychologists have found that those who have the worst mental health problems are usually those who have the worst financial health. Multiple studies report people with mental health problems are more likely to be in debt. And those with addictions are most likely to be at issue. A great example of action is how UK challenger banks Monzo and Starling are helping customers to give up gambling by offering a block to prevent their financial accounts accessing anything related to gambling. There are two million people at risk of mental health issues caused by gambling in the United Kingdom so that is a good thing to be able to do.

Finally, there is **sustainability and responsible banking**, an area that the United Nations (UN) Sustainable Development Goals (SDGs) are leading with the publication of the Principles for Responsible Banking in 2019. Sustainable finance, I think, is best illustrated by Ant Forest. Ant Forest encourages users of Alipay in China, of which there are 800 million, to play a game of growing virtual trees. To grow a tree, the system encourages users to avoid doing things that increase carbon emissions. For instance, if you take a bus to work rather than a taxi, you get points towards planting your virtual tree which, when you get enough points, becomes a real tree in real life. You get more points the more environmentally friendly your lifestyle becomes, so if you walk or cycle to work, you save even more than if you take the bus.

In fact, there are nineteen changes you can make to your lifestyle to become more eco-friendly, including making online payments, going paperless in the office, using disposable cardboard cutlery instead of plastic cutlery and recycling. You can then claim carbon points for the actions you have performed every day and save them into your Alipay account. These points are used to water and grow your virtual tree in Ant Forest and, when the virtual tree grows tall enough through your constant watering of carbon points, Ant Financial plants a real tree for you. By playing a fun app whilst making payments, 500 million Chinese Alipay users have planted over 100 million real trees in Inner Mongolia and Gansu province that cover nearly 1,000 square kilometres of land. It has been estimated that this will reduce the carbon emissions of China by 5 per cent by the end of 2020.

This is where lessons are learnt by looking at new economies that had no or little historical infrastructure. We see this occurring in India, China, across Asia, Africa and South America. These countries started their infrastructure projects in the internet age and are turbocharging their economies as a result. I personally learnt this lesson when I visited Ant Financial in Hangzhou, China, as the company has a mission for mobile financial inclusion and has exported its technologies to local partnerships in Indonesia, the Philippines, Thailand, Pakistan, India and more. This is bringing simple and easy financial services to markets that have historically been ignored by banks.

My favourite example is in India. This really brings home what is happening with technology and financial inclusion. Paytm is a mobile wallet that is used across all of India. It has around 400 million users today whereas, just before demonetisation in November 2016, it had about 150 million. Because of demonetisation and other moves by the Indian government, the story of inclusion in India has risen dramatically, and much of this is thanks to the mobile payments wallet network.

Vijay Shekhar Sharma is the founder of Paytm. He is also a fan of Jack Ma and Alibaba, and wanted to copy Alibaba and Alipay in India. He went to see Jack Ma and persuaded him to invest in his venture.

This is why Alibaba and Ant Financial own a substantial part of Paytm. Core technologies behind Paytm are provided by Ant Financial through Open Banking, open payments and open financial services. Using these technologies has enabled Paytm to both grow and scale very quickly thanks to these cloud-based services. As already mentioned, Ant Financial and Alipay are not just doing this in India, but also with partners in many other countries, from Pakistan to the Philippines to Indonesia, Thailand and South Korea. Ant Financial has gone global.

It is worth nothing that Sharma is India's youngest multibillionaire today but was homeless ten years ago. He had been bankrupted by his business partners and was sleeping on friends' sofas to survive. That is what today's digital network enables—opportunity and inclusion for everyone.

We are living through a revolution of humanity through digitalisation with technology. It is a fundamental change to how we think, trade, transact, talk, build relationships and build structures. It demands a completely different business model from financial institutions and it is the reason why it is incredibly difficult for these institutions to make this change, especially if their leaders do not understand it.

But Banking Is Different

There is a lot of noise out there, saying that companies have to change. We have reached a Kodak moment. Or a Nokia moment. Or a Blockbuster moment. In banking, this is not the case. Banks are different from technology firms and retailers. They are licensed to bank. Anyone can launch a technology or offer a retail experience. Not everyone can open a bank. They have to go through a registration and licensing process that is challenging, difficult and time-consuming. Typically, registering as a bank requires $20 million of seed money and takes two years to process. That is not the same as a technology firm or retail firm setting up office, which can be bootstrapped in days.

The reason for this tough process is that banks are not frivolous. Like hospitals, pharmaceutical firms, airlines and other organisations that can have a huge impact on people's lives and stimulate life or death situations, banks are viewed as just as fundamental. They are fundamental to the health of economies, governments, countries and their peoples. That is why banks are often the oldest organisations in a country, dating back centuries, and why there are very few new firms that challenge them. When you have been at the heart of an economy since its inception, and regulations mean that very few can challenge what you do, you find yourself in a fairly cosy situation. Why would you need to change?

Of course, banks do change, but most of it is stimulated by fear of just three factors: regulators, competition and investors. If the regulator says you have to change, you change. If a competitor does something that impacts your business, you change. This is why we are seeing so many changes in banking, from branches closing to Open Banking. Banks are reducing their physical footprint because they have to deliver shareholder results. Banks are investing heavily in digitalising to increase self-service and reduce costs, and because their competitors are doing the same. Furthermore, they are offering data through code to third parties because the regulator told them that they have to do it.

What about the customer? Are banks changing because the customer wants them to? Not really, and they don't have to. Customers come into the equation of design around cost reduction, technology investment and regulatory change, but they are not the reason for change as most customers do not change their bank accounts. They are often with their banks longer than they are with their partners. Changing bank is the last thing on people's minds, as all banks are the same. They provide a utility service and, unless there is an interest rate incentive, most corporations and citizens cannot be bothered to change.

So why change? Why transform? Why go through the hassle and process? Well, one of the things that has impacted all industries is technology change. It began years ago but has increased rapidly over the last twenty years. The Kodak, Nokia and Blockbuster moments were created because those companies did not adapt to technology change.

Unfortunately, for most banks, neither have they. These institutions have been protected from transformational change because of regulatory barriers, customer lethargy, the lack of competitive heat and shareholder concerns. In fact, banks have been far more concerned with risk and the global financial crisis of 2008 than with digital transformation and technology change.

However, a decade after risk was the key metric, the digital beat has been growing louder. Every major bank is now talking digital transformation. Every bank is talking about investing billions in technology over the next few years. Some talk about mass lay-offs in the process of digital change, others talk about cost savings in the digital transformation process and a few talk about customers and service.

This reaches to the heart of how banks view digital transformation. The majority are focusing on their age-old drivers of regulators, shareholders and competition, without placing the customer at the heart of their strategy. In reviewing some bank digital transformation strategies, customers are mentioned rarely and, when they are, it is often in the context of cost reduction through increased self-service.

There is an issue with this though, as technology and digital change is not about regulators, shareholders and competition. It is about customers and service. Technology has placed the customer in control. You can see this today as challenger banks rise.

Challenger banks are rising because regulators are encouraging them—they want more competition—and investors are investing in them because they can see that the markets are changing. Challenger banks start with customer need and the customer journey. They design from scratch around customer need and the customer journey. Their technology is developed from scratch around customer need and the customer journey. They have no legacy, no background, no heritage and no mess. Banks have plenty of legacy: legacy systems, legacy vendors, legacy staff, legacy customers and, worst of all, legacy leadership.

The issue with leadership in banks is clear, as most banks are led by bankers. They are led by bankers with no technology experience or digital background. Their view of the world is steeped in regulation, compliance, risk and finance. Their world is built around maximum stability and minimal change. That is not a good recipe for digital transformation, which requires minimum stability and maximal change. This is because a bank is rebuilding what has been built for over half a century in order to be fit for the digital age of competition with challenger banks, which are built around customer need and the customer journey. It requires a new mindset, a different way of thinking and a brand-new organisational and systems structure.

Having worked in such change over the past thirty years, I have been able to identify clear elements of transformational change. It starts with leadership. Does the leadership team have the right composition, knowledge, commitment and passion to make the change happen? Many in positions of leadership have said to me that they know they need to change but just don't know what or how to change. It is much the same with innovation teams: many can have great ideas, but if they cannot execute those ideas, then they are just ideas. They never become anything.

Once you have the right leadership, then there are more elements of change around technology, customers, employees and structures. These elements of change are explored in depth throughout this book. How did banks get the right leadership structure? What did they do with technology? How did this impact customers? What did they change internally to engage their people? How are they working with third parties and partners?

These are all the elements of change and transformation but, to begin with, you have to admit that there is a need for fundamental, transformational change, not just an evolution of what has been around before. In the 2020s, we no longer deal with banking as usual but banking as unusual.

Are You in Banking or Technology?

I have had a lot of conversations with bankers and technologists, and realised something recently. That realisation is a simple but important one: dealing with technology is very different from dealing with money. Furthermore, dealing with money through technology is very different to dealing with technology through money. It may sound like a strange thing to talk or write about, but it is important as it explains why technology companies like Amazon and Alibaba would struggle if they were to try to open a bank.

Let's start with the basics. We all use technology a lot these days. Most of us have smartphones and Facebook accounts, and most of us don't get too angry if our call drops or our update only gets a few Likes. However, if our money transfer fails or our salary payment does not arrive on its due date, we get very angry. The difference is obvious: money is a key control factor in our lives but technology is not.

This is why we can upgrade our smartphone every couple of years but never change our bank account. With money, we want security and safety; with technology, we want excitement and experiences. This is also why I find it amusing to hear about technologists claiming that banks will shut down, be destroyed and disrupted by technology. It is not going to happen (as long as banks adapt and change, which they tend to do).

Adding more nuance to this, we are seeing banking and technology collide. We are seeing banking and technology meld and merge in the twenty-first century. Then, as mentioned earlier, dealing with money through technology is different from dealing with technology through money.

What I mean by this is that when I deal with technology through money, I am usually just looking to pay for stuff. So we have Square, Stripe, PayPal, Venmo, Alipay, WeChat Pay and more. They all let me pay for stuff online. Great. That is not dealing with money through technology, though; it is dealing with technology through money. It lets me pay for stuff online and on my mobile. However, when it comes to something more complex like trading and investing, corporate treasury, deposit accounts and full-service banking, it is different. It is far more complicated and comprises regulations and centuries of development. There is a reason why banking is regulated the way it is, and why banking has five times more regulation than technology.

According to an analysis of regulations by Bank of America Merrill Lynch in 2018, the average technology firm deals with 27,000 government regulations whilst the average bank deals with 128,000. There is a reason for this. Technology is disposable but money is not. Money needs to be safe and secure. Technology needs to be flexible and adaptable.

Figure 1.3 The average number of regulations (000s) faced by firms in each industry

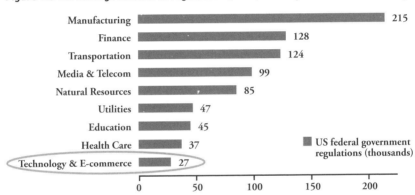

These are core tenets of the way forward. This why it is interesting as banking and technology meld and merge. Some call it FinTech—the integration of finance and technology—while others call it TechFin—the integration of technology and finance. I call it change, and I call it dramatic change.

Those approaching technology from finance will be firmly grounded in rules and regulations, safety and security, resilience and reliability; those approaching finance from technology will be firmly grounded in innovation and change, adaptability and flexibility, obsolescence and upgrade. The approaches are very different, and it is why it is very different dealing with technology through money and dealing with money through technology. They are not the same and the way in which these markets merge are not the same. Don't get me wrong. They are merging. But the way they merge will be interesting as who is right? Is it better to deal with money with the complexity of regulations or deal with technology with simplicity and ease? How do these two extremes come together?

The answer for me is that we will deal with money with simplicity and ease, but with a backdrop layer of strongly simplified regulations to keep our money safe and secure. And there is the rub. Simplifying finance and financial regulations so that we can use money as data simply and safely. It is a tough job, but we are all involved in making it happen, whether we are in banking or technology. After all, there is no difference between the two nowadays.

Trust Me, I'm a Banker

There is a lot of talk about trust when you meet with people in finance. "Customers trust us with their money" ... "There is trust in banks" ... "We are trusted when it comes to advice" ... "Our brand is a trusted brand."

I usually keep quiet as most of these conversations are pure BS. Of course, there is trust in banks, but it is not in bank brands, bank people or bank products. It is in the security of the bank licence, the government regulator and the insurance compensation scheme should anything go wrong. Just look at any Edelman survey of trust in institutions, and banks are usually near the bottom of the list. Equally, when you look at brands and trust in brands, the brands we trust are the cool ones. Nike, Apple and BMW, not Citibank, HSBC or Deutsche.

However, there are two kinds of trust. Trust in the company doing the right thing for you versus trust that the company will not lose your money. Even after events like the Barclays Bank LIBOR scandal, the Australian banks that charge dead people fees and the Wells Fargo account-opening farce, did people shut their accounts en masse? No. We may not trust the company but we trust the utility of that company to keep our money safe. So, we trust the company with our money, even though we do not trust the company. We trust the company will make our transactions happen, will be a safe store of value and will provide access to our money 24/7. Yet we do not trust the company itself, the brand, its management team or its people to do right by us, the customer.

This is the core reason why people do not switch bank accounts. Why should they? If I have a safe store of value that doesn't mess up, why would I want another one that does exactly the same thing? In fact, the only time customers do switch banks is if the bank screws up on that basic promise of being a safe store of value. What makes customers angry is if the bank does not provide access, loses a transaction, messes up their balance or cancels a cheque. Not media headlines about another bank being caught behaving badly. Banks behave badly all the time but we only care about it if it affects us personally, such as when TSB went down or RBS had a glitch.

Equally, when I have talked to people, the overwhelming view is that they do not trust the bank or its management team, but they trust the manager of their branch. They may know them personally although that is less and less likely in this mobile app internet age. Yet there is something about the physicality of a bank that creates trust.

When Northern Rock went under in 2007, what is the first thing that people did? They queued up outside branches to get their money out. If you have a problem with the bank and its promise to store value safely, one of the biggest assets traditional banks still have is that there is a place to go and yell, "Show me my money!" Being able to bang on a door, shout at a human, see the cash and know it is safe is a core reason as to why some banks are opening branches. They are doing it for trust. Not for service or advice, but for trust. It is a marketing investment.

This Is Revolution

A regular argument is whether digital is a revolution or an evolution. I firmly believe that it is revolutionary. When industries are rebuilt from the ground up with new technologies and new business models, then it is a revolution. When we are living in an age in which every human on earth can be connected through technology, then it is a revolution. The full story is in *Digital Human*, which, I suspect, has not been read by those who think that we are going through an evolution.

When you have a reinvention of humanity, you have a reinvention of everything that goes with it. It is a revolution. It is not the fourth Industrial Revolution, but a revolution of everything that humans do in relationships, commerce and trade. It is as simple as that. The only part that is evolution is how you deal with the revolution. How you adapt to survive. Charles Darwin makes it clear in *On the Origin of Species*, which is about evolution dealing with revolution, that only the most adaptable survive. If you do not adapt, you do not survive.

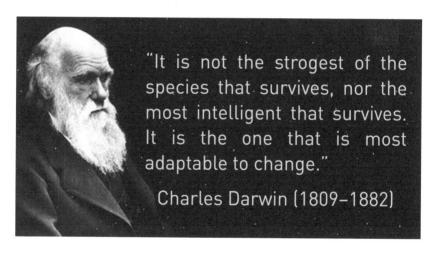

"It is not the strogest of the species that survives, nor the most intelligent that survives. It is the one that is most adaptable to change."
Charles Darwin (1809–1882)

What does adapting mean and how fast do you need to adapt? If it is a Slow Change Evolution of everything that we have always done, then it just means keeping up. It is making banking more efficient, cheaper and better with technology. A faster bank is just like a faster horse. Henry Ford famously stated: "If I had asked people what they wanted, they would have said faster horses." Of course they would have done; they had no idea what anything else was. In fact, a Victorian vision of the future was one that included a steam-powered robot horse.

Figure 1.4 A Victorian caricature depicting a steam horse on wheels

The reason why the Victorians wanted such a robot horse was because real horses left a lot of manure on the streets. The streets not only stank but were also rife with diseases unless the manure was cleared away quickly. A faster, cleaner horse made sense. Then the automobile was invented. People had no idea that it was coming. A horse-powered vehicle with an engine instead of a horse. A robot horse. Fantastic.

To begin with, not everyone got the idea of how an automobile worked but, over the decades, the automobile took over from the horse and, eventually, became affordable for all. That is why there are over a billion vehicles on the roads worldwide today, equivalent to around six billion or more horses ... and no manure. To create a world that could support over a billion horse-powered engines, we had to create a whole new world of infrastructure. Roads, freeways, interstates, motorways, Autobahns, service stations, bridges, tunnels and more have been built around the world to allow the billion horse-powered engines to move.

The radical change from horsepower to engines is similar to the radical change from analogue to digital. When banks talk about digital as a channel, appointing chief digital officers (CDOs) in each line of business (rather than one for the enterprise), delegating digital budgets to projects that the CDOs control and delegating digital rather than leading it, then I see a bank that looks like this.

Figure 1.5 How most banks see technology

The bank has the engine and it has the vehicle but, because of its limited vision and leadership, it just attaches a horse to the front. It is not a faster horse. In fact, it is a slower horse because it is lugging a heavy vehicle around behind it. Rethink the infrastructure, build roads and bridges and reinvent the system. Don't just add the new to the old and hope it will work.

It is clear from a lot of discussions around innovation and leadership that many banks are grappling with making faster banks (horses) while the start-ups are trying to create new business models (cars). Banks are trying to retrofit this shiny new technology of shared ledgers to their existing trade structures and processes. That is why distributed ledger has been talked about mostly in the context of clearing and settlement, trade finance and the supply chain and payments in banking. That is just trying to create new and more efficient trade structures rather than going back to basics and asking, is there a better way of doing this thing?

If you agree that digital is a revolution, then it means taking drastic action and taking that action fast. It is not about keeping up but about rethinking the business. It is not making a faster bank, but reinventing the business model from the ground up for a new world. The revolutionary camp sees brand-new ways of doing things. A good example is real-time financial services from firms like Trov, which insure by the hour, not the year. A good example is Ant Financial, which can provide minuscule loans to Taobao sellers for minutes rather than lump sums over a year or two. A good example is the mobile wallet in Africa, which is making many of the continent's nations cashless and enabling entire countries like Zimbabwe to run on the mobile network.

These are not products that make better versions of what we had before; rather, they are re-inventing finance with technology. It is TechFin, which starts with technology, rather than FinTech, which starts with finance. TechFin is about automobiles; FinTech is about faster horses.

Now there are some banks that get this is a radical, rather than incremental, change. Radical means dramatic action to deal with a revolution; incremental means small changes to deal with an evolution. We will meet some of these banks in this book.

Comparisons of Platforms versus Banks by the Numbers

When launching my last book, *Digital Human*, in London in April 2018, I was delighted to host Ashok Vaswani, CEO of Barclays Bank UK, and Li Wang, head of Alipay and Ant Financial in Europe, the Middle East and

Africa (EMEA), as panellists to debate the book's themes. Wang mentioned that each Alibaba employee generates RMB 100 million (over $16 million) in revenue per annum (each employee at Barclays generates around $400,000). That is a pretty startling difference. In fact, it means that even the most efficient banks are competing with new, digital players that are operating thirty to forty times more efficiently through automation. That is a striking line in the sand for digital transformation imperatives.

Now, I am not a financial analyst but a technologist and so, unsurprisingly, I got called out by some pedantic accountants over my simplistic assertion that Ant Financial is thirty to forty times more productive than banks like Barclays, as I was simply using their revenues per employee to make comparisons. Similarly, in previous discussions about platforms versus banks, using their market capitalisation per employee is also flawed. It does not mean that it is wrong, as I think platform firms like Amazon and Alibaba are truly transforming business models, but it is not an accurate comparison of productivity. So I drilled down into some more numbers and found a better way to make comparisons of companies using DuPont Analysis.

DuPont Analysis is a method of performance measurement started by the DuPont Corporation in the 1920s and focuses on return on equity (ROE) and return on assets (ROA) as a mathematical method of assessing a company's performance for investment purposes. According to DuPont Analysis, ROE is affected by three things: operating efficiency, which is measured by profit margin; asset use efficiency, which is measured by total asset turnover; and financial leverage, which is measured by the equity multiplier. Therefore, DuPont Analysis is represented in mathematical form by the following calculation:

ROE = Profit Margin x Asset Turnover Ratio x Equity Multiplier

I know that I am getting bogged down in detail but it is important to understand these numbers before we start to talk about transformation and change.

The average ROE for the largest U.S. firms is around 12 per cent, so the first thing that we are looking for is a higher ROE than this. Equally, the higher the figure for ROA, the more efficient a firm is with its inventory. ROA is calculated as Net Income divided by the Average of Total Assets. Therefore, the higher the ROA, the more income you are generating out of your assets, which is good, not bad.

Let's begin by taking the three biggest U.S. platforms: Facebook, Amazon and Google (Alphabet). Using DuPont Analysis, we get the following results:

Figure 1.6 The ROE and ROA of Facebook, Amazon and Google

	Facebook	Amazon	Alphabet	Facebook	Amazon	Alphabet	Facebook	Amazon	Alphabet
	ROE (%)	ROE (%)	ROE (%)	ROA (%)	ROA (%)	ROA (%)	Leverage	Leverage	Leverage
2017	21.43	10.65	8.3	18.85	2.31	6.42	1.14	4.74	1.29
2016	17.26	12.29	14.01	15.73	2.84	11.63	1.1	4.32	1.2
2015	8.34	4.45	13.59	7.46	0.91	11.09	1.12	4.89	1.23
2014	8.14	-2.24	13.82	7.32	-0.44	11.1	1.11	5.07	1.25
2013	9.7	2.81	14.8	8.38	0.68	11.65	1.16	4.12	1.27
Average	12.974	5.592	12.904	11.548	1.26	10.36	1.126	4.628	1.248

What you can see is that Facebook and Alphabet are similar structures: platform firms that do not distribute much (other than content), are low leveraged and give slightly better than average return on equity. Having said that, these are not boring firms, as their ROE and ROA swing quite dramatically year-on-year. Amazon, on the other hand, is a higher leveraged firm with lower ROE, but its efficiency is shown by its very low ROA. This is a sign of a low-cost distributor. Equally, Amazon has never been that profitable because it ploughs nearly all of its surplus into expanding its offerings. This is why its ROE is low and leverage is high, as it is a long-term play to create a monopolistic firm.

It would actually be more telling if we compared Amazon with its U.S. arch-rival and incumbent, Walmart. What you then find is that Walmart's results are far better.

Figure 1.7 The ROE and ROA of Amazon versus Walmart

	Amazon	Walmart	Amazon	Walmart	Amazon	Walmart
	ROE (%)	ROE (%)	ROA (%)	ROA (%)	Leverage	Leverage
2017	10.56	17.54	2.31	6.86	4.74	2.56
2016	12.29	18.24	2.84	7.36	4.32	2.48
2015	4.45	20.1	0.91	8.03	4.89	2.5
2014	-2.24	21.01	-0.44	7.83	5.07	2.69
2013	2.81	22.27	0.68	8.37	4.12	2.66
Average	**5.592**	**19.832**	**1.26**	**7.69**	**4.628**	**2.578**

Having said that, I know which firm I would invest in.

Now, let's take the top three U.S. banks: JPMorgan Chase, Bank of America and Wells Fargo. Truth be told, I found it hard to track down a decent analysis of these banks as the figures showed an above average ROE of 20 per cent before the 2008 crisis, sinking to flatlining for a few years before picking up again. Nevertheless, here are the latest statistics sourced from *MorningStar:*

Figure 1.8 The ROE and ROA of the top three U.S. banks

	JPMC	BOA	WF	JPMC	BOA	WF	JPMC	BOA	WF
	ROE (%)	ROE (%)	ROE (%)	ROA (%)	ROA (%)	ROA (%)	Leverage	Leverage	Leverage
2017	9.86	6.83	11.53	0.9	0.74	1.06	11.03	9.32	10.75
2016	10.27	6.95	11.78	0.95	0.76	1.1	10.92	9.05	11.03
2015	10.34	6.29	12.78	0.91	0.68	1.24	10.62	9.17	10.47
2014	9.75	1.71	13.68	0.81	0.18	1.36	12.14	9.39	10.21
2013	8.4	4.61	13.99	0.7	0.47	1.42	12.08	9.58	9.92
Average	**9.724**	**5.278**	**12.752**	**0.854**	**0.566**	**1.236**	**11.358**	**9.302**	**10.476**

These results show that Wells Fargo is the best-performing big bank in the United States while the Bank of America is underperforming.

All in all, what does this actually tell me? For the financial investors and analysts, it tells them which companies to invest in and in which sectors, but does it actually give me any meaningful comparisons across sectors? Does it give me a clear view of how Amazon stacks up against JPMorgan Chase?

Figure 1.9 Amazon versus JPMorgan Chase

	Amazon	JPMC	Amazon	JPMC	Amazon	JPMC
	ROE (%)	ROE (%)	ROA (%)	ROA (%)	Leverage	Leverage
2017	10.65	9.86	2.31	0.9	4.74	11.03
2016	12.29	10.27	2.84	0.95	4.32	10.92
2015	4.45	10.34	0.91	0.91	4.89	10.62
2014	-2.24	9.75	-0.44	0.81	5.07	12.14
2013	2.81	8.4	0.68	0.7	4.12	12.08
Average	5.592	9.724	1.26	0.854	4.628	11.358

Financially, yes; strategically, no.

I realise that the nitpickers out there do not like it when I say that Stripe generates twenty-two times more value per employee than JPMorgan Chase, based on its last funding round valuation, or that Ant Financial is thirty-five times more productive than Barclays Bank, based on revenues per employee. They want a DuPont Analysis of these companies so that they can point out that Amazon and Alibaba are highly leveraged, but JPMorgan Chase and Wells Fargo are strong and stable. I think that misses the point however, and the point is this: which company/companies will dominate the next century?

The Digital Transformation Journey

More and more business leaders around the world are realising that digital is a transformation project, not just an adjunct to business as usual. However, there needs to be more leaders like this. We can liken most people's thinking about digital in banking, for example, to the thinking within the media when the first digital magazines were produced. The idea was that a page flicker was added to the top right and left of each page online so that the user could flick through the magazine as though it were in print. We digitised printed media into online printed media. That is not digital content or digitalisation, it is just a faster horse, and there's the rub. Much of what I see banks doing is producing faster horses, a theme I will return to many times in this book.

This struck home when one of the big consulting groups told me about its worldwide global survey of big banking execs and how 76 per cent of them thought that they had done digital. Their response made it clear that the banking survey had found that most banking execs believed they had done digital because they had a mobile app. "That's digital," they would say. "Oh, and we have a chief digital officer—several of them actually—and we made a big point of talking about our digital investments and journey in our annual report and investor briefings. So yes, we've done digital."

In reality, these banks had changed nothing. There was no rethinking of product and service. No new ideas about how to structure the bank. No fundamental redesign of core systems structures. Effectively nothing had changed except that they had stuck an app on the front end of the banking process.

This is a fatal error and will prove the downfall of some big banks in the next decade. They will not die, but will be acquired and merged into other banks that did adapt successfully. The reason why I am confidently predicting the demise of a big bank—and by big, I mean systemically important—is that it will be acquired or broken up due to its inability to keep up. If a bank is just sticking apps on the front end, how is it meant to keep up with its competitors' deep learning projects? If a bank has not changed anything under the hood, how can they leverage internet technologies for the twenty-first century? If the management team has zero digital experience, how can it lead the bank through a digital transformation journey? Between the hordes of start-ups that want to challenge banks, along with their compatriots who want to reinvent financial services for the internet age, a bank firmly rooted in last-century technologies is clearly not going to survive in the long term.

Digital transformation demands that a bank reinvents itself in order to place a digital structure at its core. That digital structure is based on front-office apps for sure, but it is deployed in a marketplace of middle-office APIs and back-office analytics that are open-sourced and collaborative. The banks that just do the front-office app have changed nothing fundamentally. They are not ready to collaborate and co-create, but sit rigidly in their old command and control structures like King Canute on the beach trying to stop the waves. Eventually, unless they move, they will drown.

Banker: We've Done Digital! Skinner: Oh Dear

There is a huge difference between *doing digital* and *being digital*. Digital is about reimagining finance using technology and requires a complete rethinking of the bank's business model and organisational structure.[3] This is because the banking business model is built for physical distribution, whereas we are now moving to digital distribution. Banking has its heart in its back-office products, and thinks about pushing products to customers through channels. Digital has its heart in real-time availability, and thinks about using customer data to create intimacy through devices. Banking has added technology to its core products, and calls these channels. Digital is adding financial products to its technology, and focuses on access.

I meet a lot of senior executive teams of large banks and talk to them about the FinTech world of change and how millennials are reshaping banking, from Stripe, started by two brothers aged nineteen and twenty-one, to Venmo, started by two friends in their twenties, to Klarna, created by some guys who were working at a big-brand burger chain in Sweden. I talk to them about how distributed ledger technology, also known as blockchain, is reinventing the back office of banks, along with AI and machine learning, and their eyes sometimes glaze over. I talk to them about how new thinking about money is coming out of the cryptocurrency world, and particularly how Africa is experiencing changes by using mobile phones and distributed ledger technology to move massive volumes of small transactions for no charge. At this, they look a little nonplussed.

---

3   The business model discussion is a refrain in all of my books and is discussed in-depth in *Digital Human*.

Digital is a complete transformation of the fabric and foundations of the organisation.

It is obvious that digital is a massive, fundamental shift of a bank's business model. As said earlier, the bank's business model was developed in the Industrial Revolution to enable cross-border commerce with trust. This is why banks are regulated and licensed by governments, which gives them that trust, and why most banks are the oldest institutions in their respective countries. The model is based around a focus on the physical distribution of paper in the localised network focused on buildings and people. Banks controlled the whole value chain of that network, and designed and built everything themselves.

Then along came technology in the 1950s and the giant computer firm IBM, which sold big back-office boxes to banks throughout the 1960s, 1970s and 1980s. The idea was simple: get rid of the paper transaction systems in the branch and automate the ledger of debits and credits in a head-office system. This way the head office could track and trace its whole branch network of ledgers immediately. It cut costs, increased security and made the banks far more efficient.

80%

of big-bank decision-makers believe they have done digital

CGI

76%

do not believe digital requires any change to their business model

Gartner

94%

do not have any technology-related professional experience

Accenture

When other technologies came along, they were added on to this big central system. Call centres, ATMs and internet banking all followed, and all show a record of debits and credits. Then mobile banking made an entrance at the same time as Cloud Computing, Big Data, cryptocurrencies and Open Banking, and it has ripped that whole system to pieces.

This is why a twenty-one-year-old university dropout could start a bank called Loot. It is why two friends could spin out of one challenger bank, Starling, and start another called Monzo. It is why a Chinese company, Ant Financial, in partnership with India's Paytm, has become the biggest financial firm in India in less than five years.

There are many other examples, but the key to all of these is that they do not do everything themselves. They use APIs to find partnerships with other providers that can do the work for them. Loot is backed by Wirecard. Starling Bank has twenty-five partnerships through APIs to offer full-service banking, from pensions and savings to insurance and mortgages. Ant Financial offers a marketplace of APIs to companies worldwide, which are used by some of the biggest banks in the world to do the things they cannot do, such as processing payments using quick response (QR) codes.

These developments are called various things from "platforms" to "marketplaces", but I like to call it "Open Banking". I do not mean open banking in the regulatory sense, but in the sense of a business model. A bank that historically controlled everything is now open to everything.

This business model is a reimagination of the old physical one as it is built from the ground up using today's technologies to focus on delivering a customer experience that is exceptional, and through its tech devices rather than through physical interaction. In other words, the industrial-era business model of banks based on branches is replaced with the digital-era model of banks based on servers. This is a completely different business model and focuses on the digital distribution of data through software and servers on a global network of systems called the internet.

So why would a senior decision-maker in a bank believe that they have done digital, and it requires no change to their business model, when it is clearly obvious to those who know technology that digital is a massive cultural, business and organisational transformation based on a brand-new business model? The key words in that sentence are "to those who know technology". Most senior decision-makers do not know technology. Banks are run by bankers, not by technologists, except that the new digital banks also need to be technologists, otherwise they are just a bank, not a digital bank.

My statement here is backed by a recent analysis of big banks' annual reports that found that 94 per cent of their leadership have never had any professional experience that relates to technology. That is a serious flaw and is the reason why most big banks think that they have done digital because they have rolled out a mobile app.

Banking as Usual Is NOT an Option

Banking as usual is not an option. It is similar to standing in the middle of the road. If you stand there long enough, you will get run over. This is as true in banking: if you stop changing, you die. Now banks know this—they are not stupid—and have changed a lot over the past decades. Since I started in banking, I have seen the mass adoption of ATMs; the introduction, growth and move to offshoring call centres; the deployment of online and now mobile banking; the rise of algorithmic, high-frequency trading; the drive towards server farms co-locating next to the stock exchanges; and the big trends towards blockchain, cloud and machine learning overall.

This is why banks are as strong today as they have ever been, and I think that anyone who says that banks do not change or are doomed is an idiot. Banks are not doomed unless they stop adapting to change and, so far, banks have done a pretty good job of adapting to change.

Can you name one bank that has failed due to technology? I cannot think of one. Ever. I can think of many that have failed due to poor risk management, abuse of market rules or general misconduct but failing due to technology has not happened. This will only happen if a bank resists change. If a bank resists the march of time. Banks will be doomed if they resist changing legacy systems, especially those at the core.

Now when I talk about getting rid of core systems, many people ping me a note saying that it is not necessary. You can build adjacent systems that suck the data out of the legacy and analyse and use it to feed APIs and apps. In other words, you build middleware to reach into the graves of the old data processing systems and suck out their knowledge. I personally don't think this is an advisable approach to a long-term future, as sucking the data out of the dead is not really a viable strategy for the next century, is it? No. Admit those old systems are dead and replace them. That is the only way to avoid being doomed.

Currently, I think that there are two financial systems out there: the banking for the banked, and the more recent mobile wallet for the unbanked. We are now at a point where I think that we may see the end of traditional retail banking as the rising financial system, which currently complements the old financial system, could replace it in the long term. The new consumer financial system of the mobile wallet. As the mobile wallet has developed most successfully in parts of the world that were unbanked and underbanked, it is being developed by non-banks. This is the innovator's dilemma in full action.

The *Innovator's Dilemma* by Clayton Christensen argues that, when confronted with change, large institutions see a no-frills product, something that has stripped everything back to basics, and dismiss it as irrelevant. In fact, it should really be called the "Incumbent's Dilemma", as the large incumbent does not want to respond to a product that eradicates all of its existing profit and functionality. The heart of the dilemma is articulated by Christensen as follows:

"The reason [for why great companies failed] is that good management itself was the root cause. Managers played the game the way it's supposed to be played. The very decision-making and resource allocation processes that are key to the success of established companies are the very processes that reject disruptive technologies: listening to customers; tracking competitors' actions carefully; and investing resources to design and build higher-performance, higher-quality products that will yield greater profit. These are the reasons why great firms stumbled or failed when confronted with disruptive technology change.

"Successful companies want their resources to be focused on activities that address customers' needs, that promise higher profits, that are technologically feasible, and that help them play in substantial markets. Yet, to expect the processes that accomplish those things also to do something like nurturing disruptive technologies—to focus resources on proposals that customers reject, that offer lower profit, that underperform existing technologies and can only be sold in insignificant markets—is akin to flapping one's arms with wings strapped to them in an attempt to fly. Such expectations involve fighting some fundamental tendencies about the way successful organizations work and about how their performance is evaluated."

Today, mobile operators and companies like Ant Financial are developing mobile wallets that can operate across borders, globally. These mobile wallets ignore the banked, and are largely developing in Africa, India, Indonesia, China, the Philippines and other markets. They offer cheap financial inclusion and, in order to do this, offer microloans, microsavings, easy payments and low-cost digital identification. The thing is that if they offer all of these services, what is to stop them from upscaling? I made this comment the other day about Alipay. Right now, it is just for Chinese citizens but what if Alipay were to put a nice local language front end on the app? I would use it.

Then, I might need a bank for commerce, trade and investment markets but, for consumer retail banking, the innovators are already a mile down the road of taking out the banking system as we know it. The real question is, therefore, not about banks responding to change in the banking system, but whether banks have recognised the real need to change. You can adapt to change for sure, but if you are adapting to the wrong change, you then have a problem.

If this opening dialogue has yet to convince you that your bank must fundamentally transform, rather than just evolve the old firm slowly with technology, there are five clear areas that are forcing transformation on the bank: the rise of FinTech, the impact of challenger banks, the threat of the Big Tech firms, the regulatory drive for open competition through technology and the clear lack of internal readiness in the leadership team for change. I will now explore each of these five areas in more depth.

THE RISE OF FINTECH

I have worked in technology in finance all of my life and it was not called FinTech twenty years ago. It was just technology in finance. The breakthrough came when start-up firms launched technology-based financial structures using the latest technologies, focused on cloud and internet.

The Five Phases of FinTech

Having been involved in FinTech since the start, there are five clear phases of development (the dates given are a rough guide):

Phase One: Disruption (2005–2014)

When FinTech began, most of the start-ups talked about disrupting or even destroying the banking system. They wanted to replace banks. Now, that was a good idea but a bit naïve, however, as banks exist for a reason. They act as a regulated intermediary of trust with money. Without that regulated structure, the system would collapse.

Phase Two: Discussion (2014–2017)

The second phase of the FinTech wave paved the way for discussion between banks and FinTech, and banks did hackathons and innovation theatre. There was not much tangible connection into the banks—most still preferred to build than buy or partner—but at least there was a connection.

Phase Three: Partnership (2017–2022)

Today, FinTech firms are beginning to collaborate and partner with the banks.

Phase Four: Integration (2022–2027)

I think it will get interesting in the next ten years as we move from partnerships to fully integrating FinTech capabilities into the banking system through Open Banking and open APIs. While the revised Payment Services Directive (PSD2)[4] already mandates that banks must make payments data available to third parties through an open API, many banks are resisting being open. Equally, third parties have not really grasped the mantle of change yet.

---

4   PSD2 is the second iteration of the European regulations that apply to payments under the Payment Services Directive. This particular update forced banks to share customer data with trusted third-party firms, only if the customer gives permission.

> **Phase Five: Renewal (2027+)**
> When we get to truly open the platforms and marketplaces of APIs, apps and
> analytics, we can start to fully integrate banking and FinTech and BigTech.
> Finally, when that is completed, we will no longer talk about banks versus
> FinTech or even banking and FinTech. We will just talk about finance over
> the network, as it will be fully integrated as one seamless, frictionless system,
> internet-enabled, global and in real time.

For me, it is particularly interesting how the FinTech world has developed over the past decade or so. My first memory of a company that fit the FinTech world stems back to 30 March 2005. On that memorable evening, one of the founders of a technology start-up talked about a vision where platforms could connect people who have money with people who need money and have the risk managed by software. It would be like an eBay for money, he said, and the people would trust each other, knowing that the system polices the activities. That person was Richard Duval, co-founder of Zopa. Zopa has now grown into a megabrand in the United Kingdom, enabling thousands to save and borrow through a peer-to-peer network for money.

Back in 2005, however, no one understood what Duval was talking about. Things like Cloud Computing were just being discussed, and rejected by most financial institutions as too risky. After all, if third parties looked after core systems and data, it would bring down the financial system. Mind you, they did not need third parties to do that. They did it themselves.

In retrospect, we all know that the 2008 global financial crash was caused by calculated risks being taken by investment markets using instruments that had no connection to reality. Collateralised debt obligations and mortgage-backed securities were derivatives that seemed to wrap up buckets of debt nicely. Unfortunately, the markets then dumped them into other buckets of debt and caused a global debt crisis.

However, out of the ashes of the financial system came a new drive and vision from young millennials who could code. They hated the big banks, and wanted to redefine finance through software and servers. Just as Zopa had the idea of connecting savers and borrowers through code peer-to-peer, thousands of other bright young things had similar ideas.

This led to the first wave of FinTech and the explosion of peer-to-peer everything, from peer-to-peer money (Bitcoin) to peer-to-peer payments (Venmo) to peer-to-peer insurance (Friendsurance) to peer-to-peer investing (eToro). From the combination of open-sourced structures allowing start-ups to bootstrap on cloud computers and release APIs into the wild, a whole new world of finance and technology emerged, FinTech for short.

Initially, in the first wave of FinTech, much of the development was directed at disrupting the banking system through these peer-to-peer models. Then some start-ups moved into new areas, from financial inclusion through mobile wallets in African nations to crowdfunding projects and ideas across the developed world. All of these proved to be radical and new. For example, from the seeds of M-Pesa in Kenya in 2007 sprang mobile wallets that allow anyone in almost any African country to send and receive money instantaneously electronically. Kickstarter and Indiegogo created models that allow start-ups to get funded by their customers, so they no longer need a bank loan in order to find their markets. Instead, their markets find them. Other new ideas emerged, especially in China, where Alibaba, Tencent, Baidu and Ping An have all developed radical new ideas with technology.

The first FinTech wave led to huge investment in start-ups that could attack the financial structures with code, particularly leveraging apps, APIs and analytics. Big Data, Cloud Computing, mobile networks and social media all conspired to create new structures, and the banks were subsumed by these developments. Many banks got the idea of mobile banking apps, but they had not understood the gamut of technologies affecting their business structures, which left a soft underbelly for kids with code to attack.

And attack they did. Unicorns emerged, with many removing friction from the financial networks. While Stripe, Square, Klarna, Adyen, TransferWise, Revolut, Venmo and more all made successful bids for the FinTech crowns, many of the traditional institutions struggled to keep up. Then banks decided that much of what these guys were doing was actually helping rather than disrupting their business. Removing friction from financial processes with code was actually a good thing. So, banks started to collaborate with, co-create with, invest in and partner many of these start-ups.

The great unbundling of banks moved to the great rebundling of FinTech by the banks. In this process however, something started to happen that moved us from a big bucket of FinTech to a much more granular strata of different markets for different things: RegTech, WealthTech, InsurTech, blockchain and distributed ledger technology, AI and machine learning and more came into play. It was no longer the case of integrating finance and technology, but rather merging them into something completely new.

During this period, the quiet developments emerging from the Chinese internet giants also blossomed and bloomed into the financial stratospheres. Ant Financial, Alibaba's payments subsidiary, suddenly emerged as the tenth-largest financial firm in the world by market capitalisation, and everyone seemed to start talking about Alipay and WeChat Pay.

A completely different FinTech world had emerged out of Asia, and many suddenly woke up to the fact that they had not even been looking. By way of example, in 2018, Alipay and WeChat Pay each processed more dollars in a month through their apps than PayPal processes in a year. China has seen an explosion of online mobile payments, rising from $5 trillion in 2016 to $15.5 trillion in 2017 and to over $40 trillion in 2018. Compare this to the United States and you see a quiet revolution. It is not just about Alibaba and Tencent, but the whole FinTech scene emerging from Asia, Africa and South America. This FinTech scene began without the blinkers of big bank thinking and has created wholly integrated internet finance on mobile apps, or superapps, seamlessly.

Think of Amazon acquiring PayPal and Facebook, and you get the idea. An internet scene spawning giants like Alibaba and Tencent, but also Baidu, JD.com and Ping An. These are all companies born on the internet and focused on changing the world of everything including banking, payments, finance and FinTech. Add Google, Amazon and Facebook, and you have this melting pot of Big Tech platforms offering huge potential.

This is why the hybrid model brings together many players across ecosystems and marketplaces on the Big Tech platforms. I see FinTech unicorns collaborating to offer full services on those platforms. Already we see Revolut working with Xero, Sage, Fresh Books and Quaderno; Monzo partnering with TransferWise; Metro Bank working with Zopa; Wirecard working with Alipay, Ingenico and many others; and Starling Bank working with PensionBee, Wealthsimple, Habito and Kasko. These are the foundations of collaborative marketplaces of apps, APIs and analytics led by one, partnering with many, on platforms.

Banks should feel duly threatened by FinTech for these reasons because banks are control freaks by nature. Historically, they have partnered with no one, unless they had to. For a big bank to about-face and start to become an open market collaborator is a huge cultural change and, in the meantime, the challenger banks are actively building their ecosystems.

When Will the FinTech Bubble Burst?

Reading about forty or so firms being valued at billions of dollars after just a couple of years, you would think that everything is rosy and sweet in the FinTech garden, but it is not necessarily the case. For every Uber, there is a Karhoo. Lyft is losing more than it is earning, $1.14 billion lost on revenues of $776 million in the first quarter of 2019. WeWorks, with a valuation nearing $50 billion, is just a cool reboot of Regus with an app. Monzo gained a valuation at near $3 billion in the summer of 2019 and, soon after, Europe's biggest unicorn, TransferWise, was valued at $3.5 billion. These valuations do strike me as similar to the internet bubble. Is this one going to burst in the same way? Is there going to be a lot of FinTech blood on the ground?

That question has been asked a lot, and I first asked it back in 2015. My answer then was that the FinTech bubble would not burst. Just a re-architecting of finance through technology that, until it finishes, will see us moving through waves of innovation and change. I still hold this view today. That is why FinTech investment doubled in 2018, has reached record highs, continues to burn higher and sees more and more unicorns arising.

The main evidence as to why FinTech investments will continue is twofold: first, specialising in making boring old banking better and, second, serving people profitably who could not be served by boring old banks. In the former category, there are huge amounts of inefficiencies in banking, as best evidenced in the customer onboarding and know your client (KYC) processes. If every bank in the world switched to the onboarding processes of firms like N26 (8 minutes online), then we would see a huge change to banking and, of course, each bank could do this. There are plenty of firms offering innovative KYC solutions, and this is one of the major growth areas in FinTech. It will be interesting to see how many of these firms end up being invested in by big old boring banks or partnering with big old boring banks. There is still a long way to go.

In the latter category, we have only just scratched the surface of small business services, financial wellness, financial literacy and financial inclusion. There is still a long way to go on this axis as few firms are emerging in this space, but there are more and more each year. In fact, it is interesting that even the big banks are waking up to this opportunity. For example, HSBC recently introduced a service to monitor customer accounts that may be vulnerable due to the account holder having dementia.

Serving customers that the banks have historically ignored is a big growth area, as dealing with customers in a physical network created an astronomical overhead of cost that meant most people were excluded. Eradicate that cost overhead, and everyone can be included. This is what digital offers and delivers, and explains why it is such a high growth area.

One Brilliant Thing Is Much Better Than 1,000 Average Ones

One key reason why FinTech will continue to grow strongly is that many of these firms are focusing on doing one thing brilliantly that the banks do badly. From customer onboarding to online checkout, many start-up companies are finding better ways to do things with code than the ways in which banks currently do them. And they only focus on that one thing and focus on doing it well. This is why there are so many changes taking place in traditional banking as the FinTech community rises.

The first is that banks' organisational structures have to move from being locked in, proprietary and tightly coupled to open, partnering and loosely coupled. It is all about plug-and-play and open-sourcing technologies based on apps, APIs and analytics. A bank has a strong position in this space as it owns the marketplace today, and should be building the platforms to allow its customers great experiences by connecting with the best-in-class APIs out there.

From an open API viewpoint, there are thousands of start-ups focused on doing one thing really well, from making a merchant payment (Stripe) to borrowing money (SoFi, Prosper, Zopa) to investing (eToro, ZuluTrader, roboadvisors). However, as a customer, I have no idea which of these firms to choose and trust, if any. That is why banks should be partnering with the firms that they think do these things best, and bring them to me through curation.

After all, if thousands of new, shiny FinTech firms are doing one thing well, how can a bank compete when it is full of legacy and heritage, meaning that it does a thousand things averagely? Reboot through co-creation and partnering, and gradually reshape the bank for the twenty-first century by replacing the bits that don't work with a partner's capabilities that do.

This is not as easy as it may sound as many banks have dodged the legacy replacement question for decades. They think that fast following is acceptable. They believe that they are immune to technological changes. They believe that digital is rolling out a mobile app. They just don't get it. For the few that do, they do not know what to do. This means that the banks are currently stuck in the tightly coupled proprietary avenue. However, if the leadership teams do get this, they will want to move to the open street future.

There are two huge mountains to climb to get to digital: the first is to get the people on board; the second is to replace the legacy. The first thing that banks need to grapple with is culture and leadership when developing their digital transformation. They need leaders who can articulate and communicate what is going on to staff in a non-threatening way. Unfortunately, I heard one bank CEO recently talk about thousands of employees being replaced by robots. That is not the most sensitive way of articulating such a message. As Piyush Gupta, the CEO of DBS, puts it, show people that they have a great opportunity to be part of a change to make the bank digital and, in the process, they are allowed to experiment. They are allowed to try things and, even more important, they are allowed to fail. Next, the replacement of core systems is essential if the systems are based on legacy vendors or legacy architecture.

Bank leadership teams may believe that it is too huge an undertaking to digitally transform their bank's culture and replace core systems, and insist that it really is not necessary as the customer will not notice. However, it is wrong to think like that. The customer is bound to notice because there are all these really cool, new firms doing things differently. And guess what? If those new, cool firms that do one thing really well start to group together to do hundreds of things well together, how would a bank compete?

If the bank that does a thousand things averagely, cemented to its past, is not agile[5] enough to update daily and refresh its core regularly, it will be outsmarted by those that can. Those that can will then recognise that the banks are doing a thousand things averagely, and will naturally come together to do a thousand things brilliantly.

---

5   An approach to software development under which requirements and solutions evolve through the collaborative effort of self-organising and cross-functional teams, and their customer or end-user.

Figure 1.10 The emerging FinTech marketplace

Just watch as the FinTech marketplace matures and the partnering and co-creation ecosystem emerges. How many banks will be part of the endgame? It won't be many, but the ones positioning themselves into this space today are going to decimate the ones that resist.

Suits or Jeans, Canapés or Pizzas? The FinTech Shuffle Moves on ...

Finance and technology have created this hybrid market called FinTech, and this market is populated by both breeds of human. I attend many financial conferences and have come to realise that banking and technology communities are, culturally, at somewhat of an impasse. It is the meeting of two tribes, and the tribes do not mix well. One tribe is full of suits, fine wines, Michelin-star restaurants and business class jets. The other is all jeans, beer, pizza and Ryanair. It may not be quite as extreme as this, but it is not far off.

Figure 1.11 Dylan Richards and Harper Reed, founders of Modest, acquired by PayPal in 2015

Figure 1.12 Stuart Gulliver, former CEO of HSBC

Marrying the millennials of technology with the boomers of banking is a tough task, and a big challenge for a bank. A bank likes minimal risk and is organised by financial experts to provide maximum returns; a technology company likes to learn and fail fast, and is organised by youthful technology experts to provide maximum innovation. How do you bring together the old and the young, the financial and the technological?

This is a question that arose during a meeting with the senior head of innovation at a bank. I said that his bank seemed to be doing the right things to be digital, and he replied, "We are making the right actions, but the question is whether we can be digital, which is more fundamental." I asked him why the bank could not be digital, and he replied that it was due to the culture. *The culture is the hardest thing to change, and becoming a digital bank is nothing if you do not have the passion to change.*

That was an interesting comment and was followed by another discussion that worked the other way around. A friend of mine is creating an interesting blockchain company. The company's leadership team are experts in finance. They are seasoned City people who like the shared ledger structure so much that they have created a breakthrough system for banks using this technology. They have been pitching the technology around the markets, and are being regularly referred to as young millennials for *due diligence*. My friend was pretty annoyed about this, as he usually deals with world leaders and respected business figures. To suddenly be referred to as a young upstart in jeans and trainers does not fit well with such experience.

This leads to another chasm of culture: trust. The old guys do not think that the young guys understand financial markets. In contrast, the young guys do not think that the old guys understand technology. So the ideal mix is to have a company of millennials and boomers, isn't it? Let the old guys share their wisdom about money and let the young guys share their knowledge about computing. This Fin and Tech integration of boomer and millennial is not easy. The answer may therefore be that the boomer needs a millennial mentality and the millennial needs to respect the boomer's experience.

FinTech and the Parent–Child Relationship

To me, the FinTech relationship is more like that of a parent and child. The parent wants safety, security and a stable home; the child wants to run around, kick and break everything, and challenge everything that the parent thinks. That is all well and good, but it is difficult for a bank to work with a start-up when the start-up is kicking and screaming about how stupid the bank is. Like a child, the start-up has no idea why the world works the way it does and all they want to do is change it. The parent sighs, as they have seen and done it all before, waits until the child falls over and then picks them up and helps them.

This symbiotic relationship between parent and child—bank and start-up—is at the core of the current wave of FinTech developments, where banks are talking about co-creation, collaboration and co-operation. How should banks work with FinTech start-ups? Going back to the parent–child analogy, what role does the parent play for the child? It is obvious. They act as mentors, educators, nurturers and investors. They help the child to learn and grow. The child sometimes falls over but the parent always picks them up. As Confucius said: "Our greatest glory is not in never falling, but in rising every time we fall."

In this new world of partnering, co-creation, collaboration and co-operation, banks need to place themselves firmly in the mentoring parental seat. Now this is not easy when you have the daftpunk child. Some banks, because of their control freakery and arrogance, will end up in a patronising and condescending stance. They will talk down to the child, slap them, lock them in their bedrooms with no food and ground them indefinitely. These banks will fail in their co-creation, collaboration and co-operation efforts, as that attitude does not work. The child will just open the bedroom window, slide down the drainpipe and escape.

If a bank is truly serious about co-creation, collaboration and co-operation, then it needs to be completely open and tolerant of its start-up children. Yes, the children will run around, break things, argue and challenge, but that is brilliant because it is exactly what is needed. Why do you do things that way? Why not this way? Do you really need to do all of this checking? Why do you think the regulator won't approve it? Have you asked them?

Like a growing child, FinTech start-ups are moving from a developmental phase to a sentient phase. A true banking partner will be tolerant and supportive of this process, not dismissive and patronising. Banks are parents. Parents are mentors. FinTech start-ups are children. Develop the children.

What FinTech Means to Banks

There has been a lot of discussion about FinTech and what it means to banks. Initially, everyone was talking about the disruption and disintermediation of banks. Next, the discussion moved on to incumbents versus start-ups. Then it led to talking about partnering and co-creation.

Many of the FinTech start-ups have ended up partnering with banks because they are trying to make the existing business more efficient and effective. A good example is the regulatory sandboxes developed by national regulators to aid speed-to-market for FinTech start-ups. Most of the start-ups that qualify for the sandbox are focused on one of two things:
1) reducing costs and inefficiencies in the existing bank processes
2) improving the customer experience and access to information for the customer

The first camp is illustrated by firms focused on things like KYC and anti-money laundering (AML) or firms like TransferWise and Zopa that reduce costs through peer-to-peer connectivity. The second camp is all about using data better, such as how Monzo runs its financial app or how Loot delivers cashflow forecasting and personal financial management to millennials. These are faster horses.

What I see developing, however, is a new business model coming from markets that had nothing before. Because they had nothing before, they do not know what a horse is, so they have not even considered developing a faster one. They have just leapfrogged everyone with a new way of thinking. China is a great example.

Traditionally, Chinese markets did not have cheque books and plastic, and most Chinese citizens did not have bank accounts. Therefore, when the internet took off, the big innovators, namely, Tencent, Alibaba, Ping An and Baidu, simply leapt from old style bank products to mobile wallets, microsavings and microloans. Many Western pundits describe these big Chinese players as banks, but I don't see them that way. I see them as technology firms first, applying technology to create new ways of exchanging value and money.

Their vision is based on easier shopping and commerce online, and better management of money with technology. It is why China transacted over \$40 trillion through mobile wallets in 2018, over eight times the value of 2016, while the United States is still stuck in old style money. Americans transacted \$6 trillion with plastic cards in 2016, and just \$150 billion on mobile phones. The numbers are radically different.

It is not just the Asian internet giants that are changing the world, however. Firms from Paytm in India to M-Pesa in Kenya to Globe Telecom in the Philippines to Banco Original in Brazil are all reimagining finance with technology. What all of them demonstrate is the mindset of starting with technology first to address the problem faced by people who are not getting the right access to money.

It is these markets that will deliver the FinTech revolution because they are not thinking of a faster horse. They are not looking at bank products and trying to think about how they can make them faster or cheaper. Instead, they are looking at technology and trying to work out how it could be used to reach the people who need service. The FinTech revolution will not just come from U.S. or European FinTech firms, but also from South American, Asian and African start-ups.

The Endgame: Banks Become Technology Firms

Twenty years ago, I worked on a strategy for the future of banking. My conclusion was that banks would merge with technology and/or telecommunications firms and become hybrid institutions. Twenty years later, it has not happened. Will it?

It is interesting because way back then, I worked for a technology firm focused on banking that was owned by a telecommunications business. The telco was all about the network. My firm was all about banking. The two did not get on very well as banks are all about basis points differential while telcos are all about minutes on the network. Interestingly, even as the alignment of these industries converges, that mentality has stayed the same. Banks are all about risk management; telcos are all about the volume of calls and data.

However, the meme of banks and telcos coming together does not go away. Many of my banking colleagues go to the big GSMA jamboree in Spain[6] every year, and many telcos appear on my banking panels at numerous tradeshows. Many of my bank friends have had stints in their careers working for telcos, and many telco guys turn up in banks to manage their mobile banking play.

This is why I find it interesting that banks today talk about themselves as technology companies that happen to have a banking licence. First, they are not technology companies, they are banks. Second, if they were something else, they would be a telco and not a technology company. This is because the backbone of banking today is the network. The thing that banks and telcos have in common—and something that technology firms do not—is frequent customer contact. A telco is with us 24/7 and, for many, that is what they want their bank to be, too. A telco knows intimately where you are all day long and, in many ways, could probably work out what you are doing. Combine that intimacy with a complete analysis of your financial lifestyle and appetite for risk, and you have got a good method of leveraging proactive, predictive, personalised, proximate service. That is something core to the future banking offer. Deep data analytics to provide incredibly personalised service that

6   This is the largest conference in the world that focuses on telecommunications and, specifically, the mobile network. It is attended by all firms involved in mobile phone, apps and beyond.

acts as a financial blanket around our lives, and makes us spend and save smarter.

Another question to ask here is, can banks downscale? Can banks become mobile money operators? The answer is yes, and some already are. There are several banks that offer mobile services or even own their own mobile network operator (MNO). There are some MNOs that have opened banks, such as Orange in France.[7]

The symbiosis of high customer contact, location-based services, deep data analytics and financial lifestyle support make for a compelling offer, so I will go back to my prediction of twenty years ago and say it again: banks will merge with telecommunications firms over time in order to provide a hybrid service. I call this service "digilife", a term that I have intriguingly only seen used in one other financial operator's presentations. That company happens to be called Ant Financial. Just saying ...

BOTTOM LINE

About 12,000 start-up companies have gained billions of dollars of investment over the past decade to change the structure of finance with technology. Each company is focused on very specific areas to change the landscape of banking and finance. This cannot be ignored and most banks are actively trying to work out what to do with these start-ups. Do they partner with them, compete with them, acquire them or something else? It is challenging as the culture and structure of the incumbent and the start-up are very different. Eventually, the two will merge and become one and, as they do, will create the digital banking structure of online finance for the twenty-first century. Banks must adapt and change to be part of this or they will become irrelevant and acquired.

---

7   Orange Bank had over 30,000 people signed up in its first week of operation and 100,000 in the first four months. By 2025, the bank is targeting two million customers, or 2.5 per cent of the French consumer banking market.

THE RISE OF CHALLENGER BANKS

Over the past few years, there has been a lot of discussion about challenger banks. As the name implies, these are new banks that want to challenge the old world order. Their specific aim is to challenge and take over substantial market share from a traditional bank, which is why they should be of concern to such institutions. However, it is not as simple as this. After all, many refer to banks as challengers that are not banks at all, so the first question has to be: What is a challenger bank?

On the face of it, this seems a very simple question. After all, the *Oxford English Dictionary* defines a challenger bank as follows: "A relatively small retail bank set up with the intention of competing for business with large, long-established national banks."

However, it is easy to poke holes in this definition as not all challenger banks are retail. Take ClearBank as an example. The first UK clearing bank in more than 250 years, ClearBank could be described as a challenger bank to the long-established national banks.

Market Business News defines a challenger bank as: "A challenger bank is a small bank that is threatening the rankings of large banks. The term includes any new or upcoming bank that has recently gained a license. Above all, it is a small bank that is biting at the heels of the 'big four' or 'big five' banks."

And the ever-present Wikipedia states: "Challenger banks are small, recently-created retail banks in the United Kingdom that compete with the longer-established banks in the country, sometimes by specialising in areas underserved by the 'big four' banks (Barclays, HSBC, Lloyds Banking Group, and Royal Bank of Scotland Group). As well as new entrants to the market, some challenger banks were created following divestment from larger banking groups [...] or wind-down of a failed large bank."

All of these definitions have one key aspect in common: each of them describes a challenger bank as "a bank". That is to say, a challenger bank is not an e-money issuer, using Agency Banking to access banking facilities for its customers. It is a company that has received a full banking licence from its regulators. So it seems everything is quite simple: to be a challenger bank, you need a banking licence.

Yet this does not seem to be the case. If we look around, there are a lot of non-banking companies keen to be described as, or happy to be called, "challenger banks". Is this because investors like the business they are investing in to have that catchy title of "Challenger Bank"? Is it because consumers like to be able to say that they are using a "challenger bank"? Or is it just an easy term that they all understand to describe a company offering bank-like services, but not all of them. After all, it is easier than what many in the industry would call a "Bank Lite" solution.

Even then, if a challenger bank does not have to have a banking licence, what makes a business a challenger bank? Many would argue that it is the provision of bank-like services, as already stated, the most basic of which is an International Bank Account Number (or IBAN for short), a number linked to the card/e-money account (in the UK domestic market, a sort code and account number). The issue here is that if we agree to call companies like Revolut a "challenger bank", even when they are not, are we not both misleading ourselves and consumers?

We also need to recognise some key differences. First, banks take in deposits, pay interest and use the deposited money to carry out other banking activities. e-money companies cannot do this. The funds are ring-fenced and 100 per cent protected, but they cannot pay interest. It could be argued that this makes it much easier to see where the funds are from. Second, an e-money licence is very portable around Europe, allowing you to issue your cards across Europe almost instantly. As a bank, you cannot do this. You need to set up a whole infrastructure and be regulated locally. e-money is, thus, relatively quick and easy to launch across Europe.

So who is right? I would contend that we need to start an industry that tells it like it is. In other words, companies that do not have banking licences are not challenger banks. Therefore, we should stop referring to them in reports as challenger banks. The more we perpetuate this mis-description, the more we mislead the general press, and thus consumers, into thinking that companies that offer bank-like services must be challenger banks. This denigrates the great Bank Lite solutions that are live in the market today and have no wish to be labelled a challenger bank.

Are Challenger Banks Challenging?

I keep seeing headlines about Amazon opening a bank, challenger banks pulling the crown off the incumbent banks' heads, the end of old banks, the disruption of the system and the end of all traditional financial services. I do *not* believe that banks are being destroyed by technology. Challenged, yes, but not destroyed.

The traditional banks that are not adapting will end. They will most likely be acquired, perhaps even by a challenger bank in a few years, but I don't predict that many of the big banks will disappear. Part of the reason why I say this is that we have been predicting the end of the big banks since I started working in this industry, and yet the big banks have just got bigger. I recall predictions in the 1990s that Microsoft would open a bank and destroy the incumbents and that Google would do the same in the 2000s. Neither has, as many of their biggest customers are banks. Do they really want to bite the hand that feeds?

Now that many new challengers are appearing on the scene, particularly in Europe and Australia, have any of them taken significant market share away from the incumbents? Are the traditional banks losing to these challengers? Not yet. Will they? We will have to wait and see.

Either way, one thing that has impressed me is the growth of the new banks. And the fact that they are doing some things differently. For example, Monzo and Starling made headlines in June 2019 when they announced that they can block someone's account if they have a gambling addiction. It means that if a customer tries to make a bet with a bookmaker—either online or in a shop—the transaction is blocked and a 48-hour cooling-off period is applied. It is entirely up to the customer to sign up to this service.

What is interesting here is that there are now calls for these features to be available in all banks. The question here is, can the big banks respond? It is a good question, and one that I will keep coming back to. Over the next decade, if the challenger banks keep adding more and more cool features to analyse and leverage data, how will large banks respond if their systems are still batch?

These are the real battle lines. I do think banks will be challenged— both those challenging and those being challenged. The challenger banks will be challenged to get customers to switch their main accounts and become profitable before their capital dries up. The traditional banks will be challenged to keep customers' main accounts, particularly as their back-office systems are creaking and groaning into the twenty-first century.

How New Banks Differ From Traditional Banks

We know that there are a lot of new bank start-ups out there, particularly in Europe where names like N26, bunq, Fidor and Monzo stand out. Monzo, in particular, is notable. A UK-based challenger bank, it is noteworthy for a variety of reasons: it has the fastest crowdfunding of a new bank, it achieved over half a million customers before it got its licence, it aspires to be the Facebook of banking and has a devout fan base. In fact, Monzo is so loved by its users that having a pink Monzo card became a pick-up line for dates in nightclubs.

How have banks like Monzo achieved so much in such a short space of time? First, new banks like Monzo inform you. I am often frustrated with traditional banks because they only tell me what I have spent. They simply offer a transaction app of debits and credits from the past, with no information about the future. Equally, the transactions are often confusing as they only state whether it is a debit or credit. The individual transactions do not tell me about how, what, where or why that debit or credit occurred. This is one big difference with the new banks. For example, Monzo informs you. It tells you exactly where you used your card via Google Maps so that you can see the store location. It tells you the categorisation of that spend—groceries, travel, clothes or whatever— and it allows you to easily share and split bills with friends through its app. Taking this one step further, Monzo's smart systems are able to spot and report unusual transaction activity on old accounts that are inactive and enable the bank to act swiftly to protect its customers from fraud.[8] A bank should know about vulnerabilities before everyone else, if it is worth its weight in salt. Most banks are unable to detect such activity until much later because their systems are not real time.

The second reason is that these banks are intelligent about your lifestyle. They watch your spending via software algorithms and look for opportunities to help you to spend less or save more. A great example is if you use the card for specific purchases on a regular basis. Let's take a specific example: commuting. Let's say you commute to work on the underground every day. The cost is $15 a day. You could buy an annual travel card that would allow you to travel for $12 every day, saving over $700 a year, but the cost of the travel card is unaffordable at $3,000. Digital banks like Monzo are intelligent enough to recognise this habit and challenge. They will tell you that you could save $700 a year if you had the travel card, and offer you the ability to buy one. The offer is actually a $3,000 loan for the travel card but, because it is specific to your lifestyle and packaged as an informed offer, it does not appear as a loan. It appears that the bank cares. This is important as it makes these new banks very different from the way in which traditional banks appear.

This leads us to the third reason why these banks are different— they really do care about customers. I often talk about traditional banks punishing customers with hidden fees and charges. The new banks are far more transparent and alert to charges, ensuring customers are aware of any issues or potential exposures. They go further than this,

8 Monzo's Natasha Vernier wrote a blog detailing how the firm detected fraudulent activity on Ticketmaster and the steps the bank subsequently took to protect its customers. See "Protecting customers from the Ticketmaster breach: Monzo's story," Monzo (blog), 28 June 2018, https://monzo.com/blog/2018/06/28/ticketmaster-breach.

however. I was quite surprised to see that Monzo wrote an in-depth update about the link between debt and mental health on its blog. In fact, the fact that Monzo has a blog is something in itself, as many traditional banks do not have one.

On 18 May 2019, Monzo posted an item titled "Disclosing Mental Health to Your Bank". In it, the bank talked openly about how debt and mental health are closely linked. Here is an excerpt of what was said:

"Like all lenders, we have to get in touch with people who miss repayments or go beyond their lending limits and stay there for a while ... we approach this process in the most empathetic, understanding way we can. And our priority is to find out what's happened, work out how we can support you, and point you towards the right sources of advice. We'll never send you letters with angry red writing, or a barrage of calls trying to get you to pay ... if you owe Monzo money and are having mental health problems, it's useful for us to know. If you tell us, we can work out what we can do to support you – whether that's changing how often we contact you, pointing you towards other sources of support and advice, or just leaving you alone for a while."

I have to say that this honest, open and transparent approach to money, lending and customers is a breath of fresh air, and that is what new banks need to bring: a breath of fresh air. Honest, open and transparent banking will be the differentiation that new banks can bring to the market and, as they do, old banks need to take note. The traditional approach to punishing customers with fees and providing almost zero information about transactions, let alone financial lifestyles, will no longer meet the needs of an increasingly discerning marketplace.

Banks Are Losing the Data War
Furthermore, Monzo is very clever with data. Using Google Maps' APIs and other services, the bank enriches my transaction statement

so that I know when, where and what I was doing when I paid $1,000 for that bottle of champagne (I'll let you guess that one!). As a result, I have moved more and more of my activities over to Monzo. This means that my bank statement from my primary account with Lloyds, which has historically had all of this transactional data, now just reads £200 Monzo, £200 Monzo, £200 Monzo and so on, based on the auto top-up of my Monzo account prepaid card, as it was then. Today, many people use Monzo as their primary account, with its total customer base surging into millions, more than quadrupling in a year between 2017 and 2018. Amazingly, Revolut and many others, like N26, are also growing at this speed and/or scale.

One of the big things about this movement is that if the battle of the future is over customer data, then the big banks are already losing big time. A big bank with legacy architecture can only tell customers what they have spent. Their back-office systems are pure transactional ledgers of past payments. There is no intelligence, forecasting, predictive analytics or machine learning about customer behaviours because the data is all fragmented across multiple, legacy, product-focused, silo-structured systems. This is the big banks' soft underbelly and a weakness that the young start-ups are clearly focused on exploiting.

As customers find data enrichment of their transactions and lifestyles from new banks, they start to use them more and more. Soon, all of their lifestyle transactions are with an intelligent new bank and all the old bank sees is regular payments to that new financial relationship. Lloyds knows that I am using Monzo non-stop but has no idea what I am spending money on; Monzo knows everything about my financial lifestyle and tells Lloyds nothing.

Extending this idea further, what happens if there are many intelligent data aggregators out there? Apple knows all of my downloads, music and film preferences; Amazon knows all of my regular buying needs; Google knows what I am thinking before I finish entering my question; and so on.

Before long, the big banks will just see statements that read:

Amazon (auto top-up) £500.00

Monzo (auto top-up) £200.00
Apple (auto top-up) £300.00
TfL (auto top-up) £40.00

They know that I am buying things on Amazon, doing things on Monzo, downloading things on Apple and travelling on the London Underground but they have no idea what, why or where I am buying, doing, downloading or travelling.

In other words, the financial intermediaries, who never believed that they would be disintermediated, have been disintermediated by a new intermediator. A data intermediary. The lifeblood of the bank's future—customer data—has been stolen by a new middleman: the intelligent intermediator.

Of course, banks can say that this is not a problem, but if all a bank ever sees is the data from the intelligent intermediator, then they know absolutely nothing about the customer. Nothing. Nada. Zero. And that means they have zero chance of creating, leveraging or making a digital relationship with the customer.

If They Get Big Enough, We Will Buy Them

I remember years ago hearing the story about a start-up that wanted to be acquired by a big incumbent institution. The founder was struggling to succeed, and felt that an easy exit through acquisition was the best way to go. The young CEO went to the big, old incumbent company and said, "Hi there. Look at my company. We have designed the next generation of you. Why don't you buy us?"

The big incumbent asked, "How many customers have you got?" To which the CEO replied, "25,000."

The incumbent laughed a deep laugh and said, "Come back when you've got two million."

A year later, the young, struggling CEO knocked on the big, old incumbent's door again. The conversation was repeated but this time the start-up had 250,000 customers. The incumbent still laughed as it had 25 million. Again, the big, old incumbent told the up-start to come back when it had two million customers.

Another year passed, and a new CEO took over the incumbent firm. The new CEO could see that the firm was stuck in its old, traditional ways and looked around the market for a way forward. She noticed that there was a bright, young firm doing well out there, offering the next-generation service and went to meet its CEO.

"Hello," she said. "You seem to be doing well, offering the next generation of what we do. Can we buy you?"

The young CEO laughed a laugh that lasted a week. Eventually, he said, "Not by the hair on my chinny-chin-chin."

The start-up was onboarding over 250,000 customers a month, most of whom were from the big, old incumbent, and had already reached over three million customers. The start-up had grown up and no longer needed the big, old incumbent. Soon after, the big, old incumbent was acquired for a peanut and now no longer exists. In turn, the start-up has taken most of its market.

I recount this story because I get the sense that most big financial firms look at the FinTech world a bit like how the big, old incumbent looked at the start-up. They see new challenger banks, peer-to-peer lending firms, payments innovators, roboadvisors and think: They are new companies with no customers, no history and no trust. Let's just watch them. After all, if they pose any threat to our business, we can just buy them or copy them.

The trouble with this stance is that, if the young bright thing has a half decent idea, by the time they become notable for acquisition, they do not want to be acquired. In particular, if they are privately held, well-funded and can see a fast track to success, why would they be interested in selling out?

Therefore, my advice to the bank CEOs who talk about co-creation, co-operation and collaboration: make sure that if you are working with a bright young thing that could kill you, acquire it now, while you can. Don't wait until it is too late.

BOTTOM LINE

The fact that a raft of start-ups are focused on challenging traditional banks should be taken seriously and yet, often, they are not. They are dismissed for the following reasons: (a) they are too small to be competition; (b) their strategy is flawed, as they are not getting the main accounts but serving as secondary accounts; and (c) if they ever do get big enough to challenge, they will be acquired by the large incumbent banks. All three of these arguments are wrong and, in a decade, one or two of these challengers may well break through and challenge.

THE BIG TECH THREAT

A further nuance of the developing challenges that technology presents to big banks is Big Tech. Big Tech is often characterised as GAFA—Google, Amazon, Facebook and Apple—but I prefer to also include Alibaba, Tencent, Ping An and Baidu, the Chinese Big Tech giants. If you haven't read *Digital Human,* a third of the book is dedicated to the story of Ant Financial and Alipay, a company whose capabilities are unprecedented. Tech from China and the United States has now expanded substantially into financial services. Starting with payments transactions—the key focus of these massive platforms—many have now expanded by adding loans, credit cards and ancillary services to their commercial propositions. In fact, in China, Tencent and Alibaba have opened full-service retail banks called WeBank and MYBank, respectively, both of which are doing well. So, what threat do these firms present to traditional banks?

> **"**The Big Techs are trying to come downstream. We are trying to go upstream to where the interactions start. **"**
> **Derek White**, *former Global Head of Customer Solutions, BBVA*

Do You Really Think that GAFA Want to Be Banks?

Google and Amazon will probably never open a bank. The same is true for Facebook and Apple. There are two reasons for this. First, most of these U.S. giants are dependent on the financial community for their revenues and profits. Google and Facebook generate huge amounts of revenues from banks investing in online advertising. Amazon's major clients for its cloud-based Amazon Web Services (AWS) are banks. Apple's key clients in business for iPads and smartphones are financial institutions. Why would you bite the hand that feeds you?

Second, these companies would find full-service banking a difficult and unprofitable space. They are all likely to open operations that assist in their main business of commerce, and hence will offer payments and loans, but full-service banking is a thankless task with onerous compliance requirements. Such dogma of regulation would kill their innovation spirit.

Nevertheless, these firms are in active talks with the federal agencies. This comes as no surprise as Google, Apple, Amazon and a group of other internet influencers, such as PayPal, formed Financial Innovation Now (FIN) in 2016 to lobby the White House in regard to doing business online. FIN wrote a full and frank letter to then President-elect Donald Trump.

In the letter, FIN called on the President-elect to embrace technology's potential to improve financial services for American consumers and the U.S. economy. To achieve this, FIN listed seven recommendations: appoint financial regulators who value technology's potential; promote open, interoperable standards for card payment security; streamline money transmission licensing; ensure consumer access to financial accounts and data; streamline small business access to capital via the internet; help consumers and businesses manage money with real-time payments; and leverage mobile technology to increase financial inclusion.[9]

Figure 1.13 FIN's requirements for doing business online

Transferring funds between bank accounts should be as fast as sending an email...

America's entrepreneurs should have access to capital to grow their companies...

Cashing and spending a pay cheque should be easy and cheap...

Consumers should be able to make payments safely at the touch of a single button...

9   To read the full letter, go to https://financialinnovationnow.org/2016/11/30/fin-trump-transition-letter/.

In other words, the U.S. internet giants are awake to the opportunities and issues presented by banks. They are also very aware of the opportunities and methods to leverage relationships with their customers through finance.

Say, for instance, that I want to buy a $999 Apple Mac or a $1,000 camera on Amazon. Easy—simply click and it is all wrapped up in easy payments of $100 a month. I do not even know that I have been given a loan. I just used one click to buy the product, without having to shell out the money.

This is where the internet giants see their major leverage: making buying simple, easy and fun. It is not about payments, but about wrapping finance into buying and selling, which is where it should be anyway. It is very much in line with the PayPal approach to small businesses. PayPal can see what business a company is achieving through its PayPal activities, and consequently launched loans for free just a few years ago. You do pay a small set-up fee for the loan, but no interest is charged. Brilliant. No wonder PayPal lent more than $10 billion in loans of up to $125,000 each to more than 225,000 small businesses around the globe, according to figures reported in May 2019,[10] up from just $3 billion to 115,000 small businesses as reported in August 2017.[11]

What does this mean for banks? It means that the majority of bank products, particularly payments and credit, will be eaten by the internet. I do not see the internet giants becoming banks. I just see them eating into the profitable bank products. They will be specifically looking at product adjacencies and complementary areas, such as the PayPal Working Capital example above.

For a bank, that means that they are left with the expensive products, namely, deposit accounts, without the cross-selling opportunities that are used to subsidise those accounts: credit cards, loans and charges. It means that banks will have to end free banking services and start increasing fees for the privilege of having an account. It will mean that some people will find those fees unaffordable and will

---

10 Donna Fuscaldo, "PayPal's Latest Milestone: $10 Billion In Small Business Loans," *Forbes*, 29 May 2019, https://www.forbes.com/sites/donnafuscaldo/2019/05/29/paypals-latest-milestone-10-billion-in-small-business-loans/.

11 Madeleine Johnson, "PayPal Scoops Up Swift Financial in Loan Expansion Deal," Nasdaq, 10 August 2017, https://www.nasdaq.com/article/paypal-scoops-up-swift-financial-in-loan-expansion-deal-cm830415.

become unbanked. For the unbanked and underbanked, the internet giants will offer easier services to provide them with finance and payments support, and eventually FinTech firms and internet giants will pick them up with prepaid mobile wallets and easy microloans and microsavings accounts.

Gradually, this will all impact a bank's bottom line, and banks will retreat into providing the large and complex infrastructures of global finance—the smart pipes—and their large and complex corporate client services, asset management services, wealth management and investment banking. In the long term, the internet giants and their FinTech brothers will become the consumer champions, and retail banking will no longer look like it does today. Then the internet giants and their FinTech brothers will start to upscale, as any innovator would do.

In all of the above, what I am describing is being able to do banking without being a bank. That is why I do not see the internet giants becoming banks. I expect them instead to reimagine banking and finance for the internet age, and deliver it as a frictionless digital service that does not feel anything like banking as it is today.

The Amazonisation of Banking?

Name the company that strikes fear into the heart of every business? In the 1980s, it was IBM. Nobody ever got fired for buying IBM even though It's a Bloody Mess. In the 1990s, it was Microsoft. Sure, Most Intelligent Creatures Realise Our Software Only Fools Teenagers but, yes, it was taking over the planet. In the 2000s, it was Google. Everyone searching for something and finding a platform that connected them through the Global Object-Oriented Group Language of Earth. In the last decades, it has been Amazon. Amazon, the platform with tentacles everywhere that is just Amazing Everyone, or Amazon for short.

Amazon comes up almost once a month as the beast that will break into banking, and is often cited as a great example of adjacency. Adjacency is moving into other industries adjacent to your core that help your core grow. Amazon's core business is commerce, but adjacent to commerce is finance, and Amazon will move into any space that grows online business—apart from full-service banking. As already mentioned, this is because doing so would do little to improve its core business model. Payments and lending do for sure, as that helps merchants, but the over-regulated deposit account marketplace? I don't think so.

Nevertheless, when you put Amazon in the headline with banking, it gets headlines. According to David Birch, a digital identity expert, the Amazonisation of banking is very different from Amazon being a bank. The backdrop to his thinking started with a story in the *Wall Street Journal* about Amazon being in talks with major banks, including JPMorgan Chase,[12] about building a "checking-account-like" product. This set off a storm of speculation about Amazon moving into the banking business, despite the obvious fact that you do not need to be a bank to offer such a product.

One of the main reasons why speculation grew was that consumers seemed to warm to the idea. Almost half of U.S. consumers surveyed said that they were "open" to the idea of Amazon as the provider of their primary bank account,[13] which may seem surprising but is a reflection of consumer experiences of Amazon in practice. For instance, I ordered some bottles of sparkling water and some bottles of Coke from Amazon one day, and they were delivered the following morning. From the time I hit the "buy" button on Amazon, I did not give the transaction a moment's thought. It just works. And given the reach of Amazon, and the amount of money spent on it, these positive experiences could easily translate to adjacencies.

"Bain and Co estimates that a banking service from Amazon could swell to more than 70 million US customer accounts within five years, equalling the size of the country's third largest bank, Wells Fargo."[14]

12 Laura Glazer, Liz Hoffman and Laura Stevens, "Next Up for Amazon: Checking Accounts," *Wall Street Journal*, 5 March 2018, https://www.wsj.com/articles/are-you-ready-for-an-amazon-branded-checking-account-1520251200/.
13 Jim Marcus, "Will Amazon Offer The Best Digital Checking Account Ever?," Financial Brand, 6 March 2018, https://thefinancialbrand.com/71037/amazon-checking-banking-alexa-chase/.
14 "Bank of Amazon could woo 70 million US customers within five years," Finextra, 9 March 2018, https://www.finextra.com/newsarticle/31789/bank-of-amazon-could-woo-70-million-us-customers-within-five-years.

However, like me, Birch does not believe that Amazon will become a bank because Amazon does not want to be a bank in the way that JPMorgan Chase is a bank. Amazon just does not make money the way that banks make money. Look at its existing partnership with Bank of America to lend money to merchants. Amazon does not care about making some small margin from interest payments, it cares about helping merchants to increase Amazon's overall sales.

If Amazon is going to distribute financial services but not be a bank, then what will it be? It is time for another review of terminology. Let's standardise this way: a "neo-bank" is something that looks like a bank but isn't; a "near-bank" is something that performs a function traditionally associated with banks but is not a bank and does not look like a bank. In this framework, Amazon would be a neo-bank.

The neo-bank is not a new idea, by the way. In 1997, Birch wrote about the potential for new technology to assemble a banking service depending on the customers' needs, explaining how the new infrastructure would allow customers to build their own financial services "with the underlying best-of-breed products originating from a wide range of suppliers".[15] The manufacturers of financial services—banks—would "retreat to a small range of products that build on core competencies, but supplied to a global market". Amazon is precisely the kind of organisation that can take products such as unsecured personal credit to that market, which is why it keeps the people who run banks awake at night. Not the challenger banks or FinTech start-ups.

"Wall Street veterans are less worried these days that smaller startups will steal their business, but they say they're wary that big tech could invade their turf. Amazon was mentioned more than 160 times in the past year during financial industry conference calls, according to data compiled by Sentieo for firms listed in the US. That's nearly triple the typical rate in 2016, on a rolling 12-month basis."[16]

15 David Birch and Michael Young, "Financial services and the Internet—what does cyberspace mean for the financial services industry?," Internet Research, Vol. 7 No. 2, pp. 120–128. https://doi.org/10.1108/10662249710165262.
16 "Bank executives are talking about the threat of Amazon more than ever before, out of admiration and fear," Quartz, 30 April 2018, https://qz.com/1265471/bank-executives-are-talking-about-the-threat-of-amazon-more-than-ever-before/.

In Europe, there is nothing that banks can do to stop Amazon from becoming a neo-bank. PSD2 means that bank customers will give Amazon permission to access their bank accounts, at which point Amazon will become the interface between the customer and financial services. There is no reason to doubt Amazon's potential for success if it goes down this route.

If Amazon were to provide something that looked like a deposit account, but was actually a prepaid account of some kind, would people use it? Obviously yes, especially if Amazon were to offer the usual array of discounts or cashback to go with it. It has plenty of margin to trade for data. Look at its credit card that gives customers 5 per cent back at Whole Foods, for example. If Starbucks can sit on a float of over $1 billion, just from people buying coffee, imagine the float that Amazon could sit on from people buying everything. If people were to begin to hold money in the Amazon float that gave them a discount of 2 per cent on stuff, instead of holding money in a bank account that was giving them an interest rate of 0.2 per cent, funds would begin to drain away from demand deposit accounts fairly quickly.

Now imagine how quickly that might happen in Europe, where Amazon can use PSD2 to get direct access to customer bank accounts in order to instruct credit transfers to load to Amazon accounts automatically. This would be something like its US Amazon Cash service, but using modern electronic instant payments transistors and laser beams instead of Federal Reserve bills. It could be seriously big business.

Look East for Innovation

However, when we in the West talk about GAFA, we miss a trick. For example, I often talk about faster horses and how banks think digital is doing banking cheaper and faster. It is all about efficiency and effectiveness. So, I was asked the other day, "Where is the car?" After all, it is easy to call out banks for doing banking as usual but, if I cannot show them a car, what is the point?

It is a good question and, yes, I can see some cars out there. These are the ones that are carving out the next generation of retail banking in

Africa and Asia, and it is based on financial inclusion. In fact, I tweeted not long ago that today's financial inclusion is tomorrow's finance, and I truly believe this. After all, if Asia and Africa create radical new models of moving money in real time at almost no cost, why wouldn't we all use those innovations?

MNOs in Africa initially focused on payments and then gradually extended into microloans, microsavings and microinsurance. Alibaba and Alipay started with making payments and then gradually moved into investments and loans. Payments is just the start. The UN is now looking at how to manage digital identities at low cost through mobile. If we all have KYC digitally at almost no cost, why wouldn't we all use that system for onboarding?

I have written about this a lot. In fact, my last book *Digital Human* focuses almost exclusively on this subject, and includes an in-depth case study on Ant Financial and Alipay's approach to this. However, there are two examples of where the faster horse meets the car that really stand out to me. The first was in Rwanda when M-Pesa was on a panel with three banks and I asked, "So how do banks compete with M-Pesa?" The answer was telling when the M-Pesa guy replied, "They don't. They just try to copy what we do whilst we focus upon the customer."

There are those who make things happen; there are those who watch what is happening; and there are those who just wonder what happened.

The second example occurred at a conference in 2017. During the conference, Risto Virkkala, the CEO of ePassi, talked about its partnership with Alipay and put up the following slide:

Figure 1.14 How the West sees mobile wallets

West

Strong credit card penetration

Established payment players

Credit card centric approach

Traditional card readers and payment network in key role

Scattered mobile payment solutions

Virkkala said that he was astounded how banks and Western firms focused so much on cards and payments, as illustrated by Apple Pay. Apple's wallet has taken the outdated way in which we used to pay and put it in an app. It is so innovative that Apple even put a picture of the card in the app, so we can see that we are paying by card in an app. It is ridiculous. In fact, displaying the card shows that Apple, along with Western banks, focuses on replicating the old horse into the digital age as a faster horse. It is all card and payment focused, and forgets the customer.

That is why the Chinese internet giant Alibaba, with Alipay, is serving customers who have never had cards or cheques, and focuses on things in a completely different way, beginning with the customer journey. The customer journey and the customer experience is the singular beacon that shines through its app, and making payments is a by-product of the app.

The banking world and the Western world need to turn their thinking upside-down and stop trying to replicate the last-century world into this century's world. As I now often say, we all talk about GAFA and look to the West but we are all looking the wrong way as the cars are coming from the East.

Figure 1.15 How the East sees mobile wallets

East

Small credit card penetration

Skipped directly from cash to mobile payments

Opportunity for new players to build a new ecosystem

Integrated end user experience whether in homeland or abroad

China's FinTech Scene Is a Phenomenon

In particular, if you want to see the future of finance, look to China. Specifically look to Tencent with WeChat and WeChat Pay, Alibaba with Ant Financial and Alipay, and Ping An with Lufax and OneConnect. Explicitly, the United States does tech but China does it differently, because it can. Here are a few highlights about FinTech China.

First, China has transformed rapidly to mobile financial services. In 2012, the country had near zero mobile payments being made. This rose to $41 trillion being paid through mobile phones by the end of 2018, with 54 per cent of that coming through Alipay and 38 per cent via WeChat Pay, the two major payments systems of China.

Second, China's FinTech prowess is rising fast. According to Accenture,[17] China accounted for 46 per cent of all FinTech investments in 2018. More than half of China's FinTech investment came from the record funding round of Ant Financial, which manages the world's largest money market fund.

Third, not only was China the biggest investment area in FinTech in 2018, but it is also home to many of the FinTech unicorns that dominate the global lists. These unicorns include firms that most in the West will never have heard of, namely, Ant Financial, JD Finance, Du Xiaoman Financial (Baidu) and Lufax (Ping An). These four alone are worth almost $200 billion. However, this is not something new. The chart on the following page from Visual Capitalist[18] dates to September 2016 and shows that China's burgeoning FinTech economy was already dominating the global markets back then.

17 "Global FinTech Investments Surged in 2018 with Investments in China Taking the Lead," Accenture, 25 February 2019, https://newsroom.accenture.com/news/global-FinTech-investments-surged-in-2018-with-investments-in-china-taking-the-lead-accenture-analysis-finds-uk-gains-sharply-despite-brexit-doubts.htm.

18 Jeff Desjardins, "27 FinTech Unicorns, and Where They Were Born," Visual Capitalist, 7 September 2016, https://www.visualcapitalist.com/27-FinTech-unicorns-where-born/.

Figure 1.16 The FinTech unicorns

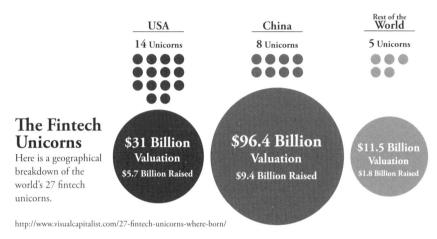

http://www.visualcapitalist.com/27-fintech-unicorns-where-born/

Fourth, the largest of the Chinese unicorns is Ant Financial, which was valued at $150 billion in 2018. That would make it the tenth-largest financial institution in the world by value. The firm began life in 2003 as part of Alibaba just to enable payments to be processed on its platform. Today, it offers much, much more. If you want to find out more about Ant Financial, I suggest you read *Digital Human.*

Fifth, Ant Financial is not just a Chinese FinTech start-up, but also a technology firm that offers a marketplace of financial services worldwide from apps to APIs to analytics. In fact, Ant Financial thinks globally and is moving Alipay into the hands of Chinese consumers across the world and, soon, all consumers. In addition, it is not just a payment app or a mobile wallet, it is a mobile world of everything from travel to investments to socialising to shopping. That is why, according to statistics from Alipay, it is now paying for more transactions than cash in China.

Sixth, there is a very different mentality in China compared to the West, due to the fact that government and regulation is very different. For example, allowing a peer-to-peer lending platform that demands young, female borrowers send naked selfies when opening an account. Why? Because if the borrower should default on their loan, their naked selfie will be released online. This is something that is unlikely to develop in Europe or the United States.

Figure 1.17 The Far East Credit Company case file

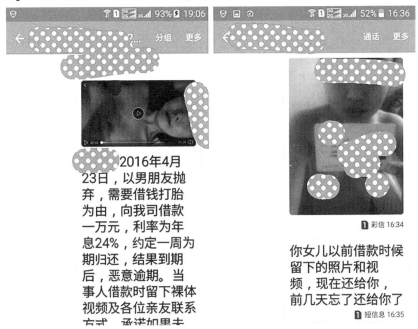

Finally, because China had no financial infrastructure in place twenty years ago, much of what is there today has come from nowhere. It has all been implemented just in the last twenty years. That is possibly why the country has the largest FinTech numbers of anywhere in the world and, equally, the most innovation.

In particular, Alibaba with Ant Financial and Alipay is the company to watch, as it is global, visionary and fast. A good example of its vision is illustrated by Singles' Day on 11 November. For the Chinese, Singles' Day is the day when singletons treat themselves to gifts and presents that they buy online. It is a fake day, like Valentine's Day or Bring Your Dog to Work Day, but it works. Invented by Alibaba, it has created an explosion of commerce in just one day.

I guess Alibaba got the idea from Amazon's Black Friday, but Amazon's Black Friday is more like a walk in the park compared to Alibaba's Singles' Day. Here are the numbers for Singles' Day in 2018:

- The Alibaba Group generated RMB 213.5 billion ($30.8 billion) of gross merchandise volume (GMV), or sales if you prefer.
- The total GMV was 27 per cent higher than in 2017.
- RMB 6.9 billion ($1 billion) of total GMV was settled through Alipay in the first 1 minute and 25 seconds.
- RMB 69.3 billion ($10 billion) of total GMV was settled through Alipay in 1 hour and 48 seconds.
- The company processed 256,000 transactions per second. Compare this to Visa, which averages 2,000 transactions per second worldwide, and you get an idea of the scale of operations.
- Over 180,000 brands participated in the day, with 237 brands exceeding RMB 100 million ($15 million) in sales volume, including leading international brands Apple, Dyson, Kindle, Estée Lauder, L'Oréal, Nestlé, Gap, Nike and Adidas.
- Cainiao handles logistics for Alibaba and delivered the first 100 million parcels in just 2.6 days, nearly five hours faster than in 2017. By comparison, the company took nine days to deliver the first 100 million parcels in 2013.
- About 97 per cent of orders were delivered in under four days.

Now, I know it is not fair but let's go back to the United States of Amazon. Black Friday 2018 generated online sales of just over $5 billion.

Even more telling is that Ant Financial accounted for 35 per cent of global venture capital investment in FinTech firms in 2018, according to CB Insights.[19] The Chinese company started in 2003 as Alipay, a payment service for Alibaba. It became the largest mobile payments firm in 2013, growing far faster than US-based PayPal in the same year, and now offers a full range of financial services including investing, credit, banking and insurance.

19 "FinTech Trends To Watch In 2019," CB Insights 2019, https://www.cbinsights.com/research/report/FinTech-trends-2019/.

China's scale is unbelievable and, if you are looking for the future of finance, the threat of the Big Tech giants and the way in which the future FinTech battles will play out, then the East is far more of an innovation engine than the West. Specifically, the Big Tech China giants of Alibaba, Tencent, Baidu and Ping An are developing full financial offerings that cover everything from payments to banking to savings to investments to loans. They are the companies you really need to watch, so just make sure you are looking the right way.

BOTTOM LINE

The Big Tech companies are moving into many areas of financial services as adjacencies to their core business of commerce and trade. Amazon is specifically seen as a threat as it has merchants with access to loans at almost no fee, payments easily enabled and gradually moving into more areas of savings and investments. However, most believe that Amazon and other U.S.-based internet giants—Google, Facebook and Apple— are far less of a concern when it comes to moving into banking than the big China-based internet giants, namely Tencent, Alibaba, Baidu and Ping An.

CHANGING THE REGULATORY STRUCTURE: OPEN BANKING

Even though I have given plausible reasons as to why banks need to digitally transform and stated where we currently are in the process, some of you may still not be convinced that it really is necessary. However, a convincer has appeared in recent years that even the digital deniers need to deal with: the regulator is telling you to do it.

Many governments around the world have seen the rapid rise of FinTech and the difference it is making, and are determined that they become a FinTech centre for their region. In particular, many countries that have active global financial centres have determined that they also need to be active global FinTech centres. That decision is a critical one, leading to London, New York, San Francisco, Singapore, Hong Kong and others to invest in their brand as a leading centre for financial innovation.

Recognising the significance of this, Copenhagen Fintech Innovation and Research (CFIR) commissioned Oxford Research and Rainmaking Innovation to identity the critical factors that allow a regulator to create a vibrant FinTech centre. The resulting research report concluded that six key factors are needed in order for a locale to become a FinTech hub:[20]

1. **A vibrant FinTech start-up community:** At grass-roots level, there needs to be a lot of events and activities, which can help the establishment and growth of start-ups.

2. **Active established players:** It is crucial that large established FinTech players invest in innovation and in leveraging the FinTech potential. Start-ups cannot build a world-class FinTech hub alone.

3. **Access to risk capital:** The access to risk capital is critical to fund the establishment and growth of innovative companies.

4. **Political support and a "friendly" regulator:** Central public bodies

---

20 "Study and recommendations for making Copenhagen a Nordic FinTech hub: Full report," Oxford Research and Rainmaking Innovation, September to December 2015, https://oxfordresearch.dk/publications/copenhagen-fintech-hub/.

need to support the FinTech sector and announce their support publicly, and regulators need to change from a reactive to a more proactive and collaborative mindset.

5. **Access to talent:** FinTech is a knowledge-intensive sector that is highly dependent on access to highly skilled specialised labour.

6. **Brand as a FinTech hub:** To attract international talent, investors, businesses and so on, a strong brand needs to be built around the FinTech hub.

The big financial centres of old have made critical investment and developed management programmes within their centres to ensure that these six factors are met, with many others such as Berlin, Dubai, Tel Aviv, Mexico City and São Paulo following their lead.

In addition, one of the big changes in governance and regulation of financial markets in the past decade is the switch from regulators and regulations discouraging competition and innovation to the regulator actively encouraging new entrants. There are various methods that the regulators have used to achieve this, from light regulation for start-ups that offer lower capital barriers and faster access to market, to actively creating their own innovation programmes and dedicating regulatory staff to these areas.

The UK's Financial Conduct Authority (FCA) led this change when it created the regulatory sandbox, a fast-track project to get new entrants to market, often working with banks as supporting partners. This was copied by regulators of several other countries, and it is now notable that most leading economies have some form of regulatory innovation programme in a sandbox. The reason it is called a "sandbox" is that it is separated from the main business as a play area for trial and error. Children play in sandboxes, and the start-ups are fledglings that need to experiment before they can grow up into the main business streams.

Consultative Group to Assist the Poor (CGAP) defines the "regulatory sandbox" as "a framework set up by a financial sector regulator to allow small-scale, *live testing of innovations* by private firms in a *controlled environment* (operating under a special exemption, allowance, or other limited, time-bound exception) under the regulator's supervision."[21]

However, in talking with many market players, start-ups and banks, there is a danger that the regulatory sandboxes may have become regulatory sandcastles. It may be possible to get into the sandbox but getting out of it and into the mainstream is just not happening. It is good in theory but, in practice, when the bright young start-ups jump into the sandbox, the regulator does a pretty good job of building a wall around them so that they never get out. That is why I often use the metaphor "from sandbox to sandcastle".

In fact, when I was told that the head of the regulatory sandbox in one country had just been elevated to be its new Start-up Commissioner, someone in the meeting room muttered, "More like the Shut-down Commissioner." This was followed by general laughter around the table. However, it is no laughing matter. If regulators stifle innovation, then you end up with stagnant markets where the big get bigger (and lazier and more complacent) and the small get smaller (and angrier and more frustrated). Regulators do need to exercise governance of financial markets, and should not be open to all and license everyone, but the enthusiasm for regulatory innovation can be quashed if the regulator does not get it right.

Again, it comes down to leadership and commitment. In fact, the criticism of banks regarding leadership and commitment to converting to digital apply equally to regulators who want to encourage competition and digitalisation. Most countries are running regulatory innovation programmes in their efforts to become a FinTech hub. However, many ingredients are needed to achieve this goal: a young talent pool, banks willing to partner, investment and capital availability, regulatory support and more. However, the most important ingredient has to be government commitment.

Governments control the regulators who control the markets. If the government is not wholly committed to financial innovation and technology start-ups, then nothing moves. It just stagnates. And

---

21   Ivo Jenik and Kate Lauer, "Regulatory Sandboxes and Financial Inclusion," CGAP, October 2017, https://www.cgap.org/sites/default/files/Working-Paper-Regulatory-Sandboxes-Oct-2017.pdf.

commitment is more than creating an innovation programme and a regular sandbox. It is about getting out there, getting your hands dirty and having a start-up system that supports and encourages, rather than constrains and discourages. You have to go from sandbox to mainstream, not sandbox to sandcastle, if a regulatory programme is going to be truly successful.

Open Banking Has Arrived, whether You Like It or Not

Another critical development from the government and regulatory position is the drive towards Open Banking. In many markets around the world, regulators are encouraging innovation, start-ups and more competition by telling banks that they have to open up their resources and, specifically their data, to any company requesting such access if the customer gives permission. This is a huge change requirement for banks, which have traditionally been closed shops.

I actually started writing about the idea of Open Banking in the 2000s. Back then, I presented the concept of Banking-as-a-Service (BaaS), with the idea that anyone could find a wide range of plug-and-play software in a cloud-based marketplace, and build their own bank by bringing these pieces of code together into an easy-to-use banking service. Over a decade later, that vision of BaaS has come true, as more and more FinTech firms offer plug-and-play code in the cloud to make banking simpler and easier. What I did not anticipate is that the regulator would push this service, making it mandatory. That is what Open Banking has become.

Open Banking began as a UK interpretation of the European requirements to open up payments data to third parties under PSD2. However, the United Kingdom took it one step further by saying that banks must open their data for any information the customer wishes to share with a third party, as long as they give express permission. This interpretation of the law, named Open Banking, is no longer just a UK thing, it has gone global. Australia introduced Open Banking rules that force the banks to share data with trusted third-party providers (TPPs) in 2019, Mexico has introduced a FinTech Law while South Korea and Singapore have enforced rules around financial data sharing between banks and third parties. Even several banks in the United States are innovating around open financial structures, although there is no law forcing them to do this, yet.

What intrigues me about the market movements is that some large financial players are taking a lead in this space, such as Citibank's and Deutsche Bank's open API markets, whilst some are resisting the change. I have heard several reports in the United Kingdom that the large banks have made data sharing incredibly difficult for the customer, by making the permission process onerous and time-consuming. Equally, the implementation of European rules under PSD2 has seen several FinTech firms cry foul, as each bank has created its own interpretation, and therefore API interface, of the law. The result is that any third party wanting to interface with the EU banks has to write integration code for each bank due to the non-standard implementations across the markets.

However, these are purely teething troubles as the markets move towards full Open Banking platforms. Interestingly, those that are embracing the change are seeing positive results. For example, the United Kingdom began its implementation of Open Banking in January 2018 and, although it has been slow progress, there has been progress.

For example, Dutch bank ING offers a digital banking app in the United Kingdom called Yolt, which has been one of the first to fully implement third-party access integration. The service links to all Lloyds Banking Group, RBS and HSBC brands, as well as challenger banks Monzo and Starling. Equally, HSBC launched the Connected Money app in May 2018, allowing customers to see all of their current, savings and mortgage accounts in one space, regardless of the provider. Using Open Banking, the app links to other banks, such as Santander, Lloyds and Barclays, so that customers can see how much money they have available until their next payday. The feature is called "balance after bills", and shows how much is available in their current account until payday, once regular bills have been paid. Other information-rich services are being developed around these themes too, making the bank more of a challenger than some of the challenger banks. Speaking of which, challenger banks, like Metro, Starling, Tandem and Monzo, are all developing around API marketplaces and information services in order to differentiate their offers.

This is why the momentum is building. The Open Banking Implementation Entity (OBIE) shared figures that show there are 49 million data sharing requests monthly, as of September 2019, doubling in just seven months and up from just 720,000 requests in May 2018. There are now 180 regulated providers of APIs, up from 67 in July 2018. These are made up of 116 TPPs (44 the year before) and 64 deposit account providers (DAPs) (up from 23) in the United Kingdom.

Where this leads to downstream is a rich market of start-ups, service providers, banks and non-banks, enriching the services and knowledge about their customers in real time, all of the time. This will benefit customers, by telling them more about their digital financial lifestyles, and provide better, more personalised service. Just one word of caution, though. If banks were to ask customers if they wanted to share their bank account data with TPPs, they would probably say no. In survey after survey, I see this question being asked and, typically, 80 per cent of respondents have a negative view about data sharing, particularly when it comes to their money. What these surveys miss is the benefit that customers would get in return. If the surveys instead asked if customers would want banks to analyse their data to help them save more, spend less and generally be smarter with their money, then most respondents would say yes.

All in all, the world is moving to an Open Banking structure where banks share data with trusted third parties, if the customer gives permission, and this march for change is nigh on unstoppable today. Bearing in mind that most countries are starting to implement versions of these rules as regulations, if banks are not engaging in creating their own open structures today, then they had better start soon. After all, I can pretty much guarantee that an Open Banking regulation is coming this way fairly soon.

The True Meaning of Open Banking

More and more is being written about invisible banking, embedded banking, contextual banking, frictionless banking and suchlike, but many people have got this all wrong. What they really mean is invisible payments, embedded payments, contextual payments and frictionless payments. They need to realise that banking is different from payments.

Equally, many throw this into a big heap of homogeneous mess that they call banking, when banking is heaped with complexity and granularity that move much further and deeper than just a payment or a deposit account. There is asset and fund management, market makers and brokers, investment banking and wealth management, trading, investing, saving, credit, mortgages, insurance, assurance and, oh yes, payments and retail banking.

This is an issue in general as most commentators lump the whole lot together, as though it is one space, and call it disrupted and unbundled. I disagree with that. I agree with one thing only, which is that the world of digital—which combines mobile, social, internet, open platforms, marketplaces, plug-and-play code and more—has enabled thousands of specialist firms to remove friction from bank processes.

This is best exemplified by a firm like Stripe, which launched seven lines of code in 2011 that gained a valuation of over $20 billion in September 2018. Stripe is worth this because it is focused on one key area—merchant checkout online—and made it so simple that dropping its code into an app is a no-brainer. That is why Airbnb, Lyft, Grab, Quora, Square, Kickstarter and more use Stripe for their in-app checkout processing. However, that is just for payments, and too often people mistake frictionless payments for frictionless banking. Frictionless banking is built up of thousands of processes, of which merchant checkout online is just one.

Equally, what interests me is the thousands of start-ups, often started up by former bankers involved in these processes, that are automating all of the other processes. When I look at today's FinTech start-ups, some of which are quite mature, there are thousands of start-ups doing one thing brilliantly across the whole gamut of financial services. In fact, Philippe Gelis, co-founder and CEO of foreign exchange firm Kantox, states that:

"All services (investing, trading & brokerage; wealth management; loans, credit & mortgages; crowdfunding (equity and social); insurance; cryptocurrencies; payments; remittances & FX ...) will be provided by third parties through API, including old-school banks, financial institutions and FinTech companies."

Figure 1.18 Applying Open Banking

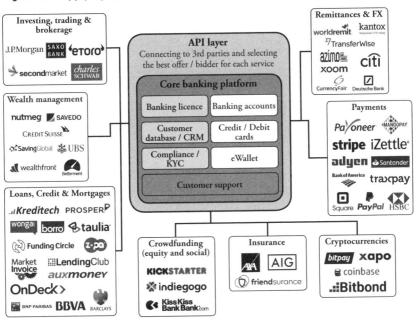

That is what Open Banking is all about, and it is gradually becoming a reality.

Large, traditional banks are finding it difficult to adapt to this forced environment, but must wake up and find the thousands of firms removing friction from bank processes and bring them to their corporate, retail and institutional clients. Customers should not have to go and find the thousands of APIs in the Open Banking marketplace that might be relevant to them or that might work for them. The bank should do this for the customer. Customers should not have to go and perform due diligence on thousands of start-up firms that are light on regulation and have little history, restricted capital and no trust. Banks should do this for them. Customers should not have to work out how to take thousands of APIs and integrate them into their ecosystems. Banks should do this for them.

In other words, banks need to be curators of open marketplaces that remove friction from bank processes, rather than developers of end-to-end services for customers aimed at controlling and retaining their relationship to the exclusion of all others. This is the only path for the future. The future is going to be bleak for the banks that think they have to control the supply chain and value chain of finance.

The Bank's View of Open Banking

A further point was raised by one bank when looking at the opportunities found in Open Banking. This bank said that it had been mapping financial moments—getting married, buying a house, having a baby, crashing the car, etc.—and had started to reimagine the whole customer experience for those moments using APIs.

A good example was crashing the car. Today, you would call your insurer (if you could remember who they were and what their number was), maybe the police (if your phone had enough juice) and probably your nearest and dearest. But what if the car could tell the network what had happened? What if it could tell the tow truck to come, inform the insurer automatically, order you a taxi (or ambulance if needed) and arrange for a replacement vehicle to be delivered to your home that evening?

Wow! However, it is not really a wow. It is simply being clever with today's technologies. Recognising that cars are on the internet and can self-diagnose. Through the same process, and given the fact that they are on the net, cars could add in all of these others features. In fact, your car will not only self-drive soon, but will also arrange its own sick days to get parts sorted out and tell insurers what is going on direct. I loved the sound of all of this and the fact that this bank—a Nordic one—had started to think out of the box thanks to PSD2 and open APIs.

Then we come back to reality. In a discussion about small business needs, it was pointed out that most banks never proactively call or give advice on how to run a business smarter using Xero or something similar. In fact, most banks give the impression that they could not care less whether the customer is with them or not, as long as the customer pays regular fees and charges. Does the customer care? Not really, as they think that all banks are the same, which is why most banks suffer from a severe lack of digital imagination.

A good example here is that I bring up my banking app three to four times a day. The bank probably thinks it is because I love it so much. I don't love my bank at all. I just keep checking the app regularly because, as a small business, I want to see if my customers have paid yet. Then it struck me. Why is there no alert setting in the app to send me a push notification as soon as any money is added to my account? The fact that the bank does not do this is because it has simply taken the old branch banking system and put it into an app, rather than thinking what it could do with the app.

It is one of the reasons why I really like new banks like Metro Bank, which are at least trying to do things better. Case in point: you cannot find your card. Is it lost or stolen? In this instance, you think that you have more than likely lost it. Most banks expect you to call them to tell them and they then reissue you with a new card. With Metro, you just bring up its app and set the card to "off". This means that the card cannot be used until you find it and set it back to "on" again or request a new card. This is better for the customer—no writing off a bank card that is actually under the sofa—and it saves the bank money. This is where Open Banking should really start, as it is all about customer focus first and foremost.

Converting the Spaghetti Bank into the Lego Bank

Assuming that we start with customer focus, there are many companies that have launched in the last few years focused on delivering Open Banking and BaaS capabilities, such as Bud, ClearBank, Leveris, 11:FS Foundry, Saxo Bank, Solaris and more. When talking with these FinTech start-ups, it soon becomes clear that anyone could launch a full-scale bank without a banking licence. I could launch a bank with a few APIs from Bud and Solaris. I could launch a full-scale investment and retail bank if I added in a few more APIs from Saxo Bank. This is something else.

In fact, if you combine the capabilities of the API marketplaces that are developing, you could develop the Lego Bank. The Lego Bank owns no pieces but assembles the pieces into different forms and shapes. The constituent pieces are all the same. It is how you put the pieces together that makes the difference. Like Lego, you can build the pieces into a castle, house or Winnebago. It is all about how you click the pieces together.

In the same way, I can take a range of APIs and build a universal bank, a commercial bank or a retail bank. It is all about how I put the pieces together from the marketplace of apps, APIs and analytics out there. This is what Open Banking is all about: do what you do best, and link to the rest. This is what typifies the new world of BaaS. A bank can be launched in a day, updated three times a day and renewed once a month based on a microservices architecture and using open-sourced services from the marketplace of bank technologies.

This is radically different thinking from the incumbent institution. An incumbent institution thinks that it has to build and control everything. The new digital marketplace institutions build almost nothing. The new institutions curate and integrate everything fast and for free. This way, they are hugely nimble, agile and free. The incumbent institutions try to manage everything, making sure that it is compliant and inspected not just once, twice or three times but all the time. This way, they are very slow, structured and expensive.

Could an incumbent institution become a Lego Bank? It is unlikely. This is because most incumbent institutions are Spaghetti Banks. Spaghetti Banks have systems built over the past fifty years that have lots of connections, interactions, dependencies and overlap. Some are there because they were built in the 1970s and are now hard to replace as they form the backbone of everything subsequently built on top. It is a core system and part of the fabric infrastructure of the bank. Changing it will be hard.

Some systems are there because the bank has grown through mergers and acquisitions over the past fifty years, and each time the bank acquired another, it did not replace the other bank's systems. The acquiring bank just merged the systems across into its own separate environment.

And some systems are there because the bank had, and has, product structures and lines of business that demanded their own operations, which inevitably became separate systems. We call them silos. Product-based silos, merger systems that were not converted and legacy core structures that form organisational infrastructure backbones are all the bread and butter of an incumbent Spaghetti Bank's operations. How can you take a Spaghetti Bank and make it into a Lego Bank?

The answer is to use BaaS to change. BaaS offers an incumbent bank a way to take any piece of the company and move it to a new API platform, without having to cut out the heart of the bank. The bank could take a payment process and open source it while maintaining its old payment systems. The bank could take a credit rating process and open source it while keeping its old credit systems up and running. When—and only when—the bank is happy with the new world can the bank switch off the old world.

This is how an incumbent gets to be a Lego Bank. A Lego Bank runs alongside the Spaghetti Bank. The Spaghetti Bank keeps its proprietary control structures operating for as long as it wants but, eventually, finds itself running in a new open-sourced structure based on hundreds of Lego pieces in the form of new APIs, apps and analytics.

The regulator is ordering the Spaghetti Bank to become a Lego Bank. The issue is that the Spaghetti Bank often lacks the vision to become a Lego Bank through lack of understanding, vision and leadership.

The Innovator's View of Open Banking

The general consensus of a lot of firms that consult, provide systems or are deploying new businesses in FinTech is that Open Banking is, first and foremost, about customer focus. For example, the customer onboarding experience is horrendous today and involves forcing customers into the branch with all of their identification documents. It would be amazing if we could take the pain out of the process by simplifying it. The question then comes down to this, how do you commercialise this? After all, if onboarding could be done in the same way that cheques can be scanned via a smartphone camera, capturing your face, passport and address, then that would become a commoditised service that no one would want to pay for but everyone would use.

Equally, how do you get customers to switch from banks to FinTech firms when they are happy with the service that they have? The biggest switch movement in the United Kingdom occurred when Santander announced its 123 account, which paid higher interest rates than any other UK bank account. This offering did get people to switch, but at a very high cost to the bank. The bank spent £1 billion a year to cover the costs, which is why Santander dropped it after a few years.

People rarely switch bank accounts, and this is the real challenge for the challenger banks. These challengers claim that the process starts with gaining customers' trust through usage. So, the challenger starts as a secondary account and then it uses the Open Banking API economy to give information enrichment. That is what Monzo, one of the leading UK digital banks, does. Over time, people find that they are always using the challenger's app and come to realise that they do not need their old bank. It is at this point that they switch banks. That is the idea but it begs the question, how many challengers will really challenge the big banks versus being acquired by them? This is what has happened with

Simple and Atom, both of which are now owned significantly by BBVA. Many start-ups want the same endgame: to be acquired by a big player at a high cost.

Bringing that back to Open Banking, there is a lot of fear, uncertainty and doubt (FUD) about the whole issue. This was evidenced by the way the mainstream UK consumer press warned that people would be hacked and defrauded if they allowed third-party access to their bank accounts, even though the regulator has forced it to happen. It is obviously not true. After all, why would a regulator bring in a regulation to make people less secure? Nevertheless, FUD works. For example, if a third party compromises your data, who is liable? Where is the burden of proof? Generally, it is with the bank. Equally, the General Data Protection Regulation (GDPR)[22] makes this a tricky one. How can you share all the customer data when the other regulation is telling you not to?

This has all been driven by EU regulations for open APIs around payments. The United Kingdom has gold-plated the regulations, and made it into Open Banking, and the bottom line is that banks are being told to open up their data and processes to third parties. But let's go back to basics: does anyone want this?

We hear a lot about banks talking about partnership and co-creation, but we have not seen much of this happening so far. There may be a lot more of it in the future, but true partnering between FinTechs and banks is few and far between today. In fact, it appears that most banks are a bit confused about what is going on. Half of the major banks were not ready for Open Banking in time, and many are asking where the business case is for doing Open Banking, especially if it demands high risk and costly investments in upgrading and replacing systems.

What banks need to ask themselves is, what does it mean if they open themselves up to data sharing through APIs, and what does it mean if their competitors do the same? There is a win-win here and, for some bankers, Open Banking presents a huge opportunity to challenge their traditional competitors and their new ones. It is all about carpe diem—seize the day.

---

22 A European regulation that means you can be fined a fortune if you are not careful with customer data.

In summary, most of the non-bank people I meet see that there are a lot of things changing around the banks, but little changing in the banks themselves. They believe Open Banking and open APIs will change banks, but it will be nibbling around the edges of the system, and that, by 2025, the big banks will be leaner, faster and cooler, but they will still be the big banks.

BOTTOM LINE

Regulators are being directed by governments to create financial innovation programmes to protect their existing financial centres and gain traction in the new market for FinTech. Key parts of these developments are regulatory sandboxes and banks being forced to share customer data with third-party providers through Open Banking regulation.

LACK OF LEADERSHIP

All in all, there are many things forcing banks to change—markets, competition, customer, regulators, investors and more—and yet the biggest issue most banks face is their own internal battles. Many banks have evolved as institutions based on strengths in investment and risk management, financial accounting and regulatory reporting. Although technology has been seen as key to the business, it has not been a core competency of many banks, as illustrated by their poor back-office structures, steeped in systems carved from decades of development and infrastructures that are more complex than spaghetti.

This challenge has not gone away. In fact, it gets more critical every day. Many banks have leadership teams that are steeped in finance but have no professional technology experience. How then can they deal with the big questions around changing core systems, deploying machine learning and using distributed ledger technology? Of course, all of this can be delegated but when these developments are critical to the future structure of the bank, it is really hard. In fact, if digital is a transformation of culture, structure, organisation and systems, can a bank's leadership team understand the implications of this if they are analogue? No.

This is clearly evidenced by research performed by the *Harvard Business Review* and the Genpact Research Institute that looked at the impact of digitalisation in finance.[23] A majority of respondents voted that they had *not* unlocked the power of digital due to key barriers, such as the inability to experiment or the burden of legacy systems and processes. In addition, less than half of financial services sector respondents believed that their companies have a clear, enterprise-wide digital strategy, and many reported split ownership between the C-suite, or the leadership

---

23 "Accelerating the pace and impact of digital transformation: How financial services views the digital agenda," *Harvard Business Review Analytic Services* study in association with Genpact Research Institute, 4 November 2016, https://www.genpact.com/downloadable-content/hbr-full-report-how-financial-services-views-the-digital-agenda.pdf.

team of the bank, and business line owners for creating that strategy. The crux of the research is that it is the absence of a clear digital transformation strategy and fragmented leadership that prevents firms from *doing digital.*

What is clear is that there needs to be an enterprise digital strategy for transformation and a leadership that is steeped in digital capabilities. This became clear as I interviewed the five banks for this book project. Three of these five banks are led by someone steeped in technology and banking. Francisco González, the head of BBVA for almost twenty years, began life as a programmer; Piyush Gupta, the CEO of DBS, spent years running technology and operations for Citibank India; and Jamie Dimon, chairman and CEO of JPMorgan Chase, realised the importance of technology when he was working in the trading rooms of Wall Street. As for the other two banks, ING learnt digital banking years ago, with the launch of ING Direct, and CMB was launched as a bank based on technology in the 1980s.

All five of these banks have technology in their DNA, but most banks do not. This is a leadership challenge. A good example of this leadership challenge is clear in BBVA where the executive leadership team—the people who run the bank—are half digital and half banking. The team has a head of Data, a head of Customer Experience, a head of Engineering, a chief information officer (CIO), a chief operations officer (COO), a CEO and chairman, all of whom have digital in their DNA. Is half of your leadership team digital? Clearly, this is different but if a bank wants to be *a digital bank*, then half of that phrase is "digital".

Are You Really "Doing Digital"?

There are a series of questions that should be asked when considering if the leadership team is fit to change the bank to be digital. First, does the bank's leadership team talk about digital, digital banking, digital investment and digital transformation? Second, has the bank actually made any visible changes to be digital? Third, are those changes fundamental or incremental? The bank has a brand-new opportunity to launch a cloud-based, designer-led, customer- and user-focused bank, with all of the latest tech from open markets using APIs. Has the bank done this? Has the bank launched a clean data architecture that uses these technologies to be more competitive with Amazon and Alibaba than with Barclays and BNP? Fourth, how does the leadership team talk about digital? Do they talk about it as a major business change programme to reinvent the bank or do they talk about it as a project, or number of projects, led by CDOs?

Many avoid answering this last question as they think it is a trap—which it is. You see, if the answer is the latter, then the bank is not going through a transformation. It is just cost-cutting services and getting customers to self-serve more. The former is the critical requirement: does the leadership team walk the walk, as well as talk the talk? If the discussion falters here, then follow up with the final sucker punch: have the chairman and CEO appointed digital people to the leadership team? How many digital people report directly to the CEO? Who are they and where did they come from? What have they done to prove themselves to be digitally capable?

Many banks fail to answer these questions adequately because the majority of banks that *claim* to be doing digital are actually doing stuff that is digitally related, but missing the mark. They are doing apps and redeveloping services, but they are not really committed to transformation or to reinventing the bank for the twenty-first century in order to compete with Amazon and Alibaba.

From Innovation Theatre to Real Innovation

During a discussion about innovation among a group of innovative bankers, the conversation focused on how innovation has changed over the past decade or so. Before the financial crisis hit, innovation was big on the banks' agendas. In the annual reports of the world's top one hundred banks, the reference to "innovation" had risen from an average 1.3 mentions in 2000 to 6.2 in 2006. Yes, innovation was big on the banks' agendas, but they were not really innovating.

Most innovation was in a laboratory, separated from the business. If the person running the lab got frustrated because the bank would not let them play in the big boys' room, then they were told to leave. I think most CIOs that I knew back then had an average lifespan of eighteen months. My comment would usually be that innovation was like a virus that had entered the organisation and challenged it. As with any virus, the white blood cells soon gathered to squeeze it out.

Then the global financial crisis hit, and most banks moved into survival mode. During this period, innovation was of no interest. Living was the focus. During that period, a whole raft of new start-ups began to pop out of the woodwork and the FinTech world began to evolve. With most banks hated and unable to innovate, the innovation focus moved outside the banks and into the private equity and venture capital world. That was the springboard for so much of what we see today as innovation.

When the banks got through the worst of the crisis, they then noticed that everyone was trying to disrupt and destroy them. Their reaction was to scoff and laugh at first, then sit and watch and, finally, invest and focus. It was, therefore, around five or six years ago that banks started their innovation theatre. Let's run hackathons and innovation days, and invite these upstarts to come and show us what they've got. Let's have some pitch battles and demo discussions and offer prizes. Let's do some stage work to make it look like we are hip and cool ... when we're really not. Those innovation days and roadshows lasted a year or two until a few banks finally started to say, "Silicon Valley is going to eat our lunch! Let's do something about it."

Given that $10, $15, $20 or even $25 billion a year was being invested in FinTech start-ups, the banks could see that things were actually changing. Not just innovation or theatre, but real change. It was, therefore, around the mid-2010s that the biggest banks began to get serious about innovation. They started to look at partnering, investing and working with start-ups, and they started to take a long hard look at their own business, and its ability to change. At this point, a bridge was built. The bridge joined the sandbox to the bank.

Now, the innovation dialogue has moved up a notch, from being a play area—a sandbox or lab—to a testing ground to prototype and try new ideas to then build and grow. That is why most banks today are talking co-creation and collaboration. They finally get it. Innovation is not about messing around and tyre-kicking, but really about learning to fly and not crashing.

Run the Bank or Change the Bank

This commitment to technology and digital transformation is clear from the hiring practices of the big banks. JPMorgan Chase now has more developers, designers and engineers than Twitter and Facebook combined. Of its 250,000 employees, 50,000 are now technologists. Even when the bank does hire bankers, a mandatory part of their induction programme is to code. "Coding is not for just tech people, it is for anyone who wants to run a competitive company in the 21st century," stated Mary Callahan Erdoes, head of J.P. Morgan Asset & Wealth Management. "These are skillsets of the future ... by better understanding coding, our business teams can speak the same language as our technology teams, which ultimately drives better tools and solutions for our clients."

This reminded me of a comment made by Marcus Schenck, former co-head of Investment Banking at Deutsche Bank, who stated, "I don't think we're far away from saying that whoever wants to work in a bank better speak English, and better be able to code." Similarly, Goldman Sachs claims to be a technology company that happens to have a banking licence and, in recent times, has advertised for new employees who are engineers, rather than bankers. Generally, in the last year or so, one in four of its jobs advertised had the word "engineer" in the title.

What I find interesting about all of these examples, and there are many more, is that banks are pivoting from being branch-based structures to digital structures. Between 2016 and 2018, Barclays Bank shed a third of its workforce and that trend is being matched by most big banks. Some of this is down to branch closures, but a vast swathe is coming from the trading rooms. As machines trade, humans disappear. This is well illustrated by Goldman Sachs, whose U.S. cash equities trading room employed 600 people in 2000. Today, there are just two equity traders left. In 2017, Marty Chavez, the then chief financial officer (CFO) of Goldman Sachs, claimed that the bank had found consistently that four traders could be replaced by one computer engineer. Unsurprisingly, a third of Goldman's 36,000 employees are now computer engineers.

This is an irreversible trend, and Marc Andreessen, the whale investor in technology start-ups, wrote in 2011: "software is eating the world". It is now full steam ahead. There are huge impacts on the banking world, with major changes taking place. Banks are not only shedding staff, automating jobs and hiring coders, but are also partnering with start-ups, investing in innovation and opening to a world of data.

What is interesting in this space, however, is that only a handful of names, notably, JPMorgan Chase, Goldman Sachs and a small clan of others, are taking this seriously. I still find that many banks dodge the hard questions about laying off staff, shutting down offices, changing outdated systems and moving to the new world of Open Banking. By way of example, there are frequent headlines about banks' online systems and apps not working. In our world of connections, being unable to provide access—for even a few hours—grabs major headlines.

As already mentioned, this is a reflection of old systems, written in the 1970s and 1980s, that are still the backbone of many banks' operations. Reuters found that 43 per cent of the big bank systems in the United States run in COBOL, representing 220 billion lines of code and over 80 per cent of transactions. This shows the conundrum of today's bank change: developing new code and being open to real-time operations while keeping old code that is closed and running in batch overnight updates.

My friends in the big banks call this challenge "run the bank" while "changing the bank". It is not easy. "Run the bank" is keeping the lights on, having the systems up and running, not having downtime and maintaining infrastructure from the last century. "Change the bank" is opening to code, creating digital structures, closing branches and buildings and attracting new talent and partners.

Ten Chairs: How to Change the Bank

When discussing how to change the bank, there is a boardroom issue. According to research, nine out of ten bank boardroom members have never had a job in technology.[24] How can a bank convert to a digital bank if there are no digital people in the decision-making team? The issue is greater than this, however.

Imagine that the leadership team in a large bank has ten chairs. The ten chairs are filled by a variety of people who have got there by being good at their roles. The CEO is a banker, the COO is a banking operations person, the CMO is a banking marketing person, the CFO is a banking financial person, the CRO is a banking risk person and so on. They are all banking people. They got to their chair by being a good person doing what banking has always done. In other words, their chair was given to them for loyal service. Their chair will only be vacated if they leave, retire or die. There is no other way that someone else will get their chair. And if their chair does become vacant, the CEO will only replace them with someone else who has been with the bank all their life and is the most similar to the person vacating their chair. In other words, another banker.

So how do you get the digital people into the bank boardroom? How can you convert the bank to be a digital bank if all of the leadership team are bankers, who have never had a job in digital or digitalisation? That's a tough call. After all, no one in the leadership team would vote to give up their role to hire a digital leader. They got to their chair after years of doing the job that they have always done, and they are not going to stop doing it now.

This is why so many banking people are talking digital but not doing digital. They are banking people, and have always been in banking. They are not technology people who understand technology. This is a core conflict in most banks: the fact that they are led by bankers. If you are in a bank that is led by only bankers, how will you ever become a digital bank? A digital bank is half digital and half bank. How can you ever become a digital bank if you only have bankers leading and changing the bank? How can you ever become a digital bank if you only have leaders who understand banking?

24 "Bank Boardrooms Lack Technology Experience," Accenture, 28 October 2015, https://newsroom. accenture.com/news/bank-boardrooms-lack-technology-experience-accenture-global-research-finds.htm.

I guess this is why there are so few banks that I can point to that are truly converting to be digital banks. The few that I talk about— BBVA, DBS and JPMorgan Chase—have people at the helm who truly understand technology and digitalisation. It does not have to be the case that they have worked all the time in technology—Jamie Dimon is not an IT guy—but they do show an understanding of how technology is changing the bank. This is why these few, selected banks demonstrate major change with technology and have technology people in their leadership teams. Those ten chairs have been restructured with intent to ensure that two, three, four or five of those chairs are filled by people immersed in digitalisation.

Change the Bank or Change the Leadership

Banks are being fundamentally challenged by the digital transformation process. A lot of bank leaders think that they are keeping on top of things because they have rolled out a mobile app and completed a blockchain proof of concept. Their IT guys have said that there is no need to change core systems—they work and aren't broken, so why change them?—and there have been a lot of tests using AI. Open banking is under way, and so too is the FinTech incubator programme. So, what is the issue?

The issue is that all of the above is fine and dandy, but none of it has got anything to do with digital transformation. The above are all activities and projects, not a change to the core of the bank's culture, systems, organisation and processes. And digital transformation demands a change to the bank's core everything.

This is because banks were built in the industrial era for the physical distribution of paper money through buildings with humans; the digital era needs banks built for the digital distribution of data money through software and servers. It is a completely different business model, and has no relation to the existing and historical bank structures. As a new business model, it requires new organisation and thinking, a new culture and a new design. You do not get that from doing projects.

In fact, the project-focused structure of digital—rolling out apps, doing proofs of concept and testing AI—is just doing what we have always done, but cheaper and faster with technology. The new digital bank structure is completely rethinking what we have always done—with technology.

This is why it is a leadership challenge and not a technology challenge. It demands bank leaders who understand digital, have digital in their DNA and can change the bank while running the bank. These leaders have to bring their people with them—people do not follow leaders because they are told to but because they believe in them—and purely through their passion and belief in the digital transformation journey. They have to change the organisational structure, which means displacing several people including some of their direct reports, and bring in new blood who are digital people, not bankers. After all, how can you become a "digital bank" if you only have bankers leading the bank? You need digital people in the leadership team and diversity. Leadership is needed to execute cultural change and change is most resisted by the "frozen middle". The middle management fear change the most, particularly digital change, as they believe it will mean losing jobs and losing status.

The bottom line is this: who are the bank leaders out there? There are plenty of bank *managers*, but who are the *leaders*? Which bank leaders are driving radical change to deal with the digital revolution, rather than making incremental changes because they believe it is just an evolution? If digital really is an evolution, why are more changes happening faster and more dramatically with technology than we have seen since the last revolution, namely, the Industrial Revolution? The Industrial Revolution took place over decades and radically altered work, trade, finance and life; the Digital Revolution is taking place in dog years on speed—for every seven years of the Industrial Revolution's developments, think seven months in today's world—and it is getting faster. The real concern here is that the bank managers who are doing digital projects to evolve their industrial-era bank structure may be sleepwalking their banks into oblivion.

Do Bank Leaders Really Need to Be Digital?

Back in the 1980s, Walter Wriston, the then CEO and chairman of Citibank, said, "Information about money is becoming more important than money itself." His successor, John Reed, said, "Banking is just becoming bits and bytes." A quarter of a century later, this vision of the future of finance has come true. By way of example, the cryptocurrency Litecoin processed a single transaction valued at nearly $100 million between two users in April 2018. The transaction took just over two minutes to process for a cost of $0.40.[25] On a similar note, the move to Open Banking means that most banks are now managing a marketplace of apps, APIs and analytics, with disappearing branches and humans.

The relentless move to automation is moving at a pace. Traders and investment bankers are disappearing and being replaced by algorithms while tellers and call centre workers are being replaced by mobile apps and chatbots. Is it any wonder that the forecast long term is that banks will be run as automated structures without people? By way of example, Opimas, a U.S. research company, forecast that 230,000 jobs could disappear in capital markets by 2025 thanks to AI, and the former CEO of Deutsche Bank, John Cryan, announced in October 2017 that half of the jobs at Deutsche Bank will be removed by technology because most of the humans are "just abacuses".

The march of technology is unstoppable. Bearing this in mind, it' surprises me how nonchalant many bank leadership teams are about technology. The reason I say this is that back in the 1990s, I remember key presentations from the leaders of several tech firms. One particular presentation was delivered by Ken Olisa, who was then CMO of Wang Laboratories. In a speech in the early 1990s, he talked about the network effect of technology and how it would mesh into a world of networked systems requiring every business to have a technologist at the helm. Another was the head of financial markets for NCR who, in the mid-1990s, predicted that every bank board would have people with technology experience leading the charge forward.

---

25 I recently received a cheque from an American client for $15,000. It took my bank *two months* to process and cost $200. This is due to the fact that the bank had to exchange funds through the SWIFT network and verify receipt of funds before it would credit my account. This shows the true disparity between the digital age and the analogue age, and that only Americans send cheques in the post these days.

Twenty-five years later, it is starting to happen, slowly but surely. What is amazing here is that, based on these predictions from the 1990s, banks' executive team members are only now getting the message. For example, when Barclays Bank announced the formation of a new board for the ring-fenced retail bank, one of the key requirements was that "candidates should have experience of organisational transformation, particularly with a focus on customer, digital and technology". However, when it announced the new boardroom team, not a single technology person was on the team. There was a retailer, an accountant, two investors and a banker.[26] This is surprising as most of us would have expected a former CIO of a bank or a CEO of a technology firm to have been in the team if the bank were truly appointing someone with real experience of digital and technology.

Take a step back and ask: does the bank board really need to know digitalisation, technology and transformation? According to many respected regulatory and oversight organisations, the answer is no. The board is there to oversee the leadership team of the bank—the people who do the day-to-day management—and ensure that the team is fit to maintain the bank's stability, is not taking excessive risk, maintains the bank's strong balance sheet and is responding to the strategic requirements for change. In other words, there is a major difference between the boardroom and the management executives of a bank. The board is there to oversee the bank's management leadership team, and the management is there to deliver the day-to-day needs of running the bank.

The C-suite must be fit for digital transformation and the board must provide the oversight to ensure that the management team is balanced with the right level of skills to cover digital transformation. However, my contention would be that if the team at boardroom level has little digital transformation experience, how can they vet the management team of the bank and, specifically, know that their digital leaders are the right people? More particularly, if the massive changes of technology

---

26 This particular banker had, admittedly, overseen the finance of the digital transformation of a bank but that, to me, is not a technologist. A technologist is someone who has implemented the transformation and made a success of it, not overseen the cost of it.

and digitalisation predicted twenty-five years ago by leading bankers and technologists are held true, surely both the management and the board need to have digital intimacy?

BOTTOM LINE

Banks know that they need to digitally transform but many bank leaders—the CEO and chairman, in particular—do not know *what* to do or *how* to do it. They do not know how to lead digital transformation and so, instead, make digital change. They invest billions in projects, people, programmes, systems and structures but duck the big issues of organisational overhaul, cultural change, management reorganisation, restructuring systems, replacing core systems and so on. The reason is because the latter is risky and difficult, and these leaders do not understand that the digital revolution requires them to do this. The banks with such leaders will cease to exist in the next decade. They will not *die*, but will be acquired and merged with the banks that do get it.

PLANNING
TRANSFORMATION

In the first chapter, I discussed why banks need to digitally transform. It is clear that this has to happen as the most valuable companies in the world today are platform companies that connect people who have things with people who need those things.

Figure 2.1 The rise of digital corporations

Top 5 Publicly Traded Companies (by Market Cap)

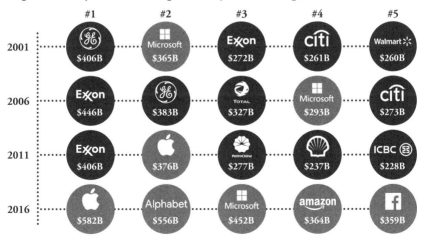

What is interesting is that these companies make nothing. They just connect everything. I need a journey, use the Uber app; I need answers, check out Google; I need a bed, swipe Airbnb; I need to buy something, here is Amazon. This is why the new digital platform firms employ few but have high valuations.

Figure 2.2 Digital companies run platform infrastructure rather than physical infrastructure

FIRM	ESTABLISHED	EMPLOYEES	MKT CAP
BMW	1916	116,000	$53B
Uber	2009	7,000	$60B
Marriott	1927	200,000	$17B
Airbnb	2008	5,000	$21B
Walt Disney	1923	185,000	$165B
Facebook	2004	12,691	$315B

Here, we can clearly see the difference between an industrial-era company and a digital-era company. An industrial-era company made everything, controlled everything and distributed everything; a digital-era company makes nothing, controls nothing and distributes nothing— but they connect everything. That is the critical point.

This clearly defferentiates the industrial-age firms from those for the digital age. In fact, someone asked me recently to define "digital transformation" and this was my reply:

"Most companies were born in the industrial age and are trying to evolve to be digital. However, the truly digital companies were born on the internet. For industrial-era companies to transform to be truly digital, they have to completely transform their business to have its core foundation built on the internet. Businesses cannot evolve to be digital, as such strategies leave the core foundations to be firmly industrial."

For any industrial company, this is a big issue. For any bank, it is a huge challenge. In fact, when talking about the challenges of creating a digital bank, the greatest challenge is the organisational transformation.

A transformational bank process—where the whole bank's business model is turned on its head to move from physical to digital foundations—is just too difficult for most. It is also too risky for most. Hence, they fudge it. They add budget to invest in digital while also investing in dusting up their branches, adding more people in compliance and audit, and juggling the sale of non-core assets while also thinking about the acquisition of new assets. In other words, they are banks that are spinning plates.

The trouble with such a bank is that plates can often drop and, if too many plates require too much focus, then this is even more likely to happen. This is what I think is happening with big incumbent banks that are thinking about an evolution to digital. As I keep saying, they know that they have to change, but do not know *what* to do or *how* to do it. Here, I will look at what to do.

What Banks Do Not Get

JPMorgan Chase spends $11 billion a year on technology, of which $3 billion goes into new projects. Citibank and Bank of America invest similar amounts in digital transformation. The question this prompts is, why are banks spending $3,000,000,000 on new tech when they could probably get better results spending $3,000,000 on a brand-new start-up set-up?

The issue here is that it takes a lot of effort to roll out a brand-new bank app system. Take, for instance, Finn, a digital bank by JPMorgan Chase that was designed for the under-thirties but shut down a year later. Bearing in mind that the bank already has millions of customers on its existing platform, introducing a new platform leads to a big challenge of cross-platform cannibalisation, where customers are *stolen* by the new service from the old service. The balancing act of launching a brand-new start-up bank that competes with the existing bank is, therefore, a challenge that needs to be managed carefully.

Equally, to build incredibly smart AI systems that can eradicate lawyers and traders takes some heavy investment in tech. Yet the amounts being invested in new bank start-ups by large incumbent banks are shockingly high when I see new challenger banks in the United Kingdom getting through the gates with $100 million or less. In addition, their offers are incredibly comprehensive, considering that their budget includes getting a banking licence, which costs around $30 million on average. You can go a long way with little investment nowadays. Social media, cloud and the network have made the difference to the reach we have today. Every day, I talk to over 100,000 people through various social media platforms. Twenty years ago, it would have cost me a fortune in telephone and postal costs. Today, it is free.

It is, therefore, frustrating when people who work in small banks say that digital is not for them. This is because they think that digital is complex and expensive. They point to the big banks that are spending billions in this area and believe that they can never compete with them. They whine about the challenge digital creates and wonder why things can't go back to the way they were before. These people do not get digital at all. They have grown up in an era when technology was complex and expensive. In other words, five- or ten-year projects that cost millions and took out a large chunk of the bank's operational expense. That is what they have cemented in their heads: technology is complex and expensive.

Many small banks come up with a multitude of barriers to change. Here are some examples:

We have too much to do: Yes, small financial firms are busy bees, and have a lot on their plate. Products are changing, customer needs are moving, regulations are updating and finding enough resource and bandwidth to keep up is virtually impossible. Tough. Make it so.

It is going to cost too much: No, it is not. Where are you from? The 1980s? It no longer costs a lot to adapt and change. That is why FinTech firms are bootstrapping on a few thousand dollars and gaining momentum. Just look at Stripe. A company based on seven lines of code that is now worth $35 billion (as of September 2019). It does not cost anything to make change these days, so just do it. Make it so.

We have to build it: No, you do not. You only think that way because you have always done it that way. If you always do what you have always done, you are always going to get what you have always got … less some. These days, anyone building everything is a fool. Build what you are good at, buy what you cannot do and partner with anyone who is doing it better than everyone else. Make it so.

The regulator won't allow it: Really? Do you know this for a fact or are you just making it up? Have you actually asked? I know plenty of regulators who are happy for credit unions, community banks, thrifts and small financial firms to innovate the hell out of the big banks using tech, so start trying harder. Believe. Make it so.

The big banks have the advantage because they are big: No, they don't. In fact, the big banks have the disadvantage because they are big. The bigger the bank, the harder it is to change. The smaller the bank, the more nimble you should be. And if you are not, why not? Work out what is stopping you and change. Make it so.

It is hard to change: Of course it is. It is hard to run a marathon, but people still do it. If you do not think you can change a teeny-weeny bank, then what are you doing there? After all, there are massive banks that are changing and they have a thousand times as many challenges as you. Just get on with it. Make it so.

This list could go on and on, but you get where I am coming from. Most of the barriers to small financial firms seizing the digital opportunities are created by negative thinking.

What they do not get is that it is actually simple and cheap if you can code. How do you think so many FinTech start-ups started up? They use AWS, partner with firms that provide APIs and focus on the one thing that they want to do brilliantly. Often, these firms are bootstrapped by incubators and angel investors, and become successful with investments of little more than $20 million, sometimes even less. Surely a budget of $20 million is affordable for a small bank? Of course it is, if it has the right leadership and vision to see where it should be invested.

In other words, the big hairy-scary banking corporations (HSBCs) can frighten little guys and start-ups with their investments of $3 billion in new projects. Let them get on with it. A lot of that investment is just going into maintaining the banks' hierarchies and structures. I do not mean maintaining old systems; a big bank will often waste 20 to 30 per cent of its investments on internal politics. In contrast, a small bank can be more nimble, agile and visionary if it has the right leadership to make it happen. And a start-up can create something radically new and different, as it has no existing operations, politics, hierarchy or legacy to deal with.

Breaking Through the Barricades

Banks need to change and adapt. If they do, they will not die or be destroyed. Banks that do not change and adapt will be destroyed. Banks that do not fully embrace change will be severely challenged.

In the twentieth century, we had an industry with massive barriers to entry. There were **regulatory barriers** that required immense levels of capitalisation to get a banking licence. Then, if you were lucky enough to get one, you had huge overheads in maintaining regulatory oversight. Then, there were **technological barriers** because setting up a bank required huge investments in systems, structures and infrastructures in order to get it off the ground. It precluded most players, apart from the richest, to even consider opening a new bank. Finally, there were **physical barriers** to entry. Most banks believed that their branch networks precluded new entrants and, to a certain extent, that was and still is true. With no physical presence, you do not have the same levels of trust, and pure-play digital banks were far and few between.

The thing is, all of these barriers have been eroded over time. The regulators want more competition in banking, especially after the 2008 crisis. Consequently, they have brought down the barriers to entry, offered light licences and created sandboxes to mentor start-ups to market in a fast-track cycle.

Technology is now cheap, and we have unlimited bandwidth, storage and networking. Cloud, APIs and apps make it really easy to launch a decent bank service in a few months, or even days. A bank-like front end to a thousand API services could even be built in a day. So, technology is no longer a barrier. Yes, it used to be. It used to be that you had to buy a lot of technology at a really high cost to get something up and running, and it would then take years to pick up. Today, it is fast and almost free. That is a big technology change.

There has also been a huge sea change within the physicality discussion. Customers used to want a physical presence, and some still do. However, many of us are becoming so comfortable with our devices and apps that it is no longer a prerequisite. As a result, the banks that have high physical infrastructure costs are facing pressure from those new services that have no physical cost. The ability to launch a pure digital play and offer 200 basis points better differential between debits and credits becomes quite compelling in an age where banks are disliked immensely, and price sensitivity is at an all-time high.

In other words, all of the things that used to provide comfort to banks as barriers to entry, namely, regulations, technologies and physical structures, are now the bane of banks' lives and are creating unwarranted overheads which now make it hard for them to compete. The challenger banks with no legacy, regulatory support and highly efficient cloud-based services, curating a marketplace of APIs with zero physical overheads, are becoming a serious consideration.

Bank Reincarnation: The Best Way to Become a Digital Bank

Nothing is simple in the digital financial world of today, but the easiest path may well be to reincarnate the bank with a new, clean start instead of trying to resuscitate the old, broken bank. To begin, the bank has to get the terms and understanding right. Many have the wrong terminology. They regard digital as a channel so appoint a head to run the digital function and assign the function a budget. Job done.

The thing is, the job is not done as this is a core foundation of the future bank, not an adjunct. It is neither a channel nor a function. The problem is that banks like to assign things to boxes, or plates, to continue my prior metaphor. So, you have the digital bank plate; the retail bank plate, which looks after the branches, something that is separate from the digital plate; the regulation plate; the compliance plate; the payments plate; and so on.

All of these plates are spinning separately, and all require attention. As a result, some plates may fall, but that does not matter as long as you can pick them up and start to spin them again. For instance, the digital bank app has already been rolled out and now someone is demanding that you roll out the next service: the wearable app, the internet of things app, the data analytics programme, etc. You can simply start spinning a new plate and things will keep on going.

However, this tactic will not work in the long term as the new FinTech world isn't spinning plates. Instead, new start-ups are a plate to themselves. They are attacking the business by having just one plate on the table. It is not spinning and, as a result, it works non-stop to disrupt all of those spinning plates.

This is precisely what is happening with these thousands of new companies out there focusing just on digital, the retail user experience, payment and so on. This means that the multi-spinning universal bank is dropping its plates faster and faster thanks to regulation and innovation. So, what's the answer? Start a new bank, of course. Reincarnate. Business Reincarnation. It is a rather dramatic term, especially if you do not believe in reincarnation, but it does help to visualise the idea. Like a phoenix rising from the ashes, a bank needs to die and reincarnate itself in order to survive this digital revolution. The real question is, should a bank launch a new bank or try to transform the old bank to be digital? The answer is that the bank has to do both.

You cannot just invest in a new bank launch and leave the old bank to rot. You must do both.

Launching a new bank is not the best answer to the challenge of how to keep up. The difficulty with launching a new bank is commitment. Commitment to let it flourish and grow, without interfering. Commitment to let the new bank steal business from the old bank, and not fight back. Commitment to let the new bank cannibalise the old bank's products and services. Commitment to fund it effectively and give it the time to complete its journey, without cutting costs halfway through as the returns are not showing. In fact, this last point is probably the most important one as banks are caught between the devil and the deep blue sea. The devil is how to maintain the bank's existing margin and profit, in an ever more crowded and competitive marketplace. The deep blue sea is how to grow a new bank, and fund it, when the old bank is struggling to maintain margin in an ever more competitive market.

I guess that the saving grace is that the old bank's market share has not changed much, even with new competition, as few customers are switching their main deposit accounts across to new players, at least not yet. Given time, however, things will change, and they are changing already. All in all, this means that:

1. A bank must change its core systems, fabric and foundations to become digital over the next five years, which is a huge internal change programme.
2. A bank can launch a new bank to cater to the digital world, but it will dilute resources and capital.
3. If a bank launches a new bank, it must be committed to let it fly free, without interference, and step on the old bank's toes as much as it wants or needs to.
4. However the future looks, the old bank and the new bank need to ensure that they are adapting fast to survive.

I see a lot of incumbent banks feeling the frustration of needing to run the bank whilst trying to change the bank, and the difficulties of spinning too many plates. Rather than change the bank, they are investing in launching NewBank instead. NewBank gets a big budget and spins out of the OldBank.

A good example of this is Hello bank!, an offshoot of BNP Paribas. Hello bank! was launched in May 2013, with the ambition of gaining 1.4 million customers by 2017 in Germany, Belgium, France, Italy and Austria, of which two-thirds would be new customers to BNP rather than existing account holders. BNP invested €80 million to launch the bank and, by the end of 2017, had 2.9 million customers across its five original markets, although a large portion were existing customers, particularly in the eighteen to twenty-eight age bracket. Nevertheless, these are impressive numbers and show that BNP and other successes, like First Direct (HSBC) in the United Kingdom, can be spun out of the old bank and flourish.

However, there are an equal number of failures like Finn, the digital spin-off of JPMorgan Chase. These failures occur because the existing organisation wants to protect the existing infrastructure and underlying processes, and the existing organisation's management team members want to protect their empires and bonuses.

The only way an offshoot can really succeed is if it runs as a completely separate bank with a completely separate management team and a completely separate budget. It cannot just be a pilot, project or offshoot adjunct that is run under the core bank umbrella. This is what differentiates First Direct and Hello bank!

Whether the bank transforms or launches a NewBank, neither approach is easy. It all comes back to leadership. Does your leader have the stomach to make the change happen? Equally important, does your leader have the backing, the budget and the board behind them to make the change happen? If yes, you are good to go. If no, what are you doing?

Reincarnate or Die?

It is interesting to hear bank CEOs talk about the threat of technology to their business, and the fact that more and more CEOs are talking about it. Francisco González, the former CEO and chairman of BBVA, has discussed this for years and, in 2013, forecast that fewer than fifty banks would survive worldwide.

"In two decades, we will go from 20,000 'analogue' banks today worldwide to no more than several dozen 'digital' banks. Diverse niche businesses will exist, but most will be mere 'suppliers' for the much-reduced number of digital banks acting as 'knowledge distributors'. They will own the platform through which products and services are channelled to the end customer."[27]

Now this rallying call has been picked up by many other bank CEOs from John Cryan, former CEO of Deutsche Bank, to António Horta-Osório, CEO at Lloyds. In a 2018 article, Dave McKay, CEO of Royal Bank of Canada (RBC), made some interesting comments around how banks need to reincarnate and rebuild their business models and turn into platforms, rather than just focus on banking. According to McKay, the idea is that RBC will expand its services way beyond finance into accountancy, home moves, starting up a business and more.

"RBC aims to offer more end-to-end services—or 'ecosystems'— covering wider customer needs than only financial, such as when they want to start their own business, sell their house, or find a new car. For instance, the bank is offering a service for entrepreneurs to register their start-up company with the government, provide it with cloud-based accounting software, supply a branding service and send it letterheads and business cards, all before it has lent the company a cent. For people looking to buy or sell a home, it offers to research neighbourhoods, move furniture, remove garbage, paint a house and even decide which bins to take out each week. Many of these services are supplied by partners integrated into RBC's digital platform."[28]

27 Francisco González, "Banks need to take on Amazon and Google or die," an opinion piece in the *Financial Times*, 2 December 2013, https://www.ft.com/content/bc70c9fe-4e1d-11e3-8fa5-00144feabdc0.
28 "Royal Bank of Canada warns on Big Tech threat to banking," *Financial Times*, 13 June 2018, https://www.ft.com/content/e70c827c-6f13-11e8-92d3-6c13e5c92914/.

He also makes a key point as to why the bank has to do this. Historically, banks have been the place where people would go when starting a business, buying a home or expecting a child. This is because they would walk into the bank and ask for advice. People do not do that anymore. The first place they now look for information on these life events is Google or Facebook. As a result, there are online players that are far better positioned to service those needs than the banks, which are still reliant on the old ways of communicating. This is why banks need to create better life event ecosystems. Now this is something that has been talked about for over two decades: servicing customer journeys during life events rather than focusing on transactional moments. However, it is the first time that I have heard a bank CEO talk about creating a financial ecosystem around those life events. It makes sense.[29]

So much resonates with my own views about the Big Tech giants getting regulated and banks becoming data vaults and curators of marketplaces of apps, APIs and analytics. However, the new addition to this is the serious consideration of how to build that ecosystem focused on end-to-end services for customers' life events. This is the future of finance: wrapping a financial cushion around the customers' lives in order to be relevant to them in times of higher stress and higher value. It is a whole new world.

> ❝ Five years ago, we identified four core capabilities that are going to be required for success going forward. First, we very explicitly recognised that we needed to be good at developing digital services. This was something that was historically outsourced for cost reasons. We first had to retain the expertise to create a core capability for development. Then design is the other element that is critical to provide the good digital experience. In order to kick start that practice, we incorporated outside talent from Spring Studio, the design shop in San Francisco. That design shop is now embedded within BBVA, so it's no

---

29 For more on this, see "Fintech threatens to eclipse banks that do not adapt digitally," *Financial Times*, 11 June 2018, https://www.ft.com/content/731bcdc8-6810-11e8-aee1-39f3459514fd.

longer a stand-alone shop but a really big design practice
with hundreds of designers incorporated as a key part of
our business. Data is the third key element. A few years
ago, we made a bold move to have a global head of data
reporting directly to the CEO and now to the chairman.
This is really to provide focus on what is the key ingredient
for success in the digital world, which is leveraging data
for value-add. The final key is the people, talent and
culture. In the last five years, we have transformed in
a huge way how this company operates. It is a lot less
hierarchical and much more agile. **" "**

Carlos Torres Vila, *Group Executive Chairman, BBVA*

What Is Your One Move?

Finally, banks have traditionally done everything for everyone. They offer
a full range of end-to-end services across the value and supply chain.
This must change in a digital structure, as there are thousands of start-
up companies doing one thing brilliantly. Banks should look to work with
these firms if they aren't already doing so. Here is a great story about
choosing that core competency:

A ten-year-old boy decided to study judo, despite the fact that he
had lost his left arm in a devastating car accident. The boy began
lessons with an old judo master. The boy was doing well, so he could
not understand why, after three months of training, the master had
taught him only one move.

"Sensei," the boy finally asked, "shouldn't I be learning more moves?"

"This is the only move you know, but this is the only move that you'll
ever need to know," the sensei replied.

Even though he did not understand what the sensei meant, the boy
kept training because he believed in his teacher.

Several months later, the sensei took the boy to his first tournament.
Surprising himself, the boy easily won his first two matches. The third
match proved to be more difficult but, after some time, his opponent

became impatient and charged; the boy deftly used his one move to win the match. Still amazed by his success, the boy was now in the finals.

This time, his opponent was bigger, stronger and more experienced. For a while, the boy appeared to be overmatched. Eventually however, his opponent made a critical mistake: he dropped his guard. Instantly, the boy used his move to pin him. The boy had won the match and the tournament. He was the champion.

On the way home, the boy and sensei reviewed every move in each and every match. Then the boy summoned the courage to ask what was really on his mind. "Sensei, how did I win the tournament with only one move?"

"You won for two reasons," the sensei answered. "First, you've almost mastered one of the most difficult throws in judo. Second, the only known defence for that move is for your opponent to grip your left arm."

The boy's biggest weakness had become his biggest strength.

It is extremely hard for a bank to change culturally, become marketplaces, curate FinTech partners and offer a platform for inclusion of all. In particular, one of the critical factors in all of this is recognising the bank's core competency. What is the one thing that your bank does really well? Is it product, process or people? Are you a great manufacturer, processor or retailer?

Once you work out what you are really good at, drop the rest. This is a tough thing to do. After all, most banks think that they have to do everything for everyone. Focus just on that one thing—that one core competency—and drop the rest. Let the others do the rest. Just focus on your one best move.

BOTTOM LINE

Banks are convinced that they have to change but find it hard to work out what to change or how. In working out what to change, the bank has to have clear strategic focus. It must focus on core competencies and key areas of internal focus, and then complete its structures through partnerships with others. This is a big structural change and a challenge, but it is an imperative for survival in the digital age.

DOING DIGITAL: AN INTERVIEW WITH PIYUSH GUPTA, CEO OF DBS, SINGAPORE

When researching this book, I performed more than twenty one-to-one interviews with bankers from around the world, not to mention all the phone calls, emails, Skype chats, online research and more. However, the interviews provided the core content of this book. These interviews were direct meetings in Amsterdam, the Netherlands, with ING; Madrid, Spain, with BBVA; New York City, USA, with JPMorgan Chase; Shenzhen, China, with CMB; and Singapore with DBS.

They were all great interviews, but the interviews with DBS really stood out because I met many of the executive team. DBS has won many awards for its digital bank transformation programme, including World's Best Bank in 2019 and World's Best Digital Bank in 2016 and 2018 from *Euromoney*. Therefore, I have included the full interview with Piyush Gupta, the CEO, as our discussion not only gives a great backdrop to responding to the challenges outlined in the opening chapters of this book, but also all of the lessons learnt in the sections that follow.

Figure 3.1 Meeting the CEO of DBS, Piyush Gupta, in Singapore

The best way to start is to ask, "What do digital banking and digital transformation mean to you?"

I think you've got to start with recognising that the way human beings are living life is changing fundamentally. I think that's the basic consideration.

Each one of us: the way we consume news, the way we buy things, the way we listen to music, the way we hail taxis. All of these things are changing the way in which we interact with our service providers. We are changing our notion of what it means to get immediate service. We are changing our notion of what it means to get informed service, through use of data. We have higher and higher expectations of the vendor—the supplier—knowing us better, so on and so forth.

Our basic premise is that when users change consumption patterns because of technology, they will also change the financial services consumption patterns. So, digital to me is just a reflection of how you reimagine customer journeys. How do you reimagine the jobs to be done? How do you reimagine the way you can fulfil these customer needs in a way that is fundamentally different from anything that's been done in the past? For us, the transformation agenda really had two big things: the hardware construct and changing the heartware construct.

The first is the technology agenda, where the digital part of it is quite clear. You've got to get the technology right. This is a fantastic once-in-a-generation opportunity. Banks have forever found it really hard to keep pace with technology because they are stuck with old core banking legacy systems. In many cases, they are fifty years old or more. It's all hard-coded. It's all done in COBOL or C++, and that technology has been really hard to change. But, in the last ten to fifteen years, the nature of cloud-enabled technology, open-sourced systems and commodity hardware has allowed you to make the transformation.

So, one big thing is the opportunity we had to really re-architect our technology. That is, not just the tools we used, but the way we ran technology. We were able to move from Waterfall to Agile and all the rest. The second big piece you can change is your heartware. If technology is hardware, you can change your heartware at the same time and, by heartware, I mean change the organisation itself.

Again, it's not new. Banks have actually done more work on the heartware side to improve service value and create a service culture. How do you put the customer first, at the heart of the things that you do?

Today, with the change in technology, it allows you to fundamentally rethink the customer expectation. It also allows you to change the internal functioning of the company. How you work. Moving from hierarchical organisations to flat organisations. Moving to collaborative workplaces. Moving to enable people to be the best that they can be. All of this is not new. That's always been there in management literature, but technology is now letting you approach it in a very different way.

To me, the concept of the organisation is changing the hardware construct and changing the heartware construct in the company at the same time, allowing you to deliver these completely different outcomes to customers.

I can name only a handful of banks that are doing digital transformation well. How did you approach this and what are the key things that you did?

I want to reflect on one or two important things. One is, I think most of the banks in the West were so consumed with the global financial crisis (GFC) and the challenges of Basel capital liquidity all the way up to 2015 that they were not looking at the forward battle. They were looking at yesterday's problems. I think some banks, China Merchants Bank is one, were not impacted by the GFC and were therefore able to get a head start as they didn't have to deal with those problems.

However, as an industry, most of the Western focus was on fixing the issues of the GFC. For example, I was on the board of the Institute for International Finance (IIF) until 2016. Until then, no IIF meeting had any discussion on digital and technology. BBVA and I were the only guys who kept raising our hands to say, "Hey, let's talk about this." Everybody else focused on a different conversation.

So, that's one thing. We just had more flexibility because we had less baggage, if you will. The other big thing is that the board got on board very early, which, in our case, was certainly important. A lot of my peers have the challenge of convincing the board because sometimes the ROI, or the payoffs of some of the investments, are not clear. You have to make a leap of faith. In our case, the board was willing to go along and take this leap of faith.

In fact, after I finished all of my budgeting and planning in 2013, the board gave me an extra S$200 million to go burn in the world. The board members told me to go and spend it over the next two to three years, and something good would come of it. To me, it wasn't the money. You know, we spent a billion dollars on technology. S$200 million is good, but it's not earth-shattering. It wasn't significant. It was more that the board was willing to give me the money and support. The fact that I was being allowed to run the whole exercise without necessarily micromanaging or unpicking the return that the board would get from this.

We need to go back to when we started, back in 2010 to 2013/2014.

We call those four or five years "Phase One". We achieved two really important things in that first period. One was that we were able to improve the backbone of our technology because we moved from eighteen different technology stacks and applications in eighteen countries to a single core banking app, Finacle. We did that for fifteen countries in seventeen months. At that time, we were told that we were the fastest rollout of Finacle ever made. We improved the resilience of our technology stack. We improved the capacity of our hardware. We improved our networks.

We used to spend S$700 million a year on technology. I then bumped that expenditure up to S$1 billion. I call that period a "down payment". You need to make a down payment to get to the starting block. A lot of people don't make the effort to get to that starting block.

I did take it slowly; we took four to five years to get through Phase One. Then came Phase Two in around 2014. There were a couple of things that caused us to jump on this bandwagon. One was Alibaba. We were seeing what Ant Financial and Alibaba had started to do, and their actions were a burning platform issue for us. Interestingly, no one else around the world was seeing what was happening in China with Alibaba. It wasn't front and centre.

I remember a meeting that I had with Jack Ma, its then chairman. It was quite clear to us that these people were completely redefining our industry in terms of how they acquire customers, how they want to learn, how they use data and how they do payments. It scared the living daylights out of me. The way these guys were going about it. No branches, no brick and mortar, no nothing. What they were doing was clearly going to completely change how financial services are done. That was the shock we needed to get moving, if you will.

We had a few positives. One, we had only spent these four or so years cleaning up our act. I felt that we had some technology capabilities. We insourced some technology. We had a fairly good set of resources.

Second, I guess my own background played a part. I'm not a computer scientist, but I had done a lot of work with technology over the last fifteen years at Citibank, including running the first e-commerce platforms in Asia in the late 1990s as well as running technology data centres, setting up my own dot-com and all the internet activity for Citi. I had some personal interest in this area and felt confident that I knew what was going on, and that maybe we could do something with it.

And third, we'd been trying to buy a bank in Indonesia but it fell through in 2013. This forced us, as a board, to step back and figure out that if the old way of expansion was not going to work, we would need to think of a new way of skinning the cat. That led us to think about looking at the digital strategy, and wonder if we could imitate Alibaba.

The fourth is that we actually spent a lot of time in the early 2014 period examining what was happening around the world. We spent three to four months actively looking. I went back and looked at ING because I was an admirer of what ING had been able to do in Australia and Germany. It was quite clear to me that ING Direct had really changed the nature of the game. So, we went and studied that. We also looked at a couple of the Polish banks. Our CIO, Dave [Gledhill] spent several weeks going and seeing all of the Big Tech companies like Amazon, Google and Facebook. He went and met every one of them. We came back with these two big insights.

One was that all of the Big Tech firms had changed their technology stack in the last decade. Many of them had started with bank-like technology with Big Data centres and IBM mainframes, Oracle databases and so on. After Amazon Web Services appeared as a downstream from that, many of them had started to move to modern technology and cloud.

A key insight was what these guys did with a billion customers or even two billion customers. If they could run this new modern stack, why couldn't a bank? That was one big insight: that it can be done and the Big Tech had done it.

So, we figured our frame of reference needed to be Big Tech, and not the other banks. We clearly modelled ourselves on what Jeff Bezos would do as opposed to what Jamie Dimon would do. We carried on with things and always asked, "What would Jeff do?"

The other thing that we took a bet on was the idea that we were trying to change the whole bank. We would go for the core. Jamie Dimon's trying to do it now at JPMC, and they bring it at scale. It's massive what they are trying to do. Even BBVA in their early days were into creating a separate division to do the transformation.

Most of the conventional thinking was that you cannot teach an old dog new tricks. Most would say it is better to let the old dog lie down, then get a new bunch of kids, put them in a garage, buy a start-up, create a separate division and you should be able to get started that way.

We figured that we had to transform the whole bank for a couple of reasons. One, when I was in Citi, John [Reed, then CEO and chair] created a separate division called eCiti in the early days of the internet in the 1998 to 1999 period. My learning from that was that these things fail because if they're not core to the organisation, then the core organisation doesn't want them to succeed. They keep taking potshots at them. Perhaps, more important, the people in this new division are on the side and often don't really understand the core business domain. They do a lot of things that look sexy, but they don't really move the needle for the business. My takeaway from that experience was that the business must own this. It cannot be somebody else on the side.

The second impression I had is personal. In 2013, I went back home to Delhi, where my parents live. One evening, I reflected that my dad, who was eighty-five at the time, had spent the day paying his bills online, doing his banking online and ordering something online. I thought if a guy aged eighty-five can change how he goes about things in his personal life, why do we think that people in their forties and fifties can't change in their professional lives? It was quite clear that the problem is not with the individual. Therefore, the problem must be with the company. The problem must be with the culture that we have, a culture that doesn't allow people to achieve the same kind of outcomes.

We boiled it down to two things. The first is that learning comes from doing. At home, the way my father learnt was that a grandniece or granddaughter had come and shown him what to download. She had then walked him through the process several times. In the bank, nobody lets you learn by doing. The first thing that you need to do is create an environment where it's okay to learn by doing.

The second is that the construct of risk is very different. At home, if something doesn't work on an app or something, we get frustrated but it is no big deal. In the bank, people are scared. If something goes wrong, you lose your job, your bonus, a promotion or something else negative happens. The risk environment is very different.

We decided that if we wanted to change the core of the institution and go for broke, then we would have to invest in these things. We would need to create an environment where it is okay for people to take some risk. An environment where it's okay to experiment. An environment where you give people a lot of opportunities to learn by doing. If you can do that, then you might be able to get this engagement and transformation at scale.

These are a couple of the big insights that we had early on. One, you can be a tech company if you make that your frame of reference. Second, you should try and change everybody and go for broke with everything.

The second one is more difficult than the first, I would expect?
It's not easy. I can tell you in hindsight that we learnt some of this as we went along but some of these things paid off for us. We created a transformation programme, which we called "Making Banking Joyful", on three pillars. One was the technology transformation, the second was customer journey thinking and the third was bringing a start-up culture into the bank.

When I think about it, the major pillar was being relentlessly focused on customer journeys. That was the principal tipping point. You have to work on the technology, but the biggest difference is that we started to train all of our people to think about customer journeys. We created a journey programme, a five-day programme to learn how to discover, define, develop and deploy. We trained the whole company in this customer journey thinking. We set up large areas where people could get together and start practising customer journeys. We took my entire senior management team for two days and taught them how to do journeys. We evolved and gave people targets—key performance indicators [KPIs]—and made it clear that everybody had to do a journey that year. It didn't matter what the journey was, whether it was internal or external, they just needed to make that journey.

So, we had a massive crusade around the customer journey process. This, more than anything else, kindled the belief in people that we were serious. It was clear to people that, as long as you can demonstrate that what you are doing seems to be good for the customer experience and you can change the customer experience, they would get support. That was the centrepiece. That journey thinking and journey world were pivotal in many ways.

The second thing we did early on is that we created a transformation group, and I gave them enough room to go ahead and try out a few things. They came up with this crazy hackathon idea early in 2014. The idea to run hackathons at scale.

This hackathon idea was to get two kids from a start-up and put them with eight people from the bank to form a team of ten. You give them some coaching on a Monday morning and a problem to solve on Monday evening. Then Tuesday to Thursday—that's 72 hours—they go straight into solving the problem. On Friday, they have to create an app that solves the problem. It's all about how to make customer focus groups, how to do the process flow and how to do the design, development and storyboarding. The team does it collectively. Once they make the app on the Friday, they can then go and tell their kids, "Hey, I made this app."

That releases inhibitions completely, as you figure out that this can be done. I know how to do it. It brings a lot to the party because the actual process of what needs to be done is now much clearer to all. You know what the start-up kids don't, but they can help you with the coding and so on.

So we came up with the idea of hackathons back in 2014 and set up investments which weren't that big—S$2 million to S$4 million. We also created these big innovation hubs. I was actually sort of cynical in the beginning. I thought that these hubs were going to be white elephants. I thought that nobody would use these things, but I was willing to try and see what happened.

It created an environment where people started to bring the start-up with them. They started to bring academia. They started to do their own projects. I used to join in during the first few months. I used to go to kick the tyres and make sure that the premises were being used. And it was packed all of the time. Packed with our own people, all running their own projects with outsiders, with new start-ups. They were working with internal and external people, all mixed. Doing so gives you a chance to do new things and change what you do.

Again, we had a little bit of luck when, in 2016, the KPI that we made for the whole company was to run a thousand experiments. The general theme was that it didn't matter what the experiment was, as long as you ran the experiment. As long as you could say, "This is the experiment we ran and these are the A and B results." It didn't matter whether people succeeded or failed. In fact, we weren't even that concerned about the quality of the experiments. We just wanted people to go through the motion of saying "I did an experiment" because when they experiment, they can learn to figure out how to take some risk.

We created an award, the Dare to Fail award, which indicated that it was okay to fail. In fact, we only award it to people who have tried and failed. That again goes back to signalling that it is okay to learn to take some risk.

Overall, it was a bunch of multiple tools that started to get the company moving. This was in 2015 and 2016, and the result was to make it clear that it is not only okay to try, but you are also expected to try. You are expected to do projects, expected to do customer journeys and expected to do experiments. By the end of 2016, I was really taken aback by how much this had taken on a life of its own. Talk about a thousand flowers in bloom.

Within the first couple of years, people were doing stuff in human resources and marketing and communications and compliance.

Everybody was reimagining how you could do things. The other one of my biggest surprises was how quickly people jumped on the bandwagon. Once they had overcome their first inhibitions—Am I allowed to do it? Will the bank support it? Will I be criticised for doing it?—it was quite clear that people were being recognised and encouraged to do this.

An interesting thing here was that the people who jumped onto the bandwagon weren't always the young kids. It was the older people with thirty or forty years of experience, and you realised you had caught onto something. A lot of people knew that what they were doing before didn't make sense. They just needed something to open up their imagination. It just needed someone to say, "Okay, you have the liberty to do it differently."

What are the demonstrable things that have been delivered?

I think the most demonstrable thing is solid data. Look at the Monetary Authority of Singapore (MAS) data, and you can see that between 2014 and 2018, our market share for mortgages has gone up from 24 per cent to 31 per cent. Our market share for cards is up from 19 per cent to 25 per cent. Our market share for Bancassurance insurance distribution is up from 29 per cent to 34 per cent.

I would argue that it is impossible to get such massive market share shifts if you're doing something wrong. There is something going on here that is different as all banks have the same people, the same resources. So why is DBS getting this huge market share gain? There must be something behind it.

I don't think we really have the best people for everything. I just think that the ability to reimagine the customer journey is allowing us to acquire customers at scale, and is allowing us to get a lot more activity with those customers.

Then we started to measure digital value as the second piece, when we started to measure the impact of digitalisation four years ago. We created large data warehouses. We started to track and got McKinsey involved to help us think about how we should measure this. We came up with this very simple thing about whether we were serving a digitally active customer or a non-digitally active customer. Then we started to measure the metrics.

If you're a digitally active customer, what do you do? How many times do you deal with the bank and how often? How quickly does it work?

We instrumented everything, and looked at the cycle times for everything, down to milliseconds, just like Amazon does, such as how long the app takes to load onto your screen. We instrumented everything and also started to measure the financial results from that.

That is what is showing up in our market share numbers. So top-down, it shows up in the market share numbers. It also shows up in our financial numbers. Take a very simple metric. We used to have the lowest ROE in Singapore. Today, we have the highest ROE in the country. There must be a reason for that. We have the best ROE, despite the fact that our cost to credit is not the lowest.

So, our ROE has suddenly become the highest from being the lowest, our market share has gained dramatically and, using bottom-up data from our data warehouses, we can quite clearly demonstrate that the digital activity, in terms of customer acquisition and customer engagement, has paid off by the doubling of our customer revenues for digitally active customers.

If you're achieving digital transformation, how come it doesn't show in the share price?

I've tried for about a year, Chris, to see how I could start to engage with a different investor base or try to get our investor base to figure that out, given what we're trying to do and the growth we are trying to get from digital. The valuation should be done differently but there are two challenges. First, the bulk of the public market investors are quite siloed. Second, banking investors are very different from the technology investors. The banking investors have their model, and they go into the model and look at our revenue expenses, the cost of credit equity and suchlike. They just put the numbers in and come up with a valuation, and then they benchmark us to the comparable banks.

The technology investors are willing to bet on the future of technology and the potential growth. That is why they are willing to pay thirty to fifty times more for those tech firms, but they just don't look at banks. So, I went on two big road trips to try to get crossover investors, to see people who are tech investors and to get them to look at what I call the "transformation story".

My first view is that the way in which banks are valued has to change in order to recognise when and how banks are becoming technology companies. For people investing money, they should look for the best investment opportunity through a common prism, but I think the investment industry is still somewhat of a stereotype in how it looks for investments. Different people look for different things. The fact is that even though we've seen financial improvement, based on traditional banking metrics, you don't see those financial improvements in the short term. Equally, frankly, you could make that case for any tech company, whether it's Amazon, Facebook or Netflix. You've got to keep hanging on in there for ten, twelve, fifteen years before you see the exponential payoffs. Tech investors are willing to hang on in there for ten to fifteen years whilst the banking investor base is not prepared to do so.

Second, you do see some advantages. If you look back at our history, we used to have the lowest multiple of all the Singapore banks, price to book ratio. Now, in the last two years, we have the highest multiple. It's not dramatically different, but we've gone from being number three to being number one. We used to be 1.1 to 1.3, now we are 1.4. So, you can see some shift, it is there, but it's not like a tech company.

The one company that has made that shift and been able to attract the right investment profile is Ping An in China. Ping An has done that because they've been able to create Lufax with a FinTech start-up profile. This is part of the whole thinking of Ping An, which is that they are not a bank but have many diversified businesses in there. They put Good Doctor in there, and Good Doctor (Ping An Health & Technology) has got a market cap of S$6 to S$7 billion. They put Lufax in there, and Lufax's market cap.

We think that perhaps the only way to do this is to create ancillary entities that people would value differently from the way they tend to value a core bank. That's the upside, and I think there are a lot of upsides to running an integrated financial services offering. The downside is that if we start to peel off pieces of our operations like this, it gives up the competitive advantage that we have of running an integrated bank. So, do we want to peel some of these things off?

A lot of people are thinking of launching a whole new digital bank rather than changing the big old bank. What do you think?
There are two challenges. One is that you don't change the existing bank. If you look at the scale of any big bank, your new bank will always be small when compared to the existing bank. So, you've given up the big dinosaur and gone for something new that may change in time. The other challenge is that, in most countries, you won't get two banking licences. In most countries, the regulator loathes to give a bank another licence for the separate bank. That means that you cannot create a separate entity, with its own set of investors and own set of financials. It's quite complex.

If you were reflecting and writing your own book about how to change a bank, what would you highlight as key?
It's focus on the customer. I keep going back to that. Even before the 2014 change, digital had taken us in a different trajectory. SMU [Singapore Management University] runs a customer survey every year across every industry, not just banking, and DBS always used to be last. The lowest. Now, we're consistently in the top tier, and number one for customer satisfaction within Singapore.

That happened in Phase One but, back then, we didn't refer to it as the customer journey. We started a customer experience group and began process improvement events, or PIEs. We started the PIEs in 2010, and again we created our own process improvement methodology. The basic message was that we have to focus on customer experience.

In 2010, we also came up with the concept of RED, which is our value proposition: to be Respectful, to be Easy to deal with and to be Dependable. And again, we spent a lot of time taking that message across the company. We gave people the liberty to say, "If it's right for the customer, go ahead and make changes. Just do it." So, we started to get some momentum around these ideas, even in the first phase. That was a big lesson to me. The principal thing was to focus on the customer and, second, put some resources behind it.

I also realised that a lot of people try to do this on the cheap, or they try to look for the return on investment first, which is clearly hard to justify. I just did things that were not expensive or hard to justify, but made sense and made change happen faster.

First, I put twenty to twenty-five people in a team to create the Customer Experience Group. Then, I created the Innovation Group, a twenty-person team. In both cases, I had to be willing to make a bet that they would pay off because I didn't know if they would. You have to take such risks, and I was willing to put a few million dollars behind them. That way, the initiative has value and will pay off in the future.

So those are two big lessons: focus on the customer and create some core teams that will change things. Don't make the core teams do the work. I told the Customer Experience Group: "Your job is not to improve the customer experience. Your job is to create the conditions in the company such that everybody's focused on it." I told the Innovation Group: "I don't want you to innovate a thing. I want you to create the conditions and the culture in the company so that everybody else is intent on innovating for you." That's what you need to do. You have to create the core people—the engines—who will drive the processes in the company to enable these things to happen. Then you have to change the measurement systems.

We created a balanced scorecard back in 2010, balanced across time, short term and long term. We balanced across many things, including financial and non-financial metrics. We made it a religion, to make sure that all of our strategic goals were being captured on the scorecard. And then it cascaded down to every business and was shared across all of the businesses. This meant that everybody was marching to the same tune by 2014, when we started the digital transformation.

In 2014, we modified the balanced scorecard and created a whole section in the middle of the scorecard called the "transformation metrics". These were tactical metrics aimed at getting 100 per cent of customers acquired digitally, measuring the amount of transactions that are done digitally, measuring how to convert to more digital engagement with customers, focusing on how to use digital value capture in terms of financials and more. What is the progress? How many journeys have we committed to? How many have we done?

We measured and evaluated everybody on those transformation metrics in Phase Two but the other key factor is to ensure that people can manage what we measure. You've got to give people the resources. You've got to integrate the scorecard with the KPIs, and fully into the measurement and evaluation process.

Finally, the other big thing is obviously technology. Dave [Gledhill, the CIO] and his team did a fantastic job with this technology transformation. A lot of times, with all the best intentions, you don't get the outcomes you want because technology prevents it. However, realising that technology today can change, and you don't have to rip and replace, meant that we could do it at the margins.

One of the early decisions was not to just go and hire young kids who know how to do Python, and let all of the old technology people go. The truth is that old people know the systems. They know the technology. They know the domain. I remember seeing the head of technology at Netflix being interviewed on YouTube. Somebody was talking to him about all of this tech change and asked where he was finding the people to do it. To which he replied, "I'm hiring the people you are firing." To me that was remarkable *and* logical when you think about it. These are people who know banking, COBOL, C++ and all of the other hard languages. What makes us think that these people can't learn newer languages and newer tools if they can learn those hard languages?

We put some money behind our scheme and gave everybody S$1,000 to spend on self-education. We also told them to learn one thing that they could come back and teach. We made this an entirely internal thing. You have to go and learn and then come back and conduct classes for people in the company.

Regarding all the new projects that we did, we shared them. It wasn't new people doing new projects, but old people doing new projects. We had core teams of existing people who did the whole thing together, and that just blew us away.

We gave ourselves four years to try and move to cloud-enabled technology. Our goal was to get 90 per cent of our systems in the cloud; we moved 85 per cent of them in four years. Just the speed at which it could be done took me by surprise.

Another benefit of internally moving to cloud was the cost implication. Let's say that our IT spend was S$1 billion. We spent 80 per cent of that just to keep the lights on so only 20 per cent was left for new development. Cloud-based technology costs so much less if you can make this change. You can actually save money on keeping the lights on, and then you have that much more money to invest in new developments. Thanks to our move to cloud, our budget is now half and half. We spend half on keeping the lights on, which means we can spend S$500 million on new developments. So, the technology part was a really crucial part of this transformation as well.

You have said quite a few things that I don't hear from other CEOs. For example, supporting change without a business case. It's an order of magnitude. We have a total expense bill of about S$5 billion a year. When I say we've got to take some bets, the willingness to put S$5 or S$10 million into an initiative is not a big bet, but a test. It is also the kind of advantage the board is making.

My board told me to take S$200 million over three years to change the bank, after our failed attempt to acquire a bank in Indonesia back in 2013. Effectively, I was given the licence to make a bet.

I based the whole thing around how we needed to digitise and that there needed to be some major changes in order to digitise. I presented my budgets and plans for 2014, and then the board asked me, "If you do all of this, will we start to catch up with Alibaba?" I replied that I didn't think that we could catch them. The board's initial reaction was, "You're wasting your time" but then proceeded to say, "Okay, let's see what happens."

So, we took a couple by setting up a Customer Experience Initiative and an Innovation Group. If I had needed to make S$100 million, I would have thought a lot harder. I would have looked harder at the business case and return on investment. But I had the freedom to not have to think that way.

Now, we do this in our technology products. We have platforms and give the platforms budgets, and we say that as long as you work within your platform budget, you're welcome to spend it in whichever way you think is sensible. If the project is going to be more than a certain size, then we do have some review processes in our community so that people understand what's going on and agree that it's a sensible way to spend the money. So, we'll take some bets. In instances where people want to put in a little more investment, there's a little more rigour in the process.

The other operation of cloud that is important to understand is that, today, just over 5 per cent of our activities are actually on public cloud, on AWS or Azure, but what we have found is that once you have enough scale, you can mimic what Amazon has done by creating a virtual private cloud. The real value you get is from the shift in the technology to automate DevOps, to move to commodity hardware, to virtualise the server stack, to look for open-sourced software. That's what Amazon does.

How Amazon got to be so good is because that's what they do. They got rid of the big mainframes and moved to commodity hardware. Then they do massive virtualisation. It's like having a different cell for each application, and they shrink the whole thing and virtualise it. They shrink the footprint of the whole data centre when they do that.

We're big enough, so why can't we do the same thing ourselves? The big difference when we moved to a private cloud is that we now get about 80 per cent of the cost efficiency that Amazon can get. That means that we are leaving 20 per cent on the table. If we were to move completely to the public cloud, I think that you could get the extra 15 to 20 per cent but data privacy, regulation and the concern of committing yourself to a single provider are issues if you do that as a bank. A particular concern is whether or not you have data portability in the future, as you could become too concentrated with a single provider. These are quite important considerations. That is why we focus on creating our own private cloud, to get 80 per cent of the value of what we could get externally. That's good enough for us.

If you left DBS and were hired by another big bank to be digital, what would be the first things you would do?
You asked a similar question earlier. Much of what I said there applies here but another blessing that DBS had is that it is "a Goldilocks size". DBS was neither too big nor too small to change; it was just the right size. The bank was big enough to have the right level of resources and small enough to make it able to change with 26,000 people. I think the bigger challenge is when you have 250,000 people and you are in 180 countries or more. Therefore, if I were advising one of the bigger banks, my first thought would be to wonder if you could actually achieve this with 250,000 people? Could you really create a 250,000-person start-up?

I would then look at the core of the business and see if there were manageable pieces of business that I could try and take through this transformation, either by geography or through some lines of business. If you're starting from ground zero, it is easier, but I'd try to get a handle on something that you could make part of the core of the business whilst still being something that you can get your head around.

The second thing that I would do is engage with the board. These kinds of strategies and changes must be brought back to the executive decision-making, which means that the board must understand what you are trying to do and be committed to supporting such change. They must understand that there will be ups and downs. There will be times when you don't have a good quarter. That is one of the biggest challenges for the CEO. If there is a big bad quarter and the investors are baying for blood, then the board could say, "Hey, you know we can't afford to spend" and pull back.

If you have pull-back strategies, they just demoralise the team, so you've got to get the board fully behind you. The same is then true of the senior team. The leadership must be onside so that you've got a shared vision for what you're trying to create and where you're trying to go.

The first task is to find a manageable thing and the second is to make sure that you have a really committed shared vision at the top of the house, that is, where you want to go and what it will take to get there. Then the third piece is where I'd go back to the three pillars that I mentioned earlier. You know, where are we in the technology stack? What can be done to start moving to a new technology stack? What can be done to make customer experience the centrepiece? What can be done regarding other cultural changes?

For example, I have been a big resister of hot-desking. I hate the idea. I have always believed that if you spend so many years in a company and if you make that employer-employee relationship so transactional that they don't even give you somewhere to sit, it is not right. I want to win people's hearts. You've got to make employees feel that they are part of a family.

Then, one day, someone asked me, "When you were growing up, did you have your own room in the house?" My answer was no. I didn't because we were a middle-class family and so I shared my room. He then asked, "Did you feel that your house was your house? I replied that I did. "See," he said, "that's the thing. I'm going to make sure that everybody feels that this is their house, but they don't need to have their own rooms in the house."

How can you create such an environment? Well, he came up with the idea of "joy space", which he then marketed to everybody, asking them about their way of working, and whether it would suit them. The aim was that everyone can create a space that makes sense for them and, today, one third of our spaces are of that nature.

It is these cultural things that matter: how people work, what liberty you give them, the flexibility to experiment, how to do innovation.

I would do the same three things, but I'd first try to make sure that it's manageable and ensure that the top-house team and board are aligned.

When you're trying to deal with a board member who just doesn't get technology, how can you change that mindset?
We didn't have a lot of technologists on the board. Actually, when I think about it, we had none. Seven of our ten board members were ex-bankers. Having domain expertise on the board is really important.

A lot of banks have board members who don't even understand banking, and if you don't understand banking, then I'm grappling with two problems. One, I'm going to grapple with making you understand the banking business and, on top of that, I'm trying to get you to think about how it can be done differently using digital. I was lucky in that I didn't have the first problem.

Most of our board are ex-bankers, so when I talked to them about their own disciplines, about payments or whatever, they understood where I was coming from. Then when I told them that things could be changed in this way, they got it. When I told them that we could change the way in which we distributed products and services, they got that. When I talked about how we could change SME onboarding and SME credit underwriting using digital capabilities, they understood that. For me, it was helpful that the board domain expertise was there.

The second piece is actually converting these people to get the digital thing, and that requires education. We did spend a lot of time with the board, between myself and Dave [the CIO]. We also brought in external people to talk to the board about the future. I created a Technology Advisory Council to work with the board. We appointed people from around the world so they could talk to the board about what was happening in different realms of technology. We did make a lot of effort, but were helped immensely by the fact that the board understood banking in the first place.

How do you see DBS moving forward into the future?

The thing that we've been able to demonstrate is that it is possible for a legacy company to transform. Have we finished the transformation? Of course not. When I compare us with Big Tech, we are clearly nowhere near the finishing line and, on top of this, some of the other players are doing better than us. Capital One do the best job in data, for example. So, there are areas where we still have a lot of work to do, and we're behind in some areas when we look at some of our competitors.

If I had to give ourselves a score on the overall scheme of things, I think we've done a pretty good job of transforming the company. If you ask people if DBS is different today, then I think most would say yes. Ten years ago, DBS stood for "Damn Bloody Slow". Today, they will tell you that it's a "Different Bank in Singapore". That just speaks to the fact that we've been able to get some transformation.

The second thing is that we are one of the few companies that is trying to transform the whole, right to the core. That's an interesting story because it is a transformation where we are really trying to change all of the people.

The third part is that we really focus on both sides of this transformational challenge. We are working on both the hardware transformation—namely, the technology—and the software transformation—namely, the culture. Doing both of these things is not easy but I think it's critical because you can't get one without doing the other.

Finally, how do you see the future of banking?

The nature of banking or financial services won't change very much in the next ten to fifteen years. People will still have money they need to save and invest. They will still need to move money around to pay for things, and people will still need to borrow money and credit to be able to invest. This is the core of banking. You save, you move it around and you invest it. I think those fundamentals don't change in the short or medium term. Even if we do get to a future world where value changes, and everything moves to cryptocurrency, it's not going to happen anytime soon.

How these activities are performed and the notion of saving or moving money around are changing. The players who perform these functions are also changing. So, the act of who raises and collects money and moves money around is where the biggest changes are going to come. Google is doing it. Facebook is doing it. Apple is doing it.

In India, the fastest growth in payments is through WhatsApp and Google Pay. They have half of the market share for all payments. In China, it's WeChat and Alipay. So different people are participating. You get different players. Is there room for traditional banks? I think there is because the reality of banking has always been a fragmented industry.

Look at the U.S. market, for example. There used to be more than 13,000 banks but they've been consolidated into about 6,000 banks. Look at most countries. There is a long tail of banks, and even the long tail of banks make a decent return. So, banking and financial services have a lot of players and we will see a lot of new players, but you'll also see a lot of old players who've been able to transform and convert.

If you're JPMorgan, you bring a lot of things to the party. You bring trust, you bring capital, you bring knowledge of the domain. You bring a lot of things to the party that Apple doesn't bring. It's not the case either that JPMorgan would always lose to Amazon. I don't think that's valid at all. However, some of the players will succeed and, if you don't transform, you will fail. If you don't give the customer a new and more convenient way of working and they find a more convenient way of working through a technology company, the customer will leave. So, then the question is, how do you disrupt yourself and transform yourself? How do you ensure that the customer has a viable proposition with you? That's where we must focus.

DOING DIGITAL: LESSONS FROM LEADERS

As mentioned at the start of this book, I know that banks are not dumb and decided to pick five banks that are doing digital well, from an external observation. These five banks are in the United States (JPMorgan Chase), Europe (BBVA and ING) and Asia (DBS and CMB). Each bank gave me open access to its senior executives for interview. From these many discussions, I identified over thirty lessons in their digital transformation projects that we can all learn from. Some are in a particular order, for example, you need vision and leadership up front, while others span all aspects of change, for instance, you need to reassure people that they can be part of the change. These lessons are shared here.

Does Anyone Know the Way?

❝ The past CEO and the past chairman were ready for and wanted change. They just didn't know how to change. It's easy to say let's change, but then what, where, how? **❞**

Karen Ngui, *Head of Group Strategic Marketing and Communications, DBS*

Many banks think that digital is a project for a function with a leader and a budget. In reality, digital is a mindset change to create a new culture through leadership dedicated to make that change, not allocate a budget. Some banks do understand this. In fact, some very big banks not only get it, but are doing it. They are making the change. They are transforming the business. They are making the elephant dance, as IBM's former CEO Lou Gerstner would say. However, it is not easy.

For example, I talked to a CxO of a bank that was actively engaged in "doing digital" but neither she nor the rest of the bank's executive team knew what "doing digital" actually meant. I was a bit surprised at this admission and gave her my spiel about the logic of digital change. To which she replied, "We don't need to have someone explain that we need to transform to be digital. We know this. The issue is not that we need to change, but we need to know *what* to change and *how* to change."

As the conversation went on, it was clear from her commentary that all of the executive team had got the message about digital transformation, but they could not work out how to do it. From my observations of banks that are doing digital transformation successfully, there seem to be four phases:

- What to change
- How to change
- Change
- Change better

The first phase is learning. Who do you think is digital? Who has transformed to digital? Who do you respect for being digital? What is it about them that you like?

Despite the range of questions, the firms listed in the answers usually boil down to Amazon, Netflix, Spotify, Alphabet, Alibaba, Tencent, Ping An and more. Firms that are transforming may include Microsoft,[30] Walmart,[31] JPMorgan Chase and more. When you have made your list, go out and meet these firms. Find out what makes them tick. See how they are organised. See what they have done. Doing so will give you the answers to the "what to do" questions.

---

30 See "Lessons from leaders: Satya Nadella, CEO, Microsoft," Finanser (blog), 16 May 2019, https://thefinanser.com/2019/05/lessons-from-leaders-satya-nadella-ceo-microsoft.html/.
31 See "What banks can learn from Wal-Mart," Finanser (blog), 18 May 2017, https://thefinanser.com/2017/05/banks-can-learn-wal-mart.html/.

Once you know *what* to change, you need to work out *how*. This is the second phase. Work out how you need to organise the business based on the lessons learnt from your first-phase explorations. How are the benchmark firms organised and, if you were going to be more like them, how would you need to organise yourself? What changes will need to be made to people, structure, products and services? How radical a departure is this from the current business structure, and how will it impact both careers and the organisational and business model? How would you implement the changes and over what time period? So on and so forth.

Now that you know *what* to do and *how* to do it, *do it*. This is phase three. This is the hardest phase because it is all about implementation and execution. Nevertheless, don't be rigid and don't be worried about failure. Allow failure and adapt. Be flexible and focused. Don't try to do things too fast; do them in your own time. In addition, don't allow things along the way to stop you proceeding to where you want to go. You need to acknowledge that you will get things wrong, there will be resistance, there will be challenges and there may even be tears. Let it be. Let it happen. Adapt and change.

In particular, as this phase is the most challenging, give it time. Sorting out all of the bank's systems and structures has to be a slow burn and often takes more than five years to achieve. First, sort out the basics. If there are known issues in the organisation, such as old technologies that need a refresh, do those things first. Sort out the problems before implementing the vision as you won't be able to move forward if the company is hampered by heritage.

Second, implement the new structure. This is not simply changing systems, but changing the company, and involves far more effort than sorting out the basics. The sorting out of basics might be a system upgrade; the implementation of the vision might be a refresh of the complete system. It is much easier to refresh the organisation once it is working properly than try to refresh a broken company.

Third, drive forward towards the vision. Now that you have the goals, systems, structure and measurements in place, it is time to turn it up. It is time to turbocharge the refresh.

Now these three steps may sound trite in the five hundred or so words it took to write but, bearing in mind that this is a three- to ten-year journey, these steps are incredibly challenging and complex. Many people believe that they can jump straight to implementation because that will sort out the basics. It seems that such thinking is wrong. Sure, you can refresh one part of the company, but not all in one go. As you go on your way, you will have reached the final phase before you know it: do it better.

Digital transformation is not easy and it does not stop. Once the changes are implemented, you will find that there are things you have learnt during the third phase that you want to go back and try again. Equally, there will be things that you did not know about before that you can now try to do, like moving rationalised systems into Cloud Computing. That sort of action could not have been done *until* you rationalised. In fact, there are likely to be a lot of things that you cannot do until after you have implemented the first wave of change. Now you can focus on changing better, not just making the change.

These are the things that I learnt and observed from talking to banks that had digitally transformed. I hope it helps. The CxO said that it did, and was already walking away to book a trip to Silicon Valley and China.

> **❝** In the late 1990s, digitisation was a way to do things more efficiently. It was the start of the digital change of tech operations. The core focus was to deliver more efficient banking to save cost through tech. In the last few years, digitisation is dictating customer interaction. It has changed a lot, in the ways we interact with our customers. Now, the firm belief is that the only way to distinguish yourself from competition in banking is through digital customer interaction. **❞**
> **Vincent van den Boogert**, *CEO, ING Netherlands*

THE LEADERSHIP CHALLENGE

" I'd point at four key elements of leadership skills that are essential for digital transformation. The first one is courage because there are decisions to be made and you need the courage to sometimes let part of your business go to someone else, because it's not profitable and would require too much investment for the coming ten to twenty years. I think it's courageous because you need a very strong story to explain this to the market outside, a determination to do this in the long run and dare to probably go against the opinion of the crowd. A second key element is balancing long-term and short-term interests. Of course, you need to deliver in the short term, yet balancing the efforts which are made, and which are not delivering anything in the short term. Nothing is visible. It's all underwater. For example, if you change your IT system in order to improve data analytics, all those things are cost. I remember when we were faced with adding the mobile phone to access the bank. I remember all those discussions. Why should we do mobile? Why should we be interested? Where is the business case? Will it really be profitable one day? I think we need to go away from the logic of what the short-term business case is and move to create a vision, and that vision must start from the top, which needs to be courageous to do this. Thirdly, you need humility, acknowledging any moment when you actually don't know all of the answers. You don't know what the future will look like, whether a technology will be there to stay, whether you allocate your resources in the most effective way. Finally,

being open, connected to your ecosystem, looking for the best solutions, partners and distribution networks will be essential to be successful in an economy which no longer will be linear but rather platform-based. **"**
Benoît Legrand, *Chief Innovation Officer, ING Group*

Before starting digital transformation, you need to check that the leadership challenge has been met. As mentioned in the last section, many bank leaders—the CEO and chairman, in particular—do not know what to do or how to do it. They do not know how to lead digital transformation and so, instead, they make digital change. This is because they delegate the project instead of leading it. Therefore, there are three tests to check that you have the right leadership mindset before embarking on digital transformation.

The first test is to wonder if the bank has the whole leadership team on board or if the team has delegated digital change to a project, a function, a budget, a person. Has the team delegated the future of the bank? Is the accountability with the CEO and their direct reports, or are the CEO and their team passing responsibility down the leadership chain?

Any bank that treats digital transformation as a delegated project is going to fail.

Now, let's assume that this is accepted and understood, the second phase of transforming the organisation to digital is even harder. This phase involves working out how to rebuild the bank from the ground up and making it happen. What to do, how to do it, doing it and doing it better. These are the four phases that digitally transforming banks move through. It takes time and it is not easy.

The key to this phase is to give the executive team the latitude to do it. Many leaders are so focused on the boardroom, investor and shareholder needs that they do not have this latitude. The banks that are successfully transforming have breathing space to focus on the customer, systems and change rather than having to focus on cost, income and the shareholder.

The second test of whether a bank "gets it" is to see whether the bank is truly changing into a cohesive, enterprise operation or whether it is being run product by product, function by function. The bank that is transforming the whole organisation in a co-ordinated manner is going to succeed. This is because a lot of the next decade of competition will be between the Big Techs, FinTechs and banks, and the bank that is not rationalised to be a co-ordinated enterprise will fail.

The third phase is making the change happen. Having worked out what to do and how to do it, this is the doing it and doing it better phase. It is when the bank transforms the organisation and not just the systems. It is when the bank changes the culture and mindset, not just the systems and structures.

It is demonstrated by banks reskilling staff, reducing staff numbers, shrinking their physical footprint and building a digital platform. It is when you can see, in practice, that everyone is being encouraged to challenge and change. That innovation is no longer a token word but a real way of thinking. That Open Banking is being seen as an opportunity and not a threat.

This is why the third and final test is to ask if the bank is still a control freak, wanting to build everything itself and avoid partnering with others, or has it truly changed to be a curator, offering its banking platform to work with start-ups and third parties with no fear of compromise, but excitement at opportunity?

These three tests are not comprehensive or exhaustive. However, they are good tests to see if the culture and mindset of the bank are ready for true organisational change and simply not doing what they have always done. In summary, transforming the organisation to be digital is just as important, if not more so, as changing the systems to be digital.

❝ It comes from leaders that are not satisfied with the status quo and who are not satisfied with the business that we have today. It comes from leaders wanting to grow existing products and business lines, but recognising key future trends and wanting to experiment with them, whilst being comfortable with failure. So much of it comes from that leadership at the top. Once you have leadership at the top, it's then getting the right talent to join them. We describe it as having creators because a lot of banks have brilliant bankers with banking in their DNA and their education and their profiles. Many of them have learned how to run businesses, to monitor, to analyse, to document processes and to measure them. Bankers are brilliant at that. The digital world is different, however. The digital world is moving to speed and scale and, in order to have speed and scale, you have to have creators that know how to create in a digital world. The banks that are lagging are those that have not recognised the very basics of what is required in the digital world, often because they have not got the right leadership. First, you need the leadership recognition of the need to change and then it's making sure you have the right human capital to invest. You can identify a vision, a strategy, projects and you can invest financial capital, but if you don't have the human capital who are creators versus the people running the existing business, then you have a problem. **"**

Derek White, *former Global Head of Customer Solutions, BBVA*

The CEO and Chair Make Digital Banking Work

"It starts right at the top. None of the work that we do would be possible without the board endorsement and all management. Without that senior support, alignment of strategy and pushing all these experimentations and culture changes through the organisation and telling people it's okay to experiment, you are not going to get anything done. **"**

Chng Sok Hui, *Chief Financial Officer, DBS*

Most of the banks embracing true digital transformation are led by people who understand technology. They have a leadership team who are passionate about digitalisation, and see it as the raison d'être of the bank's future. Not just an add-on. When comparing JPMorgan Chase, BBVA and DBS with a few others that are not as forward thinking about digital, namely, HSBC, Deutsche Bank and Maybank, you find that the executive team structures and leaders are different, particularly when looking at the operational management of each bank. Not the board or the lines of business, but the CEO and their direct reports. What are their backgrounds? Who are they? Where do they come from? What technology experience do they have?

Starting with JPMorgan Chase, the only person on the team with a dedicated technology background is Lori Beer, the CIO. However, I would say that Jamie Dimon is a technology guy. You may disagree, but he was the man who insourced the outsourcing contract from IBM when Bank One and JPMorgan Chase merged. The reason?

"We believe managing our own technology infrastructure is best for the long-term growth and success of our company, as well as our shareholders," explained Austin Adams,[32] JPMorgan Chase's then CIO, on behalf of Jamie Dimon who, bear in mind, came from the trading floor and saw the strategic advantage that technology could make to the investment markets operations. In other words, the leader of the most admired bank in the world sees technology as a core business and competitive advantage.

BBVA's executive committee includes Carlos Torres Vila, former CEO and now chairman, who is an alumni of the Massachusetts Institute of Technology (MIT), a former partner at McKinsey and was head of BBVA's digital banking programme. Onur Genç, CEO, began life as an engineer and joined American Airlines as the financial controller for IT before joining McKinsey. The heads of Customer Solutions, Engineering and Data are also represented on the leadership team in roles dependent on technology by background.

DBS's management team has Piyush Gupta, the CEO, who formerly

32 Dawn Kawamoto, "JPMorgan Chase cancels IBM outsourcing contract," CNET, 15 September 2004, https://www.cnet.com/news/jpmorgan-chase-cancels-ibm-outsourcing-contract/.

ran operations including technology for Citibank India as chief of staff. David Gledhill, former Group CIO, spent his life in technology and operations in JPMorgan Chase before moving to DBS. Shee Tse Koon, Singapore Country Head, was previously CIO and Head of Technology and Operations for Standard Chartered in Singapore.

Having done this analysis, the operational leadership teams of these three banks do not appear to be all that different from the teams heading the less digital banks. HSBC, Deutsche Bank and Maybank have similar teams. The only difference I can really identify is the CEO and chairperson.

The CEOs and chairs of JPMC, BBVA and DBS, respectively, have worked closely together to make digital transformation happen and each of the CEOs fundamentally believes that digital is core to the future of the business. Without digital transformation, they wholeheartedly believe that the bank will fail in the future.

In contrast, the CEOs and chairs of HSBC, Deutsche Bank and Maybank talk digital, but do they walk it? Have they internalised it in the way that Jamie Dimon, Carlos Torres Vila and Piyush Gupta have? It does not appear to be the case from external observation, and there is a clear difference between leaders who talk digital and walk digital. The former do it for investor relations and because they feel they should; the latter do it for the future of the bank and truly believe that it has to happen.

Either way, it is those two roles—the CEO and chair—that make the real difference. The chair needs to be on board to get the board's backing and protect the bank from shareholder resistance during the transformation process. The CEO has to be on board to get the leadership team, management and people aligned to the vision of where the bank is going.

In particular, the CEOs of the banks embracing digital transformation tend to have had considerable involvement in technology during their career. Jamie Dimon knows that technology is mission critical, which is why he will not outsource everything; Piyush Gupta was hands-on, having run the IT operations of Citibank India; and BBVA's former chairman,

Francisco González, started his career in programming mainframe systems as a developer. That is the real difference: a CEO and/or chair immersed in technology at some point in their career. Other than this, there is very little difference between a digital bank and a traditional bank.

> **❝** One of the biggest challenges is getting the boardrooms to have a sense of urgency. After all, what is their motivation? If you are going to retire in two to three years, you may not have the motivation to start transforming your business. There's a possibility that you don't take a lot of risks for very low upside. This is a key challenge to create a sense of urgency in the company but, more importantly, also in the supervisory boardrooms. This is where the biggest question should be asked. Do we have the right management and people, who have the motivation and the willingness and the passion and the energy to build the future of banking for the coming ten to fifteen years in that boardroom while delivering value in the short term? Do we have people who understand the business, who know about the challenges, who know a lot about technology? **❞**
>
> **Benoît Legrand**, *Chief Innovation Officer, ING Group*

Doing Digital Needs the Board's Mandate

> **❝** That mandate has been very important. It has given us a lot of strength to push changes that were not easy. If you look at the reorganisation that took place at the bank, that was a huge change of half of the leadership team. It took a lot of guts on the board's side to go with that and it was a statement that yes, we want transformation to happen and we are not going fast enough, so we are putting all engines on fire to do this. **❞**
>
> **Carlos Torres Vila**, *Group Executive Chairman, BBVA*

Another key factor in building a truly digital bank is commitment. Commitment from the top, and by the top. By this, I don't just mean the CEO and the leadership team, but the board of the bank as well. Quite often, the digital transformation of a bank requires years of commitment, during which time shareholder return takes second place. A bank that is only focused on shareholder return will fail in the process.

I have heard this quite often from the leaders of digital banks. Specifically, it was the support of the chairman and commitment of the board that allowed them to embark on what, for some, is a perilous journey of change. After all, we are talking about major investment in new structures, a complete replacement of core systems and a determined focus on building anew.

Interestingly, the commitment and decision of the board to radically change the bank were often sparked by disappointment. For example, I have encountered examples of when the banks tried to refresh their systems in the last decade and failed. They had undergone huge projects that cost millions to upgrade mainframe structures, but these projects were over budget and overdue. Big consulting companies had promised that the refresh could be done by X for Y dollars but, instead, it would actually be X times five years and Y times \$100 million.

Now imagine a board and chairman being told that Y dollars had been spent to get a new upgrade finished by X but it would not happen unless they spent Y times \$100 million for delivery five years later than scheduled. The disappointment and let-down of such delays triggered a new view within the bank's executive teams, and sparked an alternative way of thinking. Think about it. I am talking about the end of the last decade. What was happening then? Cloud Computing. Big Data. APIs. Banking-as-a-Service.

What amazes me is that a very small number of truly visionary bank CEOs got it way back then. Most are just waking up to it now. Most have only just understood that digital banking is not a project, but a change. However, these few understood that ten years ago and are now truly becoming digital banks. It may have taken them ten years to get there, but they are getting there, and it never stops. They are now continuing on their change programmes going forward.

Interestingly, most of these banks have had the same CEO and chairman during this time, and they have steered the banks through this turbulent change period. What they did is quite incredible really in that, instead of giving ABC Consulting a billion dollars to upgrade their creaking old systems over five years, they developed their own bank structure through transitioning to cloud, piece by piece, programme by programme.

What is more, the more they moved to cloud, the lower their cost and the more agile they became. That is what digital banking is all about. Creating a fast, flexible, new bank that is unconstrained by creaking old systems and no longer tied to a big consulting company or big computer company to do everything for you. No wonder these banks are starting to move away from the crowd and prove that digital does not just deliver a better bank, but a more efficient and profitable bank too. One that increases shareholder returns by having an on-demand systems structure, rather than one with huge capital overhead.

However, a bank needs the protection from shareholder return, quarterly results and the traditional financial metrics to allow that digital transformation to happen. That means that the board has to give the CEO and chair the backing to make it happen, and give them the relief to focus on the change and not on the financial metrics. Intriguingly, many of the banks still delivered the financial results during the transformation. However, the fact that this took second place allowed them to focus on the outcomes, and not the results. This is critical.

> **❝** It started with the relationship between the top team and the board. It is a very symbiotic one. We have a hugely supportive chairman and board. They gave the team the support, and encouraged us to take risk. Another key stage was architecting the bank and the process that's been happening, particularly on the whole technology side. It was

just the case of watching how the world is changing. These days we do everything on our phone. Another factor is just realising why we exist as a bank. As cliché as it may sound, we realise that our role in people's lives is to help them live better lives. That's why our new campaign is all about making banking invisible so that you can Live More, Bank Less. **"**

Karen Ngui, *Head of Group Strategic Marketing and Communications, DBS*

Digital Transformation Needs a Burning Platform

" One of the biggest challenges was how to change the organisation. A lot of companies want to trial and error this and do it in a smaller way. The issue is that if you just start with one department and the others are not involved, it cannot work. You have to start the whole company at the same time. That is a really big transition, but that's what we did. We went through a process where everybody applied for their new job, and everybody started at the same point in this new squad, in this new tribe, in this new department. It was a really big bang, because we changed the organisation in total with everyone at the same starting point. **"**

Vincent van den Boogert, *CEO, ING Netherlands*

I started working in business process re-engineering and transformation a while ago, before most millennials were born, and learnt a lesson early on. Transformation will never work without a crisis point. You cannot make the whole company change if profits are good, objectives are being met, customers are happy and bonuses are fat. There must be some compelling threat—a burning platform—to make the change.

In many cases, this is the near-death of the company. For some banks, this has been the case in recent times, due to the global financial crisis. However, I don't think that many banks have really achieved digital transformation because their burning platform was not the technology but the operations. The products, services and culture of the banks were considered rotten to the core as crisis after crisis hit. First, there was the meltdown, then there were the accusations, then there were the fines, then there were the court cases and so on. These issues are still with us today. I have seen more banks radically restructure and refocus their products, services and geographies, but I have seen very few that have radically transformed their technology stack for digital transformation.

A few visionary banks embarked on these changes even before the global financial crisis, but they were spurred on by it. They specifically saw early on that technology could be a game changer when cloud, analytics and APIs appeared on the horizon. They were specifically spurred into action when investors started piling billions of dollars into start-ups to exploit cloud, analytics and APIs to attack the incumbent banks.

Jamie Dimon heralded the call for change when he declared that "Silicon Valley ... [they all] want to eat our lunch." Many banks around that time, in 2014, began talking digital. That is what many banks were doing—talking—but they were not doing digital. Doing digital is making the core of the bank digital. It is not just adding it as a channel.

Talking with DBS in Singapore, the head of consumer banking said that there was a moment when everyone knew that they had to change. I asked what it was, and the answer was that the company had decided to launch a brand-new stand-alone digital bank in India. Not only was this a bold move, it also signalled to all the management that digital banking had to be taken seriously. Not just in India—it was a big bet by the bank on digital being the future. It forced everyone to wake up and think, Hey, if I don't get into digital banking, I might not have a future in this bank.

For others, it is a call to the grass roots of the bank. When the crisis hit a decade ago, many banks said that it was a chance to reboot their bank. Some of them took that chance. Some, however, had too many fires to put out first, and have only just got round to doing it.

It is intriguing to look at the difference in bank attitudes towards digital and change. I know that change is hard and getting everyone to understand it is tough, but if you don't put a rocket up the backside of every member of the firm—a burning platform—then you will never transform the firm. You will just get more of the same, perhaps delivered a little bit faster and a little bit cheaper.

> **❝** The CEO said this is a priority, and then followed it up with the iconic move. With that iconic move, I saw that every business manager, who had previously not been interested, got the message, namely, I'm going to be left potentially behind. And it started changing the culture. **❞**
>
> **Sandeep Lal**, *Group Head of Digital Bank, DBS*

And a Compelling Vision

> **❝** The CEO came up with a big heavy audacious goal and told us, 'Guys, competition is at your heels, if you don't change, you die.' If you don't change, you die—that is the message to everybody. It's that burning platform. When you have that, it's not just about fearmongering, saying that if you don't change you die, but also about how we lead the troops there, having such a big audacious goal. Let's aim to be the best digital bank in the world. That became a galvanising goal. Having a big heavy audacious goal. Having a goal is not everything. Once you have a goal, you need to deploy it to your entire management team. Everybody must buy the goal. Are you signing up or aren't you? How do we make it happen? When a lot of companies do something like that, it's probably within the front office, maybe a particular business. Here it's pervasive. It is the goal of the entire bank, including HR. How do I become digital? How do I support the organisation to become the best digital bank? **❞**
>
> **Lee Yan Hong**, *Managing Director and Head of Group Human Resources, DBS*

A compelling vision is needed along with a burning platform. People need to know where to go when they are told to go. That is an obvious message, but many transforming firms only provide the fire and not the destination. It requires strong communication skills and clear direction, which is why digitally transforming traditional banks have leaders who can communicate well.

When you think of great leaders, you might name people like Steve Jobs, Barack Obama, Nelson Mandela and Winston Churchill. What these people have in common is that they are all great orators. Their speeches are marked in history, and often cited as inspiration. That is why their vision is compelling.

This is what banks need. Leaders who can communicate a compelling vision, as well as give a reason to change. People don't follow leaders because they are told to. People follow leaders because they want to. Because they inspire them. Because they lead them. And it is their ability to articulate complex ideas and instil them in people's hearts, and in people's heads, that makes them great leaders.

Great leaders harness and use simple language well. They can inspire us by appealing to our basic instincts. It is their gift and something that they do well. Does your company have such a person? Who inspires you? Think about why they inspire you. Is it their success, their personality or their use of language? It may be all three, but their language will be a critical part of why and how they inspire you. After all, to lead people you need to have a vision of where you want people to go. Then you have to share that vision with passion to get them to follow you. This is what leadership is all about and why we have so few great leaders. However, a compelling vision communicated as a strong internal process of change is what is needed for digital transformation to succeed and to bring everyone on board in the process.

It is not easy to communicate a vision well. It is particularly difficult because most people can only remember two or three things that you say. If you talk for half an hour, you are lucky if people remember anything that you have said. That is the reason why most presentation courses advise you to tell people what you are going to say, say it and then tell them what you have said. Try and get one or two basic messages across. Do not try and make ten or twenty points as they will be lost along the way.

Therefore, most of the banks succeeding in digital transformation have an easy-to-remember vision based on phrases and acronyms for staff to use. I encountered this leadership method way back when, with one CEO using the mantra "Happy people make happy customers make happy business," and another using acronyms to share his vision. The importance here is that it is not just an acronym but a way of working, with KPIs, measurement systems and rewards geared towards these structures. After all, what you measure is what you get and what you measure and reward first is what you get first.

Here is an example from one of the banks that I studied a few years ago. The bank wanted to be the first choice for its customers. "First choice" means being Friendly, Informed, Responsive, Service-oriented and Trustworthy. Being Friendly, Informed, Responsive, Service-oriented and Trustworthy is measured by customer feedback in branch and online, as well as key structured systems that monitor how staff are delivering service to customers.

This is illustrated well by BBVA, which measures all of its business performance systems in real time on a global basis. This means that the CEO and leadership team can access business visualisation tools from their mobile devices, and see not just the digital sales and service metrics in Spain and Argentina, but can also click down into the performance of individual people working in Spain and Argentina and see how well or badly they are doing. Sound scary? Not really, as it is not used as a punitive system but as a nurturing system, helping people to progress towards better digital delivery. It is also why BBVA knows its performance right to the last minute:

> "BBVA's commitment to technology has translated into an increase in the number of digital customers, which now represent

more than 50% of the bank's total customers, as well as climbing digital sales, now comprising 41% of all sales. But this digital journey means much more. Digitization has also contributed to greater customer satisfaction and a diminishing drop-out — 47% lower among digital customers."[33]

It reminds me of when I first got into technology and we offered a private videotext service to UK businesses. One of my clients was a retailer and the CEO loved the fact that he could call a store on Monday morning and either congratulate or commiserate them on their Saturday sales. Real-time performance management makes a big difference.

DBS in Singapore has taken this truly to heart, with KPIs incorporating critical digital delivery measurements. The bank has traditional KPIs:

Shareholder metrics measure both financial outcomes achieved for the year as well as risk-related KPIs to ensure that growth is balanced against the level of risk taken, including compliance and control.

Customer metrics measure DBS's achievement in increasing customer satisfaction and depth of customer relationships.

Employee metrics measure the progress made in being an employer of choice, including employee engagement and people development.

The bank also has focal metrics around regional services and skills. However, 20 per cent of its measurements are based around digital, covering:

Ecosystems: measure the progress made in developing meaningful relationships with ecosystem partners.

Acquire: measure the progress made in leveraging digital channels to acquire new customers with increased digital channel share.

Transact: measure the reduction in manual efforts by driving straight-through processing and instant fulfilment.

---

33 "Digitization means more closely connected and satisfied customers," BBVA, 6 February 2019, https://www.bbva.com/en/digitization-means-more-closely-connected-and-satisfied-customers/.

Engage: measure the progress made in growing customers' digital engagements with the bank.

Value: measure the progress made in driving digital behaviours of consumer and small- and medium-sized enterprise (SME) customers in Singapore and Hong Kong, and increasing the income from digital customers.

Experiences: measure the progress in embedding how DBS is achieving the delivery of superior customer and employee experiences.

Culture: measure the progress in rewiring mindsets to be a 26,000-person start-up anchored on its PRIDE! values, namely:

- **P**urpose-driven: creating impact beyond banking
- **R**elationship-led: building long-lasting relationships and teams
- **I**nnovative: embracing change to add value
- **D**ecisive: our people have the freedom to think, act and own
- **E**!: Everything Fun! We believe in having fun and celebrating successes together

This is the critical factor. You cannot just create a crisis—a burning platform—and ask people what they are going to do about it. You have to create the crisis and then provide the direction to solve it. There must be a way forward, a clear vision, a destination to head towards and a way of bringing everyone along with you in that direction. You then need a way to measure the journey, monitor the direction and ensure that people are moving in the right way.

It is this combination of vision, communication and measurement that monitors the heartbeat of the organisation and the way in which it is working towards the future, not just creating a concern, leaving people to deal with it and having no idea of whether it is working.

> ❝ When we talk about our vision and values, number one is the customer comes first. What that means is that we behave with integrity of course. We are also empathic and put ourselves in the shoes of our customer. Also, that we resolve the problems they have when and if they have

them. We act upon it and solve the need that the customer has. Those are the three behaviours we want to promote in that first idea of putting the customer first: integrity, empathy and action. Second is that we think big and thinking big means ambition. Thinking big means breaking the mould and promoting change for the sake of change itself. This leads back to this idea of accelerating the pace of change internally. It is very important in a bank like ours that we promote change and we actively encourage changing the status quo. The third idea of thinking big is surprising the client. We want to surprise the client with the amazing magic that technology brings. This is another of our key values: think big, make changes, surprise the customer; and it's thinking big in terms of what we can accomplish. And the third idea is that we are One Team. One Team means a few things, but we summarise it in that I trust my teammates without needing them to demonstrate that they are trustworthy because we are in the same team. I trust them from the outset. Secondly, I'm committed. It's not that I just come to work to pass the time and make some money, but I really believe in the purpose that we have. That purpose is to bring opportunity to everyone. Bringing opportunity means that we can really solve a big problem that one has around money. Finally, that I behave responsibly with the resources of the bank as if they were my own. 🟊🟊

Carlos Torres Vila, *Group Executive Chairman, BBVA*

It Is Only Words

As I visit many banks, I am always struck by their similarities and differences. To be honest, there are more similarities than differences. Most have big corporate offices, with great views over their home cities; their branches are well-lit stores with open counters; and their apps all offer, at least at first glance, the same things: balance, payment, statements and suchlike.

Another similarity is that they all have values. Not values as in a market valuation of $152 billion, but values as in "We love our customers" or "Our people are our greatest asset". Often, these values are displayed on a big poster board in the middle of the main reception or halfway up the building on the executive floor. These boards often contain phrases like "Respect, Excellence and Passion", "Caring, Ambition and Responsive" and "Friendly, Informed and Flexible". Sometimes, the words that represent the firm's values create acronyms like RISE, LOVE and FIRST. My favourite is the bank whose values are Leadership, Integrity, Pride and Service, or LIP Service for short.

Now, many banks display such posters depicting their values and missions, but the executive leadership team does not deploy them well. They are just words, or lip service, and not something wired into the DNA of the bank. Mission statements and values are meaningful but only if we give them meaning through leadership. In fact, if you were to ask a CEO or their direct reports to tell you what the bank's values and mission statement are, and how they convey them to people in their daily work, many would struggle to do so.

They could probably give you some, or possibly all, of the bank's values because they have the acronym to remember. However, how do they measure those values? How are people trained in those values? How are those values embodied in the everyday banking experience? They could also probably give you a version of the mission statement. However, could they tell you how they have internalised that mission statement for themselves? What does it mean in regard to how they behave and work? How do they get colleagues and friends within the firm to live and breathe those words alongside them? Can they do that?

Some banks and bank leadership teams do this well. Some really work their values and mission, and have KPIs, Critical Success Factors (CSFs) and management dashboards to make them live and breathe. Does yours? Is it in the DNA of the firm? Or is it just lip service?

Figure 4.1 Working on the bank's mission

> **❝** My first question would be, 'Why go digital?' If you just say, 'Let's go digital,' it sounds like brainless enthusiasm. You should always understand the why: what is the aim of going digital? If you don't have the belief to do something, don't start. The second thing would be to go digital under the radar, at a very small scale, by small initiatives. Start small because the small projects can give you proof points, and then you get the growing enthusiasm of people that want to join these projects and make them work. Equally, start small as you don't want to over commit too early. You may also have people whose aim is to not make it work, so you need to have some small themes that have proof points. Then agree with the top board to do it massively in the future. Third, look at other companies that are inspirational. For example, Airbnb, Netflix and Amazon.

How are they doing it? What are inspirational proof points?
Then set a date that you can't escape. It's important to set
a big milestone, as that will remove resistance by selection.
Remember you can carry people with you who are not sure
of the change or are afraid to lose power, so you should
almost exaggerate the change to get them to shift and move
along. That's what a clear deadline does. **"**

Vincent van den Boogert, *CEO, ING Netherlands*

BOTTOM LINE

Banks need strong leaders who can communicate well, have a
compelling vision of where their bank needs to go in their digital
transformation and a strong reason for changing in the first place—a
burning platform. These factors need to be well thought out before
starting the transformation process, and must be clearly changing the
metrics of measurement, incentives, bonuses and structures of the
bank to align with the vision, and not just be words.

THE TECHNOLOGY CHALLENGE

> **ff** The leadership must be aware that technology is very important. Use technology to innovate. At the same time, you also have to maintain your existing systems and ensure that they are very reliable and stable. The skill is that you know how to manage the technology, especially at the executive level. You have to know, otherwise you invest in the leading-edge technology and you will hesitate. You will be afraid of destroying your reliability, your stable system. So, you've got to know how to use innovative leading-edge technology. First is the support from leaders. **JJ**
>
> **Kunde Chen**, *CIO, CMB*

For years, I have wondered why people in business operations could not align their needs with the people delivering technology in the organisation. The CIO would sit outside the business, watching and responding to requests. The requests would get prioritisation and be delivered in sequence over time, sometimes over a very long time. The businesspeople would get frustrated that the technology people did not deliver exactly what they needed, and would argue about getting reprioritisation. And so the circle went round and round.

In the last century, most technology developments would take years, involve hundreds or even thousands of developers, come with a large consulting and technology team hired from the likes of Accenture and IBM and eventually be delivered on a Monday morning looking slightly weird and wrong. For some, this has changed dramatically. In talking with banks that understand digitalisation, they do not operate this way. Instead, they operate in a microservices structure where teams have designers, coders, developers and techies integrated with product and service people, customer-focused people and businesspeople all in the same group. They go around the round, debating and developing in real time using cloud-based services and Python. They use containerisation and have that lovely term "kubernetes"[34] buzzing around the company.

This is nothing like the old, traditional bank. It is instead a FinTech bank. A FinTech bank does not isolate the *Fin* from the *Tech*, but integrates it. It is an eye-opener when you see this in action. Although few do this at present, the FinTech bank does not let technology do its own thing. It embraces it or, rather, it embraces IT. Technology drives the organisation and the organisation drives the technology. There is no separation, as it is symbiotic.

We have known for decades that technology and business must be aligned, so it seems odd that they were separated into such distinct groupings in the past. I remember working for one large, global bank a decade ago, and my job was to help the company with its new integrated technology and operations group. The group had elected a small number of individuals to be relationship managers (RMs). These RMs were not for customers, but to be the interface between technology and operations and the business.

This was because business did not understand technology. It was very complex, involving mainframes and code that no one could write, except the people in technology and operations. Likewise, the technology and operations people did not understand the business. The business was all about maximising share of customer wallet and shareholder returns using complex terminologies around collateralised debt obligations (CDOs) and Masters of Business Administration (MBAs), interest rate differentials and cross-sell ratios. How was a person immersed in COBOL supposed to understand that? The two groups sat at opposite ends of the spectrum, staring at each other and having no idea what the other did, and needed someone in the form of an RM to bridge the divide.

---

34 Kubernetes is a term used to describe many small teams working on code in what are called containers. Each container performs a function, such as an API or a process. For example, you could consider many of the players on platforms like Stripe a container, as in it is open-sourced, plug-and-play code that you interoperate with your containers of code online. Kubernetes is then the method of co-ordinating these containers of code, using open-sourced systems to achieve this. It allows a bank to have many teams working on code at scale, as well as many partnering firms developing code alongside those teams, and all co-ordinated in a simple way.

This is no longer true. The move towards rapid cycle development using low-cost systems, easy internet services and cloud means that the technology people are being thrown out of their warehouses and caves and being deployed into the business. In turn, the businesspeople, who previously looked at these developers with suspicion, have now discovered that they are human. The result is that ideas can be brainstormed on Monday morning, designed on Monday afternoon, trialled on Tuesday morning and released on Tuesday afternoon. The businesspeople are no longer constrained by slow developments that may take years to deliver and meet their needs in a manner that just misses the mark. Instead, they can now have their needs developed in near real time and be part of the process of designing their next-generation services.

> **❝** 'Tech is business, business is tech' is our mantra. It used to be that the business guys wanted to do something and then threw it to the tech guys. We would say, 'We don't care. You just have to build this the quickest and cheapest way possible.' Then the tech guys would come back and say, 'We don't understand what you're trying to do.' Now we've moved into colocation. Business is colocated with the tech guys, who are dedicated to our business. Now we know exactly who we are dealing with and it's the same team of people. That means we go through the journey together. So colocation for us is very important. They participate in all our strategy meetings and reviews, and vice versa. And you know, we've also moved into a platform organisation. We're not just looking at projects, we're really looking at the different types of platforms and how we have two in a box—one for business, one from technology—responsible for end-to-end delivery of that platform. **❞**
>
> **Pearlyn Phau**, *Managing Director and Deputy Group Head of Consumer Banking Group and Wealth Management, DBS*

Technology Is Business, Business Is Technology

> **"** If you are getting your data online, 24 days after the month end is published and then reacting to that, it is too late. How could you compete with Amazon who run many thousands of real-time tests all the time on their home screen because they are getting real-time feeds of data? Look how that compounding effect has influenced their sophistication. We are seeking to get as close to real time as possible, for people to have the data at the interaction level to help them make decisions. It is not just gathering data, opening data and storing data in a data lake that is calm and flat and placid, but how do you get the data from the data lake into the interaction level of every decision you make? **"**
>
> **Derek White**, *former Global Head of Customer Solutions, BBVA*

A key nuance of the FinTech bank is the integration of business and technology. These banks think that technology is business and business is technology. This is clearly demonstrated in their microservices team structures and agile thinking. Auditors, compliance, financial and marketing people sit in teams co-creating with designers, developers and coders. Again, it quite surprised me that there is no functional structure in these banks. Sure, there are people who sit in different roles, but they do not distance themselves from people in other roles. Quite often, they will sit together and work together. In other words, they are all motivated by digital transformation to make things happen together, and are not bonused or structured to just get rewarded for what their job does.

One of the best ways to illustrate this is to look at DBS's rewards structure where traditional measurements of success are now combined with digital reward structures. The traditional measurements comprise 40 per cent of the bonus, the areas of focus another 40 per cent and the new digital indicators make up the remaining 20 per cent.

What are the traditional measurement structures?

- Deliver consistent income growth
- Be cost-efficient while investing for growth, with cost-income ratio improving over time
- Grow exposures prudently, aligned to risk appetite
- Deliver consistent ROE
- Achieve broad-based increase in customer satisfaction across markets and segments
- Deepen wallet share of individual and corporate customers
- Improve employee engagement levels
- Provide people with opportunities for internal mobility to enhance professional and personal growth
- Maintain or reduce voluntary attrition
- Achieve top quartile retention and performance in all key markets

Areas of focus measurements are based on the individual's area of expertise and may relate to personal performance, compliance with regulations, community and geographic focus.

I have seen similar approaches in the other digital banks that I talked to. For example, BBVA measures the performance of its regions, countries, managers, individuals and all of its services and sales via digital media. This is how the bank knows in near real time how customers are adopting digital services. The bank reported in August 2018 that 38.6 per cent of total sales in the first six months of the year were through customers using remote digital access, compared to 22.4 per cent in 2017 and 14.6 per cent in the first six months of 2016.[35]

In Spain, 42.4 per cent of the units sold in the January to June period were through digital channels, compared to 24.9 per cent a year earlier. In Mexico, the figure was 32.7 per cent, up from 15.5 per cent; in Turkey, 40.6 per cent versus 32.1 per cent; in the United States, 21.7 per cent, up from 17.9 per cent; and, in Latin America, 51 per cent, compared with 22.9 per cent a year earlier.

Customers who are digitally satisfied are also cheaper to serve.

---

35 "BBVA sells more than 10 million units via digital channels in H1-18," Finextra, 13 August 2018, https://www.finextra.com/pressarticle/75061/bbva-sells-more-than-10-million-units-via-digital-channels-in-h1-18.

BBVA noted that its cost-efficiency ratio stood at 49.2 per cent in June 2018, a reduction of over 8 per cent on the year before. The bank ended June 2018 with 25.1 million customers using digital channels, 20.7 million of whom use smartphones to interact with the bank. Interestingly, just five months later, BBVA reached a global digital tipping point, with more than 50 per cent of its customers accessing products and services through remote electronic channels. In November 2018, 26.4 million digital customers interacted with the bank through mobile devices, PCs and tablets, up from 22.2 million a year earlier, representing a 19 per cent year-on-year channel shift.

Technology is business and business is technology. Clear measurements of digital success are key, along with the right metrics for measuring that success, and business has to sit with technology in co-creating these services, not just sit in isolated silo units.

> **"** Back in the day, we were more departmental organised. We had a marketing department, a mortgage department, a channel department, an IT department and so on. For example, the marketers could come up with a plan to empower customers to repay mortgages online, which is fair. The marketers would go to the mortgage department to present the plan. The mortgage department would say, 'We'll think about it.' Then the marketers would go to the channel department and present the idea. In turn, the channel department would say, 'Let's see.' Last, the marketers would go to the IT department and ask if it were possible to implement. They would discuss it and say, 'Let's make it a project.' Ultimately, all of the departments would ask for a budget, and all of them would have another indication of the time needed to develop the idea. As a way of working, it is not efficient. Now we have squads of eight or nine people with sole responsibility to maintain mortgages online. Marketers, IT, design and development

people are all put together in this squad and together they decide what they are going to work on. When it's ready and good enough, they develop and do production, but they also maintain and improve. So, a lot of coordination is gone and people like it a lot more because they are able to have an idea, to test it, to build it and to maintain it. It takes fewer people and much less coordination and oversight. **"**

Vincent van den Boogert, *CEO, ING Netherlands*

Digital Banks Look More like Big Tech and Vice Versa

" Traditionally, in banks, you have the business and the business tells the application technology teams what to do. Then the infrastructure guys are just running around with instructions. What we learnt from the Big Tech firms is that the infrastructure is the most important part. What we did is invert the structure such that infrastructure is now in charge. Infrastructure tells the application people what to do. **"**

Dave Gledhill, *former CIO, DBS*

Many of the banks focused on digital are studying, visiting, talking to and hiring people from the Big Tech firms. People with experience at Netflix, Alibaba, Amazon and Tencent are in strong demand, especially those who can code. As stated earlier, a former senior member of Deutsche Bank's leadership team, Marcus Schenck, recently said that the ability to code is now becoming as important as the ability to speak English in business. That statement is becoming increasingly true.

Interestingly, many of the banks that are committed to digital are signing up their bankers to attend training courses on Python, and they are advertising new jobs with the titles of "data engineer" and "data scientist". In a reverse play, the Big Tech firms that are trying to get into the low-hanging fruit of financial services are hiring bankers. They do not want them to code, but to explain the dynamics of how credit and payments markets operate, how the profit is made and to assist in designing new hybrid products that allow Big Tech firms to operate financial products with light regulation.

What this tells me is that technology—digital—and finance—banking—are merging. I predicted this back in the 1990s but was way too early off the mark. Some twenty-five years later, it is now coming true. I wonder what will happen in another twenty-five years?

If I were a betting man, I would put a marker down today to say that it will be very difficult to tell the difference between a Big Tech firm and a bank in 2045. Structurally and operationally, they will look very similar. Their human resources and management will look the same. Their buildings and offices will be identical. The only difference will be their products and services. By no means is this a wild statement, but rather a result of the fundamentals of the digital revolution. I could just as easily have made the above statement about a retailer, entertainments business or any other services-focused company. They will all look the same as Big Tech firms, apart from their products and services.

And banks will still be around in twenty-five years. Given that banking is a heavily regulated industry, it is easy to see why. However, the way in which banks make money, store money and manage money will be completely different. There won't be any trading desks or branches, there will be far fewer relationship managers and private bankers, and there will be almost no masters of the universe. Instead, there will be a loosely coupled operation of thousands of people working in small teams to develop cutting-edge technologies to save, spend and invest. You might say that is what the whole FinTech bubble has been about. As *Fin* and *Tech* merge, we will think very differently.

Equally, the follow-on is that management theories and structures have to change substantially to keep up. Just-in-time processing, hierarchical structures, command-control and all the things that worked for the Industrial Revolution will fail in the digital revolution. What we now need is real-time processing, flattened organisations and coach-counsel management.

❝The Big Tech firms are frenemies. We often collaborate greatly with them. We are a great partner with Amazon. We have a high degree of respect for all of them. There are going to be things that we are going to collaborate on and there are going to be things that we will compete on. How can we be smart about that? We study them rigorously and we try to really make sure we understand what's evolving on their platform. Obviously, it is important for us to maintain the view that we are the innovator in our customers' eyes, which is another reason why we try to keep up with them. Obviously, some of them will choose to enter into the banking domain and some will not. Many of them are wary of the regulatory regime that would bring. How do they deal with that? That is when we want to be there to partner with them, when it makes sense for us and for them.❞

Bill Wallace, *Head of Digital for Consumer & Community Banking, JPMorgan Chase*

Two-Pizza Teams in a Microservices Structure

❝Agile means making the organisation much flatter and organising all of our work as much as possible. All of our work is delegated to small teams that have the autonomy to make decisions and solve a problem in a very short time period, typically three months. The fact that these small teams are truly autonomous means that they are owners of their own destinies. They set themselves goals and then it is down to them to meet those goals. That works a lot better than having the traditional hierarchical chain of command, where the bosses are telling the next layer in the organisation what to do. It feels different. It feels much more authentic, much more tied to the problem, and that's more authentic in that people are solving the problem they find. They are not just coming to work to do what a job description says. They are coming to accomplish a mission in a short time frame together, with their teammates. That's what makes it a very special cultural transformation. **"**

Carlos Torres Vila, *Group Executive Chairman, BBVA*

One of the key areas where bank structures are changing is how they develop and design systems. The new structures are called microservices, where each team owns its code. The old structures were monolith, where every change to every line of code had to be signed off by a hierarchy of management. When comparing monolith versus microservices structures, it is similar to comparing how an old car was built versus a new one. Old cars were made of metal and welded together into a solid machine where, if any part broke, you had to replace the whole machine. The machine was unwieldy, slow and hard to change. A new car is moulded and put together as a network of components. Each component is independent of the machine and can therefore be taken out quickly—and easily—and replaced. The machine is fast, easy and speedy to change.

This resonates with the two themes that can be identified in banks that are successfully transforming. The first is how they organise their developer teams using Amazon's two-pizza approach as a focus.[36] Each Amazon development team is small enough that it can be fed with a maximum of two pizzas for lunch. For Jeff Bezos, small teams make it easier to communicate more effectively, stay decentralised and fast-moving, and encourage high autonomy and innovation. This is clearly the case today in an API marketplace structure that demands such decentralised approaches. It also plays into the containerised code structures of kubernetes, which—if you want be a fast, agile and modern digital bank—is key.

The second theme is how a bank should structure. A bank has historically controlled everything in its value chain. Banks do not trust decentralisation. They want close control as that allows them to secure everything. Security and control avoid risks and exposures so, to banks,

---

36 Janet Choi, "Why Jeff Bezos' Two-Pizza Team Rule Still Holds True in 2018," I Done This (blog), 4 December 2018, http://blog.idonethis.com/two-pizza-team/.

a heavy metal machine is far better than a light plastic one. However, if a bank continues to try to control the value chain, it will make them slow and resistant to change, as I have written many times. In today's Open Banking world, this will signal irrelevance and obsolescence.

For these reasons, a bank needs to decentralise its internal structures and open its eyes to external opportunities to source components of its value chain through APIs. Now many banks are doing this, especially the ones that market themselves as technology companies offering digital banking. For example, many banks have innovation labs and development portals like those of Citibank and Deutsche Bank. A growing number have API marketplaces like those of BBVA and DBS (nearing 200 APIs). This shows the eagerness of the banks to change, and the fact that they are changing. However, some of these banks are expressing concern about the alignment of their digital innovation initiatives and the lines of business they are trying to change and serve. This stretches to the heart of the major risk in banking today: a lack of digital leadership.

True digital transformation involves opening up through APIs and Software Developer Kits (SDKs) but, far more important, is aligning the changes to the products, services and line of business needs, and getting those line of business leaders to be aware, involved and articulating the change to their teams, clients and customers. Without the latter, it is a bit like throwing technology at a wall and hoping it will stick.

❝ We transformed the whole organisation from 3,000 people to 300 teams of eight to nine people. Small teams of people where we mingled business with IT. All these small teams, so called 'squads', have their own purpose. We have changed the decision-making process by transforming our organisation into small squads of people who are given a lot of autonomy. They just need the ability to implement and that was the aim of our changes. We did not want a middle layer to coordinate all these teams, so we ruled out a lot of coordination. A lot of middle management disappeared as a result. That way we really catered for delivering something quick and making it better. **"**

Vincent van den Boogert, *CEO, ING Netherlands*

Banks Need to be Technology Giants

" If we want to become more like a technology company, then we had better go and understand how technology companies operate and go figure out if we can start to do some of the same things. We spent a lot of time really going deep into the way some of these large companies operate. How does the Netflix recommender engine actually work? How does Amazon do scaling? How does Google do product innovation? And what can we learn from that and start to incorporate those same practices? What we gathered is that a modern technology stack, microservices, built for data, engineering for scale are all key. The point being is that if they could do it, then we can do it. This is not magic. It's not like there is some technology genius out there. It's just basically shifting your strategy focus. **"**

Dave Gledhill, *former CIO, DBS*

One banker recently told me that banking originally started with data. It started as a ledger system hundreds of years ago. Bankers kept a ledger of debits and credits, and that was one of the first data systems. It is true that the essence of banking is to keep track of money movement, once as data in books and now on computers. Today, we have cryptocurrencies replacing fiat currencies, data as an asset, digital assets becoming more valuable than physical assets and tech giants being more valuable than industrial giants.

Some banks are now organising themselves around data and analytics. In this new structure, the very design of the bank starts with the customer and their data, with the basic premise of the bank being an enterprise store of data as information, and leveraging that information through automated intelligence to win and differentiate itself from the rest of the pack. These banks are digital-first banks, and it is clear that the banks I studied for this book are aiming to design themselves in this way.

This is the essence of why data management, data assets, data leverage and data intelligence are core to banking today and yesterday. This is why some believe that blockchains could replace banks because they offer automated and distributed ledgers with no intermediary involved. However, this is clearly not going to happen in the near future as some form of trusted central oversight is needed in any financial system, even on blockchains. It explains why banks need to be digital at their core, and why they need to act as technology giants, not just financial giants.

> **❝** You've got to look at your competitor framing. Not just what other competitors are doing in the financial space, but financial players inside and outside the USA and the non-financial players, especially the Big Tech guys, and what they are doing. If you are customer obsessed, all of those little points of journey that customers interact with define what grade of service is in their mind. The minute someone launches an app, they are measuring your app against that experience. If they open Netflix and Netflix does something new, simple and intuitive, people immediately go, 'Why can't my bank do that? That seems so easy, why can't they do it the same way?' In many cases, we can. Although, in a few cases, we cannot because we are regulated. There is certain data we need. We can't just let you enter your email and a phone number and give you an account. It just can't work that way because we have to do KYC and all those things. **❞**
>
> **Bill Wallace**, *Head of Digital for Consumer & Community Banking, JPMorgan Chase*

Data Is Air

> **❝**It's moving from providing the infrastructure around money to solving a different problem that the world has around money, which is around decision-making. The infrastructure of money has been our core value proposition. It is the money saved at the bank that you can transact with in your life, in your business. You can make payments; you can collect money; you can get a loan or some interest on the money you have saved. We built all that infrastructure and now, through digital, we can enrich that value proposition. We can move from the infrastructure of money to making decisions about money. Should I spend or should I save? Should I invest and how should I invest it? What risks should I cover? Where is my money going? I need someone to take away the pain of reviewing where my money is going and so on. It is those types of services that are much richer, value-added services that digital enables. It's all about the data gain. It's all about leveraging and applying technology that provide actionable insights for people and for businesses to make better decisions around money. That's the more exciting part of the digital journey that we are in, which is really transforming the value proposition. **❞**
>
> **Carlos Torres Vila**, *Group Executive Chairman, BBVA*

Someone said that data is oil but I disagree. Oil is a fossil fuel that is valuable because it is limited. Eventually, it will run out. Data will not run out and it is not scarce. We currently generate more data per second than ever before in human history. We upload 60 terabytes of data per second to the internet. That is incredible. Twenty years ago, it would have cost millions to analyse just one terabyte of data. Now, we upload 60 terabytes a second. To put that in context, more data has been generated in the last two years than in the previous five thousand years of humanity.

The thing is that this ubiquity of data is just an overwhelming mass if it is not sifted. That is why I prefer to liken data to oxygen. Data is air. It is the air that we breathe. The thing is that if that air is polluted, we cannot breathe. That is what unstructured, unsorted data feels like to me. In contrast, analysed data is the purified air that we need in order to breathe properly and, if you are a bank, you need a lot of air. Right now, a bank's air is not just polluted, it is also being stolen by companies that are better at purification. That is why we fear the internet giants because they are so good at purifying data. Purified data allows you to see opportunities through analytics in order for you to leverage that data. Not only can you leverage the data, you can also become intelligent with it. This is where the AI endgame starts to come into play. Taking masses of data—60 terabytes a second—purifying it and working out where the true oxygen lies. Pure air.

To purify data, you not only need great analytics but also a great data architecture for analytics to apply AI.

How fit is your firm for this? I asked that question to several banks and used figures from Forrester Group to illustrate the challenge. Forrester estimates that the average firm only tags 3 per cent of its data and analyses less than 1 per cent. I asked if that is really the case. Is it really that bad?

All the banks I spoke to said yes. Data is a core bank asset and should be leveraged to maximum effect, yet most banks are terrible with data. It is locked up in different systems, none of which share or interoperate, and the idea of a single view of the customer is very hard. It can be achieved but it is difficult to do. However, it must be done as leveraging data about lifestyles is the core differentiation of today. Amazon, Google, Alibaba and Tencent all do this really well, and it is companies born on the internet that get data leverage. This is why we admire them. It is also why we fear them because they really understand how to mine data.

In fact, for years, technology companies have been urging banks to create *a single view of the customer* by mining terabytes of data using predictive analytics. Only the biggest firms could afford to do this, however, as it used to cost gazillions to mine a terabyte of data. Today, we are drowning in data, and only those who are fit to swim will survive. Being fit to swim is really about having a clear data architecture, being clear about how to mine that data, being clear about how to structure that data, being clear about how to tag that data and so on.

In fact, data is the key to survival as a decade from now, when all companies are using AI for customer marketing and service, the question will be: who is using their data the best? We know that Amazon, Alibaba and their brethren born on the internet use data well. We know that we want to be as good as Amazon, Alibaba and company at using our data. However, the question is: have we done the right thing with our data?

As banks become telecoms and technology companies, and telecoms and technology companies become banks, only the companies that have the most intimacy with customer data, and use that data the most intelligently, will win.

> **❝**We used to separate retail, corporate and investment banking, but the internet does not see any of these divisions. They put all of this together, peer-to-peer, connected all the time. All the data comes to the internet, not just from people but from all of their things. This is huge information. How can we better leverage that data than everybody else and use this to do better banking business? A lot of products will be reinvented during this change.**❞**
> **Kunde Chen**, *CIO, CMB*

How Can You Be AI with DD?

> **❝**We know that the thing that creates the most stress in anyone's life is money. That's what banking has been good at, in terms of looking after people's money. Now it needs

> to be more than that. Today, banking is about anticipating people and their needs, and what causes stress. Understanding that about humans and what influences them, and understanding how they then make decisions about money in the future, what they are checking and what they are interacting with. **"**

Derek White, *former Global Head of Customer Solutions, BBVA*

AI is all about being artificially intelligent, but how can you be AI with dumb data (DD)? How can any traditional bank compete with an Apple or an Amazon, or even a Marcus or a Monzo, with the systems mess that it has in its back office? So many banks have grown through mergers and acquisitions over the last fifty or so years. Each time this happened, they always kept the old systems running. It was much easier to keep the status quo. Why take the risk of downtime and conversion costs? This, however, is an issue that should have been addressed a long time ago. Now banks have all this data that is left unused, unloved in silo structures of product focus with zero integration from days of old. It is dumb data because it cannot be leveraged. How can you be intelligent with dumb data?

In the meantime, new banks are hoovering up all of my lifestyle spending because they are so good at analysing my lifestyle data. They show me what I spend, where I spend it, when I spend it and how much I am spending on each and every thing in my life. They have become my lifestyle bank while traditional banks have become boring old banks for my boring old bills. Boring old banks get to pay utility bills, taxes, loans and mortgages but have no idea what I am doing day-to-day in my life, which is the important data that they used to have. The data that is important. The data that tells you everything about who I am and how I live my life. This is the data that the new banks get because they are good with data analytics. The boring old bank gets all the boring old data. In other words, they get to keep the dumb data.

An example of how dumb banks are with data is when a retail

customer is also a small business customer. How come the bank does not know this? Because of silo systems and silo structures. It is the same reason why many banks do not know when a customer has a credit card, loan and mortgage with the bank. Each department sees its part of the customer profile, but no department sees the complete picture. This is because the data is kept in separate back-office systems called business accounts, personal accounts, card accounts, loan accounts and mortgage accounts. None of them has any synergy, integration or single view of the customer.

The core issue today is that banks' competitors do have this view of the customer because they are not dumb with data. They have created their structures to be smart with data. How can traditional banks compete when most are dumb with data? Ageing core systems built on legacy after legacy, merger after merger and organised around product focus, silo structures and internal politics is how most traditional bank systems are organised.

When we talk about customer focus, it is also very hard when you have systems built in the 1970s that are based around products and numbers, and not around customers and customer journeys. A great example is when a customer calls the bank. When you telephone the bank, the first thing that they want is your name, rank and serial number because they do not know who you are, even though they have your telephone number on file and should know who it is automatically as you are calling from the number that they have on file.

Then, when you do get an answer from your bank, they ask you to go through extensive security checks like the last three payments that you made—which you most likely won't remember—and six-digit passcodes, followed by a check of your address and more. Why? The bank should know who you are. The reason why traditional banks do not know who you are is because they have this mess of systems sitting at the core of their operations that do not know who anyone is. It would struggle just as much to know who you are as it would to know who the bank's CEO is. How can you be intelligent with dumb data?

The real issue is that banks have traditionally been unassailable. Their competitors are also dumb with data so they have had no reason to change. Today, there are FinTech firms, challenger banks and Big Tech giants all vying to take a slice of that space, and banks are caught high and dry. They may still feel unassailable as they have trillions of dollars of capital, billions of dollars of assets, millions of loyal customers and centuries of history, regulation and trust. However, that no longer cuts it. At the bare minimum, a bank needs to know who its customers are.

Any bank with fragmented data around its systems and processes that means it has no understanding of its customers' basic information, let alone insights about their wants and needs, has no future.

> **❝** Data is the backdrop of analytics. What is the data that we have? What is the data we need? One of the early organisations that I worked in had this idea to first fix the data. We spent three years fixing the data but with no output and no impact. Nothing came out of it because we were just fixing the plumbing. You have to start with the use case. Then look at the data, fix the data and continuously look at the use case to experiment, because most of these use cases are not about building a model and suddenly it will be magic. A lot of it is about creating a learning organisation that will constantly improve using the data. Constantly fill the feedback loop so that you can continuously improve. It's all about continuous improvement. **❞**
>
> **Sameer Gupta**, *Chief Analytics Officer, DBS*

The Secret to Success with Customer Data

> **❝** Big companies start with a revenue pool, they build the product, write the business requirements and who's accountable for what, then talk to technology and, eventually, go to market, right? The start-up starts with

what's the human-centred need of the problem?
They solve the problem and figure out how to scale
it and eventually figure out how to monetise it. **"**

Derek White, *former Global Head of Customer Solutions, BBVA*

Banks get into trouble when they try to be intelligent with data because they handle themselves badly when communicating with customers. A great example of this was ING Bank in the Netherlands, which started discussions to sell customer data to provide more personalised offers to customers in the spring of 2014. The media backlash was so great that, a week later, the chairman of the bank wrote a letter announcing that the bank would not pursue it:

> "The use of Big Data provides many opportunities, but also calls for caution. We fully recognise that privacy is a very sensitive issue, and ING's number one priority is the protection of our customers' personal information. ING will therefore never give personal information to third parties that is traceable to the individual. Customers can rest assured that ING will only use their personal information if it is permitted to do so. We will always act in accordance with rules and regulations, as well as our own business principles."[37]

Interestingly, there have been many discussions about using customer data for leverage within the banks for years, only for this to be always met with huge media resistance and, consequently, customer resistance. This is illustrated well by headlines such as these in the mainstream business press:

> "Caring or creepy? UK banks turn to alerts to keep customers loyal"
> Reuters[38]

---

37 "ING and the use of customer data," ING, 17 March 2014, https://www.ing.com/Newsroom/All-news/Features/Feature/ING-and-the-use-of-customer-data.htm.
38 Emma Rumney, "Caring or creepy? UK banks turn to alerts to keep customers loyal," Reuters, 14 August 2018, https://uk.reuters.com/article/uk-britain-banks-messages/caring-or-creepy-uk-banks-turn-to-alerts-to-keep-customers-loyal-idUKKBN1KZ1D6.

"Banks and Retailers Are Tracking How You Type, Swipe and Tap"
New York Times[39]

The immediate reaction to both headlines is negative. Don't track and trace me. Don't dig into my financial life. Leave me alone and just keep my data safe. When you read the entire articles though, they seem to make sense. From the Reuters article:

"Digital banks also plan to increasingly use customer data to recommend a variety of products, from insurance to energy. HSBC expects its alerts will become increasingly tailored around customers' spending habits in future. Some could take a more informal, friendly tone, said Josh Bottomley, HSBC's global head of digital, data and development. 'It will start to feel like your personal trainer in the gym,' he told Reuters in an interview."

From the *New York Times*:

"The way you press, scroll and type on a phone screen or keyboard can be as unique as your fingerprints or facial features. To fight fraud, a growing number of banks and merchants are tracking visitors' physical movements as they use websites and apps."

In other words, it is to secure access to financial data, and avoid fraudsters and hackers getting in. That's a good thing, isn't it? Yes, as long as banks are tracking our identities using biometric analytics of how we type, swipe and tap *with* our knowledge and permission.

This gets to the heart of the matter. If banks, or any other organisation, tap into our data without permission, then that is where the issues lie. It is all about communication. This is because, in the digital age, data is the money. It is the most secretive thing for most people. It shows their worth and how much they earn, which, in many cases, is something even their partner does not know. It is a taboo subject. You just don't go there.

---

39 Stacey Cowley, "Banks and Retailers Are Tracking How You Type, Swipe and Tap," *New York Times*, 13 August 2018, https://www.nytimes.com/2018/08/13/business/behavioral-biometrics-banks-security.html.

This is why psychologically we want data about our money to be locked away in a vault. We do not want it shared, tracked, leveraged or sold. This is illustrated well by a 2018 poll, which found that 77 per cent of UK customers were worried about their bank sharing their data with third parties, even though the UK's Open Banking regulation forces banks to do this.[40] The issue is that customers are concerned about the insecurity of others accessing their data, even though there is no risk as the regulator would not enforce an action that risked customers losing money.

This creates a dilemma for banks. They know that there is gold in that data … but how should they use it? This is where better communication skills are needed. Notably, as banks are being forced to share customer data with third parties, thanks to regulations like PSD2 in Europe and Open Banking generally. If customers knew that the bank would share their data, but it would be safe and secure and result in them getting better deals and saving money, then maybe they would consider it.

*The bank is **analysing** your data to make you more secure.*

*The bank is **leveraging** your data to help you save money.*

*The bank is **sharing** your data to get you a better deal.*

It only needs some decent customer-focused communication to win the data war.

> ❝ The thing is trust. Not from a generic terminology of trust, but recognising through human-centred design and behavioural economics that building trust in a digital banking world is entirely different from human-to-human interactions in a branch. Building trust in a new DIY world, where I am the sole person interacting with my money, is the challenge. I can't talk to anyone about it and we naturally, as humans, like to make decisions with other people. This means we must understand the psychology of how people interact with their money and how they like to involve others in their decisions. This is especially important

---

40 Matt Palframan, "Three quarters of Britons haven't heard of open banking," YouGov, 1 August 2018, https://yougov.co.uk/topics/finance/articles-reports/2018/08/01/three-quarters-britons-havent-heard-open-banking.

when it comes to their money because we get stressed when we must make decisions by ourselves and money is one of the most stressful areas of our lives. Understanding how you then help people with the greatest stress in their life is critical. How do you help them build trust and have the confidence to make decisions by themselves in a digital world? It's all about building trust in the right way and designing their experiences, designing their interactions, in a way that shows we are helping them. This builds trust with them step by step to the point where they are comfortable enough to completely trust the digital world. **"**

Derek White, *former Global Head of Customer Solutions, BBVA*

Who Owns the Data? Who Is in Control?

"There is recognition that becoming a data-driven company is more about the challenges of our people. That's a common theme, trying to get people to behave differently. For years, people have been locked out of a lot of data, as it is only available on a need-to-know basis. To become data-driven, you need to democratise data. You need to do it in a controlled and safe way, bearing in mind some of the consequences if you get that wrong. It is a fundamental change programme. On the one hand, it's about how to change the habit of a company to start using data and experimentation to drive decisions; and, on the other hand, how to start doing some of this work around analytics and being able to do this at scale. The biggest challenge is the mentality you need in terms of reaping the data. **"**

Paul Cobban, *Chief Data & Transformation Officer, DBS*

In banking, several themes occur over and over again. Will big banks survive? When will we be cashless? When will banks be branchless? Can we replace traders with algorithms? When will we have a digital identity scheme? This last question comes up regularly in discussions around data ownership and privacy. When will people have ownership of their own data? When will people have ownership of their own identity? How can people take control away from banks, corporations and governments and have it to themselves?

There is a generally held view that the current model of data privacy, data ownership, data permissions and data control is broken. Why is it that a person's identity has to be government-issued and verified? Why is it that the bank has to check, double check and then triple check a person's identity before they can open an account? Why is it that people cannot access some services without a bank account? What happens when someone does not drive, travel or have a bank account? Does that person exist if they do not have a government- or bank-issued identity?

A good example is my wife who, the bank claims, does not exist. We tried to open a joint investment account. To open the account, the bank asked us to come in with an identity document—a passport or driving licence—and at least two utility bills showing our names and address. This was no issue for me but, for my wife, it proved to be very difficult. She had stopped travelling and her passport had expired. She has a driving licence but passed her test in her home country, and that foreign licence is not recognised by a UK bank as valid ID. She does not pay any utility bills and only has a bank statement in her name. However, she signed up for electronic statements, and these are not recognised as proof of name and address, as they are not real statements.

This is why technologists are focused on moving identity schemes to put the citizen in control. In fact, the mantra of the next decade is going to be citizen, or customer, in control. It is the democratisation of the network that will achieve this, decentralising data to the point of control at the user end and not at the central points of control. It is likely that this is going to be the biggest debate of the next decade.

How do we put citizens and customers in control of their data?

Right now, too many institutions think that they control customer data.

They say that the customer is in control, but the customer has to give permission to have their data shared, so they are not really in control. They are not in control if the institutions make it so hard to share their data by using such complex permission layers that they cannot work out how to do it. They are not in control if the institutions and media put the fear of god into them to make them think that if they share their data, they are going to be compromised.

If data is centralised, it is controlled by the state, and not by the citizen. As I have just said, this will be the debate of the next decade because we are going to move to a network where data is decentralised and democratised. If it is decentralised and democratised, who is in control? It is neither the institution nor the government, but the citizen and the customer.

Digital Banks Have a Digital Core

“ Most of the challenges have to do with legacy in all senses, including the success that our traditional model has had. Legacy has this component of systems, for example, that have been added on top of each other over decades, with product sets that have been broadened as we were making acquisitions, for example, or as new products were launching to the market. You have that legacy of a big catalogue of products, a legacy of hosts of batch systems, legacy IT and so on. That is hard to transform or is hard to enable digitally for the customers to access from their mobile phone, for example, because the complexity of it and multiplicity of it is too large. The other element of legacy is the success that our model has had. Our model itself is an obstacle for change. I like to use this saying by Jack Welch: 'If the rate of change on the outside exceeds the rate of change on the inside, the end is near.' The pace of change outside right now is really, really, really high, and so the big challenge is how do we get that pace of change to be just as high internally? I mean we are a bank and tend to be conservative. We tend not to change things, and we tend not to change things if they work well. So the momentum and the notion of doing things that have always been done is very, very, very strong in the bank. Transforming that is really the major obstacle. **"**

Carlos Torres Vila, *Group Executive Chairman, BBVA*

Every digital bank that I have met has changed its core systems to move to a digital structure fit for the internet age. When I asked them how they were doing this, the general view seemed to be that you roll the systems over like a snowball. You treat core systems change or, for that matter, any organisational change like a snowball. Start small and let the ball roll down the hill, gaining speed and size, until it eventually takes all the snow off the hill. If the challenge is getting rid of legacy—legacy people, legacy customers, legacy structures, legacy systems, legacy everything—don't try to boil the ocean. Just start small and let it roll. The banks that understand that digital is a revolution start eating bite-sized chunks and roll the snowball down the hill. They see it as a journey, a continuum of change, and keep plugging away, piece by piece, chunk by chunk.

By being dedicated to a vision to convert from analogue to digital and do it fast enough to maintain parity with the internet giants, they completely transform their organisations slowly but surely. The drive to do this is to be intelligent with data. In order to be intelligent with data, a bank needs an enterprise data architecture, a single view of the customer and a rationalised and refreshed back-office system. This was brought home to me when talking with some challenger banks. They all seem to have one thing in common: refreshment. What I mean by this is that they talk about technology in a very different way to traditional banks. Traditional banks implemented their core systems in the 1970s and have layered all new technologies on top of those systems. This has resulted in the banks being encumbered by legacy that has cemented itself to the floor. All these new waves of tech come around and these heavyweight banks, cemented to the floor, try to adapt but cannot because the core underlying structures are fifty years old.

What these new challenger banks are doing is fundamentally different. One of them said that it launched its online banking in 2010. It ditched its platform in 2013, as it was not working to its satisfaction, and regenerated itself onto a new platform. It then regenerated again in 2017. The second bank said that it started in 2003 and is now working on its fifth-generation architecture. By my calculation, this bank refreshes its technology structure every three years. That's some going. The third new bank told me that it can provide core updates to its apps every day, sometimes even twice a day if necessary. Typically though, it refreshes itself every six months, and its apps every week. How many traditional banks regenerate their systems every three years and their apps every week? For most traditional banks, it would be impressive if they had regenerated anything in the last decade.

This illustrates a gulf and divide between traditional banks and challenger banks when it comes to data. The new banks begin with a clean sheet of paper, build for today and renovate regularly. The old banks start with what they have got, try to change what they have got to keep up with today and renovate the core systems hardly ever.

Do customers notice the difference? They are starting to as they can see a huge difference in the information they receive from old bank versus new bank apps. The old banks give little or no insight or analysis of the information because they are running on an old bank ledger system that purely records debits and credits. It is illustrated well when transactions are recorded. The bank records this in truncated form on the statement. For example, a customer receives a wire transfer payment and the bank tells them that it is "1987652 from ICENI LLP". This is a short form of a long trail of information but it means that the customer has no idea where that money came from or who sent it. The new bank can record every transaction, enriched with information, because they have no back-office systems from the 1970s that truncate transactions. As a result, the customer can double-click and drill down to find out not only who sent the money, but what it relates to and when it was sent, by whom, how and why. It is far easier.

The new banks have a dream. They dream that the customers should not have to think about money. They dream that their bank can run their customers' financial services for them, in a completely automated way, linking everything with everything through apps, APIs and analytics. The old banks are getting away with terrible service because no one knows the difference. The old banks provide transactional bank statements, with ledger services that record debits and credits and give zero knowledge. Eventually, customers will realise this. Eventually, people will know that the old banks are dumb with data and the new banks are cool. Eventually, things will change.

Why Banks Fear Core Systems Change

> ❝What started in 2009 was the belief that you had to have great technology if you were going to win, whether it be organic, inorganic, it didn't matter. Therefore, you had to really go to the core. As Mark Zuckerberg says, 'You've got to move fast with stable infrastructure.' Ours was weak. We spent a lot of time therefore rebuilding all the core systems of the bank. If we are going to run a world-class bank with a world-class set of capabilities, we can't have a frail banking system at the core of it. You have got to take the risk. And it was a risk, it was very volatile. The other question is, how do you justify the cost? When we did core banking in these other countries, we didn't cost-justify it. There was no cost justification. It was just a belief, just like you must have good office space and up-to-spec branches, you had to have a good core banking product if you're going to move fast. We just believed it was the right thing to do to get the bank in the shape it needs to be in. To be digital to the core. By

2014, we had fixed all the basics. We pivoted our approach in 2014 to say, well, can we take a lesson from the platform giants and the FinTechs and actually think about DBS as a digital growth strategy and not a physical, traditional growth strategy? Rather than seeing FinTechs as a threat, we determined to work out how can we embrace FinTech and become the aggregator of ideas, becoming the system integrator of FinTechs to create your banking products. **"**

Dave Gledhill, *former CIO, DBS*

A group of CIOs were talking about legacy systems. One said that it did not matter how old the systems were as it was more about whether they were maintainable and fit-for-purpose. Another said that COBOL was perfectly fine as a programming system because it was easy to learn and use, and still appropriate for some systems today. A third pointed out that core systems change was very hard and risky, as illustrated by TSB.[41] Finally, a fourth said that, having changed core systems twice for two different banks, he would not recommend doing it. His exact words were: "You spend three years changing the systems, during which time the bank is paralysed as you cannot change anything else. Then, after three years, you get exactly what you had before on a new system that cost you a fortune and could have brought down the bank due to the risk."

This is all baloney. It is a mindset from the last century when core systems change was hugely risky and costly. Today, with microservices architecture, Open Banking, thousands of FinTech start-up firms doing one thing brilliantly and the ease of using plug-and-play software, core systems change is not hard at all.

This does not mean performing a complete systems swap-out, like TSB did, but approaching core systems change in a bite-by-bite movement. After all, how do you eat an elephant? One bite at a time. Using conversion services, of which there are many, start converting the bank's core systems one process, one product, one function at a time. Build a vision of where you want to get to and start to get there.

---

41   UK bank TSB tried to migrate customers from TSB's former owner, Lloyds Banking Group, on to a new system with its new owner, Banco Sabadell, in April 2018. The migration failed and resulted in almost two million customers being locked out of their current accounts for weeks. The failed migration cost the bank £330 million in lost revenues, fines and fees and forced the resignation of CEO Paul Pester.

One of the key aspects of the vision for changing core systems should be that it is built around the customer, and not product-focused. Customer-focused systems structures should be the main reason driving the change in core systems, as we are moving from a world where business is in control to one where the customer is in control.

Core systems change is, therefore, not about code or legacy or risk. It is all to do with intelligence. No large traditional bank is ever going to be able to perform customer-intelligent marketing and service if their customer data is fragmented and stored in lines of business leveraging products. Therefore, in order to get to use machine learning for customer-intelligent marketing and service, a bank must refresh its core systems or face tough competition from firms that are doing this much better. For example, if Amazon behaved like a bank, the book division would not talk to the music division. The music division would not talk with the electronics division. The retail business would not talk with the wholesale business. The wholesale business would not talk with the cloud business. The Kindle division would not even talk with the book division! None of them would share customer information with each other and, as a result, no one would know what customers were buying, when or how.

Obviously, Amazon does not behave this way, so why do banks? Because of their historical legacy systems and organisational structures. This is the main reason why banks need cultural change and leadership to do digital, as they have to break apart these old product empires and start to act like an intelligent enterprise together.

> **“** If you look at Alipay and Ant Financial, we are different to the giant FinTech companies in that we are under strict regulation, meaning we have to maintain a stable operation. We have to have a balance between a stable operation as well as compete with other FinTech companies. As our customers have changed their behaviours and moved more of their behaviours online, it means we have to actively

accustom to their needs and move all of our operations online and use more technology to satisfy their needs. **"**
Kunde Chen, *CIO, CMB*

The Ten-Year Ticking Time Bomb

Some banks think that they can fudge the issue of changing core systems by using middleware. New competition will decimate these banks. Firms like Ant Financial, which refresh their complete systems architecture every three to four years, believe that this is the difference between a technology company that happens to do finance and a financial company that happens to use technology.

If you are tech-first, your singular focus is on agility. It is about fast change cycles in a microservices architecture using SDKs in a network of APIs. It is all about speed, change, service, updates, agility and vision. If you are finance-first, your singular focus is on stability. It is about slow change cycles in a monolithic architecture using control systems and sign-off structures that avoid any exposures. It is about risk, security, stability, control, management and compliance.

This is why, according to Reuters, 43 per cent of all core systems of the big U.S. banks are based on programmes developed in COBOL in the 1970s. These systems are proving more and more difficult to maintain as the people who understand the systems are either retired or dead. It is also why these two opposites—the agile new and the stable old—are very difficult to marry. Imagine Amazon or Alibaba having systems that were untouched for twenty years, except by operational maintenance updates. Could they function in their fast-change online environment today?

This is why banks with legacy core systems have a maximum of ten years to change. In ten years, we will be near the Singularity imagined by Ray Kurzweil, where machines are more intelligent than humans. In a world where machines are coded to talk, walk, think, see, hear, touch, smell and feel, how would an old mainframe system (the machine used for 92 per cent of banks' core systems) with a COBOL program (the code for 43 per cent of U.S. banks' core systems) feel? Well, it just wouldn't.

The banks stuck with these old machines will have to compete with FinTechs and Big Tech giants that are using such machines.

In ten years, when the FinTechs and Big Tech giants are analysing trillions of transactions per second, in real time with AI, how will a bank's core system manage if it still works in batch overnight updates? It won't. In ten years, when the competition between all industries and all industry players is about data analytics, how will the creaking old mainframe system deal with the competition? It won't.

In a decade's time, banks with legacy core systems will die. They won't literally explode, but it will be a slow creeping death by a thousand cuts of code, and the bank will be acquired or folded by regulators and competition. So, this sets the time frame for a bank's death: ten years, and its legacy core systems are its ten-year ticking time bomb.

Any bank that wants to refresh its legacy core systems will need a five-year time frame to do this. This is because it is a highly complex task. It is not risky, but it is not simple. First, the bank needs to create an enterprise data architecture. It needs to consolidate, rationalise, analyse and organise its complex data across multiple systems and silos into a single clear structure. Second, it needs to move that data to the cloud, and separate content (data) from processing (servers). Third, it needs to gradually identify what to replace and when. There is no big change here, but lots of small swap-outs. After all, you don't eat an elephant in one bite. You eat an elephant one mouthful at a time. It is this last part that requires a five-year strategy. Five years.

> **❝** If you talk to banks, you will hear: here is my anti-money laundering system, here is my sanctions system, here is my conflicts management system, here is my insider trading system, here is my marketing system, here is my best execution system, here is my personal investments approval system. So many system verticals and, as a result, so many vendor relationships, so many contracts, so many maintenance agreements. Add to this potentially duplicative

infrastructure and so on and so forth. The big thing that we did is say that platforms take a horizontal view. Think about a data layer and think about connecting the data layer with every computing capability we need. All the risks that we cover are basically computational engines, which harvest data and process the data. If you look at some of our best competitors, they'll be doing this, but they'll be doing it for AML. They may not be doing it for the entire infrastructure, but you must have that strategic sense about where you want to go and push everybody to this common architecture. Otherwise, you will always have struggles. **"**

Lam Chee Kin, *Head of Legal, Compliance and Secretariat, DBS*

It Is Three Minutes to Midnight

The problem is, do you have five years when it is already three minutes to midnight? Midnight is when it is too late for the bank to change its systems into an enterprise data architecture. It is too late when other players have grasped the opportunity the bank cannot take.

Currently, the big platform players are giving away services that banks make money from, namely payments and lending. Amazon, Alibaba and more are keen to give free loans and payments to their buyers and sellers because it drives more traffic to their platforms. As a result, they are not interested in making money from banking products and services. They will just give them away for free, if it increases commerce on their platforms. That is today.

In five years, most of these players will be leveraging open APIs to drive more service through their platforms. They will be taking all of our social and commercial digital moments and aligning them with finance. These providers will know their customers' daily routines and movements intimately, and will watch what their customers are doing and where. Based on those digital lifestyles, they will be giving customers insights for smarter spending and saving throughout the day, automatically and for free.

Therefore, in five years, banks will make no money from what they do today and will need to be competitive in this new, proactive, augmented world. What that means is that a single view of the customer will be mandatory. A bank will not survive with product-focused systems and structures or with old back-office systems focused on payment transactions, deposits and loans. At midnight, the bank will no longer be effective if it has not changed those product-focused silo systems and structures.

We don't know exactly what the world will look like in ten years from now, but we do know that the irrepressible march of change from industrial to digital is unstoppable. The platform players will have continued to dominate by building in adjacencies, like free loans and payments, and looking for data intimacy with their customers' digital lifestyles through AI and machine learning. They are already a long way down that road. The platform players are leading the march of technology to automated customer intimacy, intelligent marketing and frictionless money. How is a bank going to compete with that if it still has product-focused silo systems?

> **❝**We won't be scalable if we don't move on to the cloud, let's be real. There is no choice. If you really want to use the mass amount of data, you have to move to the cloud. If you are waiting to deploy onto your own infrastructure, it will cost you a bomb and then your benefits case will go down. So that's the key. **❞**
>
> **Sam Wong**, *Head of Data Analytics and Robotics, Group Audit, DBS*

A Shocking Image of Legacy

During the summer of 2018, a major disaster took place in Genoa, Italy, when the Morandi Bridge collapsed, killing forty-three people. In the aftermath, there were a lot of discussions about what happened, what went wrong, how it was allowed to happen and who was responsible.

The Italian government blamed Autostrade per l'Italia, the company

Figure 4.2 The remains of Morandi Bridge, after a section of the bridge collapsed

in charge of operating and maintaining the country's motorways. A news conference with the chief executive of Autostrade, Giovanni Castellucci, saw him refuse to apologise for the incident. "Apologies and responsibilities are things that are interconnected. You apologise if you feel you are responsible," he said, implying that the firm was not responsible.

"The works and state of the viaduct were under constant monitoring and supervision," the company said in a statement, and they were repairing the foundations in the weeks before the incident happened. Yet it is claimed that the bridge collapsed due to a major flaw in the supporting piles, meaning the structure could not support the weight of heavy traffic.

Six years earlier, Giovanni Calvini, then the head of the Genoa branch of the Italian employers' federation Confindustria, warned in an interview with Genoa's *Il Secolo XIX* newspaper: "When in 10 years' time the Morandi Bridge collapses, and we all get stuck in traffic jams for hours, we will remember the names of the people who said 'No'."

Built in the 1960s, the Morandi Bridge provided a vital link for the A10 motorway, which connects northwest Italy to France. It was one of the busiest bridges in the country, carrying freight and tourists to and from the port city. The technology used to build the bridge was fatally flawed, according to some engineers, and required renewal just twenty years after the bridge was opened. All in all, there are questions and recriminations across the board. However, the bottom line is that forty-three people died, and the reason? Legacy structures.

The collapse of Morandi Bridge and its death toll is a startling illustration of dealing with legacy renewal. Post-collapse dialogue was all about how the bridge should have been refreshed years ago, and how the management kept refusing to do the work as the disruption would be too great. The risk of renewal to the business was too high. The loss of profits would be too great. That appears to be the real reason why the bridge was not closed years ago, and why the technologies used to build it were not replaced. The problems were known but the tough decisions were ducked.

This is what I see in most banks' old legacy structures: tough decisions being ducked. If you ever want a reason to stir you into action, think of the collapse of Morandi Bridge.

> **"**In the old days, we sometimes had eight systems releases in a year. Now we have up to 3,000 small releases a month.**"**
> **Vincent van den Boogert**, *CEO, ING Netherlands*

Dealing with Technology Change (The Danger of the Technology Testing Hole)

> **"**You have to invest in resources, not just money, but people. You have to trust the technology guy. You have to manage the innovation business from a business perspective because innovation is always experimental.

It's a test. You have to let them try. Probably they will
fail. If you lead an innovation team, you have to let them
try. You have to give them room. This is quite a different
culture, especially for me. It's a totally different process
from the conventional banking process. We have to build
a separate innovation procedure, which is separated from
the conventional budgeting process. You need to have a
different finance procedure because of budget approval,
KPIs, measurements, agility and refinement. You have
to tune it. You have to give up some rules that are not fit
for innovation and allow them to make trial-and-error
experiments. It's a different process. **"**

Kunde Chen, *CIO, CMB*

A common response to technology is to test it. The problem with
testing technology is that it is just a test. A false implementation. It
is not designed for reality and can lead to false results. For example,
one UK bank tried testing new technologies in one branch to see if
they could subsequently be rolled out to all branches. The test involved
video tellers, biometric ATMs and many other innovative ideas. The
bank felt that some of the ideas were okay but dismissed the biometric
ATM as it was too intrusive for customers. Some years later, the bank
had another discussion about biometric ATMs and the CEO said, "Oh
no, we tried them and they don't work."

What is interesting here is that the first biometric ATM that the bank
tried was based on iris scan technology that, yes, was too intrusive for
customers who felt it involved too much hassle. However, the second
type of biometric ATM was based on palm prints, which worked well.
The challenge in such instances is to get the bank's decision-maker
to understand that these are two different things, and that time and
technology have moved on.

The big danger here is that banks test technologies all the time, and
often it is before the technology has reached prime time. As a result, by

the time the technology is ripe, the bank believes that it is not the right technology because it had already tested it three, four or five years ago.

These tests, therefore, create negative effects in internalising the advantages that such technologies can deliver. It is why some banks lag behind in technology adoption because they believe that they are innovators, always trying out new technologies, but they are actually laggards. Their tests result in rejecting new technologies and avoiding revisiting them at a later stage because of false test results on technologies tested too early. It is hard to change this position because it is a core part of some financial cultures to test and pilot. During one conference, a banker actually said that her bank had more pilots than American Airlines.

This is where the critical path occurs, and where these banks will miss out. At some point, the technology will be ready for prime time. Maybe not now, but within a year or two. And when it is, some will say, "Ah, we've already tried that and it doesn't work." Others, though, will have a different view and say, "Keep checking in with this technology to see how it's doing."

It is the latter culture that wins because they do not test and reject. They test, retest and retest until it works. This is the core difference between financial technology leaders and financial technology laggards. A leader never tests and rejects a technology. They test and see if it is something that can be internalised and, if the answer is no, they go back to the drawing board and start again. They create a continuum of testing loops that are always open. By doing so, you may have more pilots than an airline but at least you are flying.

> ❝ We are trying to be really disruptive and innovative, while being fully in line and compliant within that space. We are trying to find our way, our path and our optimum place in the market. FinTechs have fewer of these challenges. We are also trying to shift that problem by saying okay, we are heavily regulated, but that also gives

some benefits in trust and confidence. Can we use what we've learned there to apply to other sectors of our customers? Can we learn from our experiences there in terms of providing the safety and security around dealing with customers' money and innovate? The fact that we are very regulated does build trust with our customers. It's always a balance. **"**

Remco van der Veer, *Head of ING Labs*

Banking in the Cloud

" When we see a competitor with infrastructure that is twenty times the size of ours, you may ask, 'Why are we taking such a different path?' It is because if you had got to this stage of having to refresh your architecture, like some of our competitors, three years earlier than we did, you didn't have the benefit of seeing what Amazon and Netflix were doing. You would have gone to a very big hardware mainframe and, once you have made that decision, it stays with you. You can't do much with it. You must live with it. It's going to be a very expensive system. We were quite fortunate in that cycle, where we saw that Netflix and Amazon and all the others were leveraging cloud-based services. As a result, we went from a huge hardware mainframe system and data centre to about an eighth of the original size, but with far more computing power. **"**

Chng Sok Hui, *Chief Financial Officer, DBS*

" We've built out a private cloud environment and had to work collaboratively with a number of the cloud providers to get to a place where we feel okay about putting more highly confidential data in environments like that. We have an obligation to protect customers' privacy,

> data, and we've got to make sure the place where
> we put that data is up to that task. 🔊
>
> **Bill Wallace**, *Head of Digital for Consumer & Community Banking,*
> *JPMorgan Chase*

Another common feature of banks that are doing digital is that, in refreshing core systems architectures, they have placed Cloud Computing at the centre of the future digital world. I first began writing about Cloud Computing in the 2000s. Many banks dismissed the idea back then as "the regulator wouldn't allow it". Then, the regulator did allow it in some countries but banks were confused about the regulatory position. For example, if they were to use cloud services for customer data and the provider announced it had been breached, who would be liable? As a result, they still resisted moving anything of importance to the cloud. Today, the issue is still confusing to some. When can you use cloud? When can't you use cloud?

This confusion makes most financial pundits vary wary of anything cloud-related. For example, the UK regulator, the Prudential Regulatory Authority (PRA), defines cloud as "outsourcing" and informs financial institutions to comply with the same regulatory obligations as it would for outsourcing. Now, we also have European laws—GDPR and PSD2—that have requirements for privacy and controls over data.

All of this regulation makes it easy to say that using cloud services is too difficult. It is not necessarily so, however, as Cloud Computing has come a long way. Originally, it was all about Software-as-a-Service (SaaS) but now it is Anything-as-a-Service, even Banking-as-a-Service! Nevertheless, most banks have only moved a small part of their operations, perhaps 20 per cent, to Cloud Computing, typically for hardware, infrastructure and non-customer-related operations like payroll. This is also often housed in what is called a "private cloud", a cloud that the bank still controls and manages, rather than a public cloud, which is completely managed by a third-party provider like Amazon, Microsoft or Alibaba.

The banks that are doing digital well truly understand that they need data analytics on enterprise customer data stores and are doing this through private cloud services. They are placing customer data into these cloud systems on-premises in many instances, as they are aware that some regulatory requirements demand customer data is held within national borders. This overcomes the typical response to resist such change, which is to say that the regulator will not allow it.

This attitude is illustrated well by a story from Michael Harte, who was then the CIO at Commonwealth Bank of Australia (CBA). He presented the idea of moving most of the bank's back office to Infrastructure-as-a-Service (IaaS) to the executive team. The team considered it but threw it out, saying that the regulator would not allow it, and asked him to come back with a different plan. Six months later, Harte presented the same plan to the board. The CEO became irritated and asked why he was presenting the same plan to the board when it was obvious that the regulator would not allow it. At that point, Harte brought the head of the Reserve Bank of Australia into the meeting room. The head then endorsed the IaaS plan and said that it was fine. As a consequence, CBA moved to IaaS and saved 35 per cent of its operational costs, as well as became far more agile.

Saying that the regulator will not allow it is an easy barrier to changing things, and anyone doing digital should respond by asking, "Have you asked them?" Ask the regulator what they will and will not allow. Don't just assume that they will not allow it.

This is why I have met some banks doing digital that have pushed the boundaries of Cloud Computing, and moved up to 80 per cent of their operations to cloud. Why? It gives them total flexibility to move with demands of the customers and of the business. It allows the bank to manage loads, capacity and expenditure in a much easier way than they could if they developed, hosted and internalised everything. Now, I have known for ages that cloud allows banks to move to Operational Expenditure (OpEx) for their computing needs, rather than Capital Expenditure (CapEx), but I had not expected to find this consistent theme of cloud usage among the innovative digital transformers. In fact, most of the banks interviewed view the use of AWS, Microsoft Azure, Netflix Content Delivery and Aliyun, the Alibaba Cloud, as essential for Agile, another core component of their operations.

It is even true of the largest banks, like JPMorgan Chase. JPMorgan created its own private cloud in 2016 and moved some applications into the public cloud in May 2017. According to *Business Insider,* "that makes it one of the industry's pioneers, with many in banking still wary of moving data and key applications into the cloud due to cybersecurity, operational and regulatory fears."[42]

This goes back to the heart of what many in banking have yet to understand: doing everything yourself, controlling everything yourself, building everything yourself, developing everything yourself ... just doesn't work anymore. I know so many banking people who fear letting go. They worry intensely about allowing third parties to have their customers' data for fear of the regulator, while the regulator is actually okay with it. Perhaps the best way to look at this is to make it personal: do you use cloud? I never used to. I believed that all of my data had to be on my local hard disk. I was wary. Will the cloud provider look at my data? Or, even worse, lose my data? Today, I place all of my data in the cloud, as I can then pick up the information I need, whenever I need it, regardless of location, as long as there is Wi-Fi.

That is part of the beauty of a cloud-based information business. The data is available to whoever needs it, whenever they need it, wherever they need it. In addition, it overcomes issues of employees potentially taking data home because it is on their laptop. Surely, that is more insecure than storing data in the cloud and secured by the bank?

The banks that understand this model are now creating interesting hybrid structures of private and public cloud services for their infrastructure, operations, software and data that is driven by the regulatory model and central bank oversight. Those that get this have reduced their cost of operations significantly, sometimes reducing costs by as much as a half, while increasing their flexibility and agility. In the long term, that may determine which banks will be winners and losers.

---

42 Dakin Campbell, "JPMorgan is building a cloud engineering hub in Seattle minutes away from Amazon and Microsoft," *Business Insider,* 19 February 2019, https://www.businessinsider.com/ jpmorgan-is-building-a-cloud-engineering-hub-in-seattle-2019-2.

"We are now cloud native. Everyone's got a cloud strategy. Not all are the same. We see a lot of cloud lipstick. We've done one or two cloud projects, but how do you get cloud to the core? That requires some very deep engineering, which we don't see many banks taking on but, if you do, it has a dramatic impact on your cost-income ratios and your ability to execute. If you do the typical cloud project, you'll save about 20 per cent of costs because you eliminate the hardware but software still costs you the same. You've still got people running around plugging things in and developing on those things. We've moved our software to open source using Google and Netflix. This gets rid of the software costs. Eighty-two per cent of our operations are now cloud-based in 2018. Some outcomes of that, which is a real test of whether you've succeeded, is the number of servers that you need to run the business. The number of physical machines. We've reduced that number by 80 per cent since January 2013 up to today. What that enables you to do is that all the new capabilities, all the digital products and services, are working on 80 per cent less machine costs. In fact, the number of operating systems and things that we run have gone from about 3,000 to 13,000. That means we have five times more things that we're running on four times fewer physical structures. Some dramatic reduction. Then you get real cost savings of around 80 per cent."

Dave Gledhill, *former CIO, DBS*

The Bank CIO Sees Most Tech Firms as Blah, Blah, Blah

I can understand why bankers can be sceptical about what technologists say. For years, technologists have been telling them that their business is threatened by technological change. They have been shouting that they will be disintermediated, they say that the bank must change and change fast to keep up, and they argue that the bank is not investing enough in technology. Of course, their aim is to sell more. The technology guys are driven by aiming to get the banks to upgrade more often, buy more systems, enhance their software and create big-ticket projects.

The technologists' tactics are much like disturbance selling. Like life assurance—you are going to die, what will happen to your family?—technology sales are mainly based around threat—you are going to go out of business if you don't buy this, then what will happen? Everything is a threat if you do not change. That much is true. If you don't change, everything is a threat. If you don't change, you get stuck in the middle of the road and will eventually be run over, so keep moving. Most banks are continually moving forward, slowly but surely. However, the one threat that looms large is the legacy hole.

It is still the case that many banks talk about 70 to 80 per cent of their budget being sunk into keeping the lights on, maintaining systems, keeping things going. Hence, the moving forward budget is tightly squeezed. According to Celent, money going towards new investments accounted for only 27 per cent of bank IT spending in 2017.[43] The rest, a whopping 73 per cent of spending, went towards maintenance. Globally, that equates to $200 billion being spent just to keep the lights on.

JPMorgan Chase is a good example of a bank facing this challenge.[44] The bank budgeted $9.5 billion for tech spend in 2017, but less than a third ($3 billion) was for new initiatives and, of that, $600 million was spent on emerging FinTech solutions. The bank employs nearly 50,000 people in technology, that is one in five employees, while more than 31,000 are in development and engineering jobs and 2,500 in digital technology. Interestingly, 80 per cent of the bank's IT budgets were dedicated to keeping the lights on a few years ago. Today, it is more like 70 per cent, and the aim in a few years is to make that 50 per cent. In other words, half of the budget will be moving into agile, flexible, new and competitive leverage using data and systems as differentiation. Putting that into context, we are talking $5 to $6 billion a year being dedicated

---

43 Adrian D. Garcia, "Big banks spend billions on tech but innovation lags," Bankrate, 27 July 2018, https://www.bankrate.com/banking/jpm-big-banks-spend-billions-on-tech-but-theyre-still-laggards/.

44 JPMorgan Chase increased its technology spending by 15 per cent to $10.8 billion in 2018, and by a further $600 million to $11.4 billion in 2019, with most of it going towards the enhancement of mobile and web-based services in its four main lines of business: consumer, commercial and investment banking and wealth management.

to innovation within one bank. The total amount invested in all European FinTech start-ups in 2018 was $3.2 billion, equivalent to less than one year of JPMorgan Chase's internal innovation budget.

This also marks a clear delineation between a bank doing digital well and a bank doing digital badly: their technology budget and how it breaks down. If that budget is placing the majority of cost into keeping the lights on, then it is not fit for the twenty-first century.

Come the Revolution

> **"**In China, internet giants have already formed pressure and shock onto the retail businesses of traditional banks. Ninety per cent of our customers use Alipay and WeChat Pay. Being backstage, banks are losing the interface of customer services. Only by digital transformation can banks confront the shock and impact. We have made great efforts in terms of digitalisation, and we will stick to the route in the future. Through digital transformation, we hope to build a closer relationship with customers, and create greater value and a better experience for them. **"**
>
> **Min Hua**, *Head of Strategy, CMB*

Many of the financial institutions struggling with digital are struggling because they are thinking, "This is happening over there and not over here." Wealth managers think that clients still want the personal human touch from a relationship manager. Corporate banks believe that clients still need a go-to person who can sort out any issues. Insurance is still an annualised market of premiums run by intermediaries. They do not feel the urgency to change.

For example, in a wealth management meeting, a banker said that the average private banker in Switzerland is sixty-two years old and their average client is aged seventy-five. He was being a bit extreme, but his point was that most wealth is owned by older people, as young people have not yet earned it. There are obvious exceptions to that rule but, as a generalisation, older people are the ones who need wealth management and they like dealing with humans. Or so I am told.

Yet two things are mistaken in this discussion. One, older people are very comfortable with technology once someone shows them how it works. Therefore, the view that older people want to deal in more traditional, old-fashioned ways is a stereotypical view. Two, older people often have children, who will one day inherit their wealth. How will they feel about a sixty-two-year-old private banker?

Each generation has a different way of thinking, and thinking of things as generational is where real change is coming from. While the revolution in finance is ultimately being driven by the customer, technology is enabling it and opening new avenues of opportunity to all. This is why all areas of finance have something innovative happening through open platforms with code and technological change. It is the reason why so many billions are being invested in FinTech firms; they can code to address one single issue in the market, doing that one thing brilliantly. Therefore, this idea that digital is affecting other industries, from retail to entertainment, but not banking is just old school thinking.

> **❝** In the late 1990s, digitisation was a way to do things more efficiently. It was the start of the digital change of tech operations. The core focus was to deliver more efficient banking to save cost through tech. In the last few years, digitisation is dictating customer interaction. It has changed a lot, in the ways we interact with our customers. Now, the firm belief is that the only way to distinguish yourself from competition in banking is through digital customer interaction. **❞**
> **Vincent van den Boogert**, *CEO, ING Netherlands*

BOTTOM LINE

The key message here is that banks have to break away from the constraints of their last-century systems and refresh and renew their architecture. Not only their systems architecture, but their data architecture for a single customer view, and their development architecture to be microservices and not monolithic. More fundamentally, it is about changing their business architecture to integrate technology with business and business with technology. All of this is difficult. Add on to this challenge the demands of incorporating partnerships with third-party software providers, both in the sharing of data through Open Banking and in the incorporation of their plug-and-play code through a marketplace of APIs and apps, and you have a real melting pot of change. This is why banks need leadership that truly understands digitalisation and has it in its DNA, and is not just paying lip service.

THE CUSTOMER CHALLENGE

❝ Many businesses hope that a large number of clients will deliver a high aggregate revenue whilst the cost is kept low. These three objectives—large quantities of customers, great service with high-quality and low cost—are incompatible. It is unlikely any firm can obtain all the three goals. In fact, there are few traditional retail enterprises that can reach all the three objectives simultaneously. They have either lots of clients or superior experience or low cost. Some enterprises with exceptional performance can reach two goals, but no one can achieve all three objectives. The reason lies in the fact that the traditional retail model provides service for people by people or by people with the assistance of machines. The energy of people is limited. If people pay too much attention to service, then they have to reduce efficiency. So, the number of customers will be decreased. Alternatively, if we want to focus on both the service and client numbers, we have to increase the number of employees and then the cost will be raised. However, we have noticed that some internet companies can achieve the three goals at the same time as these enterprises are more digitalised than us. Digitalisation can not only provide better service for customers with efficiency, reconciling the conflicts among the three goals, but also more closely keep pace with the future trend. **❞**

Xulei Gao, *Deputy Head of Retail Banking, CMB*

Twenty-five years ago, I worked on re-engineering projects. Most of the time, I was frustrated because the banks would not take on the big projects, like the mortgage process, as they went across too many divisions. So, we would generally end up doing tinkering projects that were classified as incremental process improvement. Yes, they may have been valid to get a cost reduction of 5 per cent in the bank's bottom line, but they were incredibly dull.

The big issue for me back then—and still today—is that the bank was not built around the customer and had little customer focus. Internally, the bank was product-focused, not customer-focused, and our challenge was how to turn the bank from being focused internally to being focused externally. That is what a lot of digital transformation is trying to achieve—to focus on the external customer .

The issue in banking, for example, is that a customer does not wake up and think, I want to pay for this shirt. No, they think, "It would be great to have this shirt." However, the bank is focused on the payment rather than what the payment is for. Customers do not wake up thinking, "Hey, I need a mortgage." No, they are thinking, "I need a bigger home". However, the bank focuses on the mortgage process rather than the need to move house.

We had these discussions twenty-five years ago and the frustrating thing is that we are still having them today. The difference is that back then, taking on a massive transformation project was massive risk. It would mean reinventing the corporation and then building an infrastructure to support that organisation. Now, that is a big ask, and perhaps it is not so surprising that few bank leaders undertook such projects.

Today, that has all changed because of various factors:

- The bank knows it has a flawed business model based around physical distribution through buildings and humans, and that it needs a transformation project to design around digital distributing through software and servers.
- The bank knows it must migrate core systems to technologies that

are open API and microservices-based architectures over the next decade.

- The bank knows that digital platforms can reduce costs dramatically and make them more competitive, so why wouldn't they do this?
- The bank knows that there are thousands of new start-ups trying to squeeze their margins, challenge their products and steal their customers, so they must do this to survive.

Today, there are a range of compelling reasons for reimagining the bank through a digital transformation project, but where do you start? The answer is to always start with the customer. Look at the interactions with the customer today, and challenge whether they really need to happen in the way that they do. Why are customers forced to pay all of their bills at the start of the month? Because that is when their salary is paid. But why pay them all at once? Because then customers know how much they have left to spend for the rest of the month. What if an unexpected annual bill comes in, such as a subscription? Well, they have to handle it. Wouldn't it better if we advised them throughout the month and showed them what is safe to spend?

In fact, it is only due to having their mobile applications built onto the banks' old legacy systems that most traditional banks purely show customers a transaction history, rather than a cashflow forecast of what will happen. This is purely a reflection of the old transaction banking ledger systems, built for branch balance tracking. The trouble is that because banks have never touched those systems, they are still at the core of the mainstream banks. That is another compelling reason why banks should transform and migrate them to modern, real-time, artificially intelligent, predictive engines, obsessed with informing customers about all they need to know.

Once we have challenged the status quo and tried to tear it down, we can then see the customer structure for the future based on the customer's preferred digital interactions. Start with the design of the bank around the customer and then build processes, structures and technologies to align with that vision. In this way, we are no longer handcuffed to the old-world view.

What then becomes intriguing is the idea of moving the bank from not only being handcuffed by heritage, but also seeing the world differently. Instead of being a product pusher, only able to see as far as the interest rates and charges that can be made, the bank can become a consumer champion obsessed with giving as much value and information as possible. This is what a digital transformation project should be.

It is almost like moving from the Flat Earth Bank to the Copernicus Bank. Most banks today sit in a Flat Earth world. Their Earth is at the centre of the universe, and it is called the bank's Head Office. From that Head Office, the CEO can see various stars and planets circling around the Earth. The Moon is his accounting systems, giving him batch overnight updates; Mars is his Senior Vice President's planet, which is full of product-incentivised salespeople; Saturn is the credit risk planet, running rings around the customer; Venus is mainly full of marketing people, as it is very touchy-feely; Mercury is hot, and houses the investment guys, making money on the markets every day; oh, and then there is the Sun. That is a very shiny planet that is so far away, it is hard to see what is on it. Let's call that the Customer planet, and it feels like that goes around the Earth, from where the bank is sitting.

The Flat Earth Bank often finds that the Sun is also eclipsed because so many of the other planets get in the way. In fact, the Flat Earth Bank is often so focused on the movement of the stars and the planets that it does not actually see what is out there at all. Imagine walking into the Flat Earth Bank and saying that the shiny thing that it sees during the day is actually the centre of the Universe. "Get out of here and shut the door behind you!" would be the response.

Then look at the challenger banks, and how they are designing their banks. Each of their banks is designed to be a Copernicus Bank. They ask people a lot of questions about how they currently bank, why they bank the way they bank and challenge whether it should be that way. You need anthropologists to create a Copernicus Bank, not a customer focus group.

Once you have built your vision of the Copernicus Bank, where everything is focused on how you use the planets to circle around the Sun—the centre of the universe that is the customer—you can then start to build a really cool, new bank. The challenger banks also recognise that to do this, they need to leverage a thousand APIs from a thousand start-ups focused on doing one thing really well, rather than trying to do a thousand things themselves when they do not have the resources to do this.

As you can see, a digital transformation programme is neither a change project nor an incremental improvement process. It is a fundamental cultural, structural and technological change. The banks that are not making such a change are just digitalising their old products from physical structures to digital ones. They will never actually be digital.

> **"**Many banks are focusing on mortgages and we've taken that all the way up to where the interaction starts. That means focusing on the house search. By incorporating third-party data through high-speed APIs, we allow the customer to use augmented reality to hold their phone up against a brick wall and look through that brick wall to see the house behind. We are able to show them how liveable that place is, how affordable it is and all of the other information you need around life in that potential building. It is all integrated, all experiences integrated, into one, and only then comes the mortgage. **"**
>
> **Derek White**, *former Global Head of Customer Solutions, BBVA*

Digital Banks Are Led by Clear Customer-Obsessed Principles

> **"**I'd go back to the guiding principles. Does the culture understand and have the muscle memory to execute against those guiding principles? Starting with customer

obsession and clean sheet reinvention of re-empowering teams to work around that customer obsession. Is the culture focused on customer journeys? How does the top of the company think about those cultural aspects? What is the path to get that built into the businesses like a muscle memory, so that we can move down the path faster? There are certain things we can do. We can take senior people and educate them. We have a training programme in JPMorgan Chase called Leadership Edge. We taught a module in Leadership Edge, taking some really senior people through our thinking and showing them the power of APIs. This made them go out and search the API repositories and think about it. They all ran different businesses, but think about their business and what could be empowered in their business if they were to access these APIs. We spent all day going through that and a bunch of other things around these guiding principles. You've got to get the management to the place where they feel like they see the business value of digitalisation and they can look at this through the lens of the customer. That's the real challenge, to get people through the lens. They think they are looking through the lens of the customer and, often times, they were looking at it from their business view. **"**

Bill Wallace, *Head of Digital for Consumer & Community Banking, JPMorgan Chase*

A key factor of the digital banks that are doing digital well is that the customer is their primary focus. Not the shareholder, the investor, the quarterly bonus, the dividend yield or the cost-income ratio. The customer.

This is quite rare in most banks because the retail customer is deemed fairly unimportant in the scheme of things. The high net worth and mass affluent are worth it, but the rest are treated with a fair bit of disdain.

They are charged high fees for accidental overdrafts and generally pay more for bank services than the rest (who get *free* banking).

Hearing banks being passionate about retail customers, and their experiences and services, is therefore pretty rare. This was brought home to me when meeting with DBS in Singapore. I was talking with the bank's CFO and she was recounting how important the customer is in the scheme of things. I commented that it was unusual to hear a bank CFO talking in such a way, as usually their focus was on shareholder value, not customer value. She retorted that you get both. If you are customer and user experience focused, then the profits flow and the shareholders get their return. She then pointed out direct correlations between customer value and shareholder value. She told me that customers who use the bank's services digitally more than half of the time are twice as profitable as other customers, and twice as satisfied. This reflects in results, as the bank's cost-income ratio lowers while its market share grows.

This direct correlation is demonstrated in several of the digital banks studied for this book. In the relentless pursuit of delivering the best digital experiences for their customers, they end up customer-obsessed in the same way as Amazon. That customer obsession then delivers in results of loyalty, advocacy, market share and profitability. Happy customers make happy business.

This simple view of the world pays dividends, but there is a starting point before happy customers. Happy people. Staff have to feel engaged and part of the business. By freeing staff from the constraints of tight control, free staff become happy and happy people make happy customers make happy business. I have used that mantra for years: happy people make happy customers make happy business. How do you get happy people? Empower them and set them free and, in order to do that, you need clear principles. This is another emerging common factor in the digital banks: they are principles-led businesses. They communicate with their people in a clear way, saying that this is our aim in business and, as long as we all work this way, we will all succeed.

Again, Amazon is a clear influencer in this space. Amazon has a fourteen-point list of principles that are embedded into the fibre and being of the company and every employee in it.[45]

Whether you are an individual contributor or the manager of a large team, you are an Amazon leader. These are our leadership principles and every Amazonian is guided by these principles.

Customer Obsession
Leaders start with the customer and work backwards. They work vigorously to earn and keep customer trust. Although leaders pay attention to competitors, they obsess over customers.

Ownership
Leaders are owners. They think long term and don't sacrifice long-term value for short-term results. They act on behalf of the entire company, beyond just their own team. They never say "that's not my job."

Invent and Simplify
Leaders expect and require innovation and invention from their teams and always find ways to simplify. They are externally aware, look for new ideas from everywhere, and are not limited by "not invented here." As we do new things, we accept that we may be misunderstood for long periods of time.

Are Right, A Lot
Leaders are right a lot. They have strong business judgment and good instincts.

Hire and Develop the Best
Leaders raise the performance bar with every hire and promotion. They recognise exceptional talent, and willingly move them throughout the organisation. Leaders develop leaders and take seriously their role in coaching others.

Insist on the Highest Standards
Leaders have relentlessly high standards—many people may think these standards are unreasonably high. Leaders are continually raising the bar and driving their teams to deliver high quality products, services and processes. Leaders ensure that defects do not get sent down the line and that problems are fixed so they stay fixed.

---

45 For more on Amazon's fourteen principles, see Rachel Premack,"Jeff Bezos runs Amazon with 14 defined leadership principles," *Business Insider*, 9 August 2018, https://www.businessinsider.com/jeff-bezos-amazon-jobs-leadership-principles-2018-8.

Think Big

Thinking small is a self-fulfilling prophecy. Leaders create and communicate a bold direction that inspires results. They think differently and look around corners for ways to serve customers.

Bias for Action

Speed matters in business. Many decisions and actions are reversible and do not need extensive study. We value calculated risk taking.

Frugality

We try not to spend money on things that don't matter to customers. Frugality breeds resourcefulness, self-sufficiency, and invention. There are no extra points for headcount, budget size, or fixed expense.

Vocally Self-Critical

Leaders do not believe their or their team's body odour smells of perfume. Leaders come forward with problems or information, even when doing so is awkward or embarrassing. Leaders benchmark themselves and their teams against the best.

Earn Trust of Others

Leaders are sincerely open-minded, genuinely listen, and are willing to examine their strongest convictions with humility.

Dive Deep

Leaders operate at all levels, stay connected to the details, and audit frequently. No task is beneath them.

Have Backbone; Disagree and Commit

Leaders are obligated to respectfully challenge decisions when they disagree, even when doing so is uncomfortable or exhausting. Leaders have conviction and are tenacious. They do not compromise for the sake of social cohesion. Once a decision is determined, they commit wholly.

Deliver Results

Leaders focus on the key inputs for their business and deliver them with the right quality and in a timely fashion. Despite setbacks, they rise to the occasion and never settle.

The banks doing digital well are taking the best of Amazon, Netflix and other big tech giants and trying to make that the core of their being.

Do Customers Want Digital Banking?

Customers do not necessarily want a purely digital bank. For example, ten years after the launch of neobanks like Moven and Simple in the United States, just 3 per cent of millennials have their primary deposit account at a digital bank. That percentage drops to 1.5 per cent of Generation X and 0.8 per cent of baby boomers. In contrast, more than four in ten millennials have their primary deposit account with one of the big three banks: Bank of America, JPMorgan Chase and Wells Fargo.

This implies that consumers do not want a digital bank, but this is not true. In reality, the big U.S. banks are converting to digital, and therefore digital transformation is critical if they are to keep up with the needs of the digital consumer. It is nothing to do with giving the customer digital banking. It is more to do with giving the customer banking in a digital way. This is why traditional banks are throwing billions at trying to transform to digital. According to Bloomberg, the big U.S. banks are spending more on technology each year than the entire venture capital (VC) investment in European FinTech firms.[46]

Figure 4.3 2019 tech spending at many big banks dwarfs investments in European FinTech

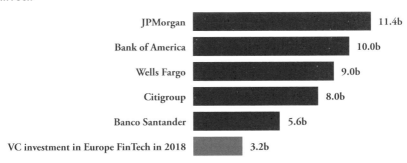

Annual spending (billions of USD)

Source: Bank disclosurses, data compiled by Bloomberg and KPMG Pulse of Fintech Report based on Pitchbook data

---

46 Jeremy Kahn and Charlie Deveruex, "Banks Waking Up to Fintech Threat Throw Billions Into Digital," Bloomberg, 10 May 2019, https://www.bloomberg.com/news/articles/2019-05-10/banks-waking-up-to-fintech-threat-throw-billions-into-digital.

Of the traditional banks, most fall into one of three categories:
- those that are truly transforming to be digital
- those that talk about transforming to be digital, but are not
- those yet to start talking about digital transformation

Banks that are truly doing digital have completely restructured and realigned their organisation, products and services around a digital foundation completely focused on the customer. Core systems have been refreshed and renewed, data has moved to the cloud and the IT function no longer exists. This is because technology is the business, it is no longer a function.

Does that sound like your bank? After all, customers do not necessarily want a digital bank. They want a bank that behaves in a digital way.

> ❝ We put a capability into a mobile app recently and didn't advertise it. It was actually buried two screens in but, in just two weeks, 100,000 people had found it because they expected it to be there, as it turns out. They found it on their own. The feature is, if they need a card replacement or they lose their card, they can turn it off. If you lost your card at home and are not sure where it is, but you think you might find it, you can just turn the card off. If you know you've lost it, however, then you can ask for a replacement. We didn't advertise it at all but customers found it very quickly on their own. ❞
>
> **Bill Wallace**, *Head of Digital for Consumer & Community Banking,*
> *JPMorgan Chase*

Changing the Bank Means Changing the Customer

> ❝ Just make sure you keep it simple and understandable for the customer. Almost every single meeting that comes across. And don't launch features for the sake of features.

Make sure that they are things that customers want
and how they want to use them. **"**
Jason Alexander, *Head of Digital Platforms for Consumer &
Community Banking, JPMorgan Chase*

" That's a really important cultural point, because
external pundits can drive functions into the app when it's
not that relevant to the customer. We try to keep our whole
environment simple. A research firm or media company
may be analysing and comparing different bank apps and
point out that someone's got more functionality than the
other. That doesn't mean it's better for the customer. It
just means it has more functionality. It's being customer-
obsessed, not other-obsessed. **"**
Bill Wallace, *Head of Digital for Consumer & Community Banking,
JPMorgan Chase*

A banking friend said that what most banks call innovation is actually business optimisation. They are just implementing incremental improvements to existing processes to make them cheaper and faster, more effective and efficient, with technology. One area in which this can be applied is customer onboarding, with many of the newer challenger banks using smartphone pictures, video and biometrics to register users in minutes, rather than demanding that they come into a branch with valid paper identification. This collapses a process of days to minutes, and is clearly better. It is not transformational, however. It is just better.

Then there is transformational change. Transformational change tries to reimagine the existing financial structures and make them radically better. For example, a transformational change is from institutional lending to peer-to-peer lending. It is completely different from what was there before but is still providing the same service, as in loans.

Finally, there is true innovation, which is completely new, and not just doing something today better or differently. An example would be Alipay and WeChat Pay, which provide a completely mobile microservice for everything from commerce to socialising to paying to saving and borrowing.

Innovations can fall into several levels of service, from doing what we do today in a completely new way to doing something completely new. P2P loans, mobile wallets and the Chinese internet giants are doing what we have done before in a completely new way, and this is transformative innovation. Transformative innovation is, therefore, what I am always looking for.

For most banks, they start with business optimisation: doing what we do today exactly the same, but faster and cheaper. They may then move into business transformation: doing what we do today in a new way that replaces the old way of doing things. Finally, there is real business innovation: doing a completely new thing in a new way that replaces the old ways of doing things.

Industrial-era companies need to strive for transformation and innovation as they change their structures and digitalise. It is no longer good enough to just do what we have always done, cheaper and faster with technology. We need to start from scratch with new thinking inspired by technology. That is what digital is doing: creating whole new structures of transformative innovation that shape the future world. That is what the P2P lenders, roboadvisors, API marketplace players and Chinese and African mobile wallet providers are doing. Creating the next generations of finance that will replace the old generations. This is what I mean by both transformation and innovation: they replace what was there before.

Now, it is fine for banks to watch these developments and deploy services to imitate or compete with such new structures, but the challenge is when to shut down the old ways. This has always been the biggest concern for most banks: they launch new things but never take out the old things. That is why they offer mobile wallets, apps and digital services but still operate branches and process cheques. When can you get rid of the paper and the bricks?

The answer to this challenge is that you have to have developed, nurtured, evolved and matured the digital models in a process that brings the customers along, before you can get rid of the old things that customers like and use. You must bring the customer along. This is the part that many are doing badly. After all, why does the media complain every time a bank shuts a branch or refuses to continue older services, like stamping passbooks? It is all to do with finding a balance between transformative innovation and business optimisation. Whether it is a transformation, innovation or both, the challenge is not to achieve the change but to achieve the change whilst bringing the customers along with you.

Are Banks Customer-Focused?

> **❝**Customer journey started as a very simple process, an improvement of events. Then we said, 'what if we create a design thinking?' It was about 2011 when we started on the design lab. The design lab was just a room back then, but at least we started doing design thinking and then built off that. Off the back of that we then developed into human-centred design, and we've gradually built on these ideas and enhanced them over time to where we are today. We think that's the right thing. **❞**
> **Dave Gledhill**, *former CIO, DBS*

I walked into a grocer's store the other day. The store had a fantastic array of fruit and vegetables, and a choice of everything. There were red, yellow and green peppers; carrots, courgettes and cauliflowers; oranges, apples and bananas, both large and small; watermelons, honey melons and mangoes; green grapes, red grapes and grapefruits; and more.

"Good morning, Mr Grocer," I said.

"Good morning, sir. Can I interest you in a lemon?" he asked.

"Well, I actually came here for a pineapple," I said.

"No, sir. I don't have any pineapples," he replied, as I stared at an array of pineapples. "You need a lemon."

I was a bit stumped at this. I didn't need a lemon. I wanted a pineapple as I was making a pineapple turnover. "I want a pineapple as I'm making a pineapple turnover," I said.

"Well, why don't you make a lemon drizzle cake?" asked the grocer.

"I don't want a lemon drizzle cake," I said. "I don't have the right ingredients."

"Ah well," said the grocer, "we can help you with that." Taking a deep breath, "LOTTIE!" he shouted. "Lottie? Can you help this guy with a lemon drizzle cake recipe, please?"

I was starting to get irritated now. "Look," I said, "I don't want lemons or a lemon drizzle cake or a recipe for lemon drizzle cake. I just want a pineapple to make a pineapple turnover, for which I have the recipe and most of the ingredients."

"Well, I can't sell you a pineapple," said the grocer. "You thought of trying a cake shop?"

I relate this story as this is how many customers feel about a bank, especially corporate customers. The bank starts with the product and tries to force that product on the customer. The bank does not think about the customer need or problem, and find the right solution. Instead, it starts with the product and internal focus and tries to force that on the customer. It may sound silly, especially in the scenario given above, but I have seen this in action. Banks classify customers into different categories: peaches, apples and lemons. If you are a lemon, you are a lemon, and that is what you get.

However, there is far more to this. If there is no cake shop in town, then you have to do the job yourself. You have to select the ingredients, buy them and bake them. You need the recipe and you have to do the work. But what if a new company came along and offered you the cake of your choice? No need to buy a lemon or a pineapple, just order the lemon drizzle cake or pineapple turnover of your choice. We may have lots of ingredients but we really just want cake!

If banks and insurance firms want to be customer-focused, they have to look beyond the product to the actual need and then present the total solution, not just the piece they deal with. This will be the delineation between those financial firms that win and lose in future.

Are You Focused on the Right Customer?

ff People think about digital. 'We should digitise?' That takes people right into that mindset of we should take what we do today and figure out how to automate it. Bad approach in my mind. You've got to step back and ask: Who is the customer? What is the customer pain point? What are they actually trying to get done? In today's world, there is a much better way to do that and start from that premise and then build from there. **JJ**

Jason Alexander, *Head of Digital Platforms for Consumer & Community Banking, JPMorgan Chase*

There is also a new generation of consumer that banks have to focus on: Generation Z. Millennials are so last decade. Who is the Gen Z? The breakdown by age looks like this:

Baby Boomers: Baby boomers were born between 1944 and 1964. They are currently 56 to 76 years old (as of 2020).

Generation X: Gen X was born between 1965 and 1979. They are currently 41 to 55 years old.

Generation Y: Gen Y, or millennials, were born between 1980 and 1994. They are currently 26 to 40 years old.
Gen Y.1 = 26 to 30 years of age
Gen Y.2 = 31 to 40 years of age

Generation Z: Gen Z is the newest generation to be named. They were born between 1995 and 2015 and are currently aged 5 to 25 years.

It is funny that we bankers talk about reaching the millennials when the millennials are now our managers. Millennials are no longer the target.

The target is Gen Z. Get them young and keep them for life. I loved these opening sentences in a recent *Economist* article that puts it all into context:

> "If you turn 18 [in 2019], you are younger than Amazon and Google. You turned three with Facebook's arrival, four with YouTube, five with Spotify, six with the iPhone and eight with WhatsApp."[47]

In other words, Gen Z has grown up digital. They cannot remember a time before the mobile telephone and internet, and they have money. A lot of it. In January 2018, it was estimated that Gen Z had $143 billion of direct spending power in the United States alone.[48] That amount will be higher today. Furthermore, they influence at least $600 billion of parental spending, if not more, according to U.S. estimates. Worldwide, you can triple those amounts, which means that there is a $2-trillion market here. How well are companies addressing this opportunity?

Some good but many badly. This is why retailers like Sears, Barneys, Toys R Us, Charlotte Russe, Wet Seal, Claire's and Payless ShoeSource have gone under in the United States while Debenhams, House of Fraser, Maplins, Jessops, HMV and more have had major issues in the United Kingdom. Like bank branches, physical stores are disappearing fast as the high street becomes a ghost town. Between 2018 and 2019, even premier brands like Gap, Tommy Hilfiger and Polo Ralph Lauren shut down their flagship shops on New York's Fifth Avenue. It is a retail apocalypse.

So Gen Z does not want shops or bank branches. They want everything digital, right? Well, it may surprise you to hear that this is not what Gen Z wants. Gen Z likes shops and shopping in a shopping centre. About 95 per cent of Gen Z visited a physical shopping centre in the United States during a three-month analysis in 2018, compared with 75 per cent of Gen Y and 58 per cent of Gen X.

---

47 "What bankers need to know about the mobile generation," *Economist*, 2 May 2019, https://www.economist.com/special-report/2019/05/02/what-bankers-need-to-know-about-the-mobile-generation?frsc=dg%7Ce.

48 "The Power of Gen Z Influence," Barkley Report, January 2018, http://www.millennialmarketing.com/wp-content/uploads/2018/01/Barkley_WP_GenZMarketSpend_Final.pdf.

Figure 4.4 Shopping like the Olds

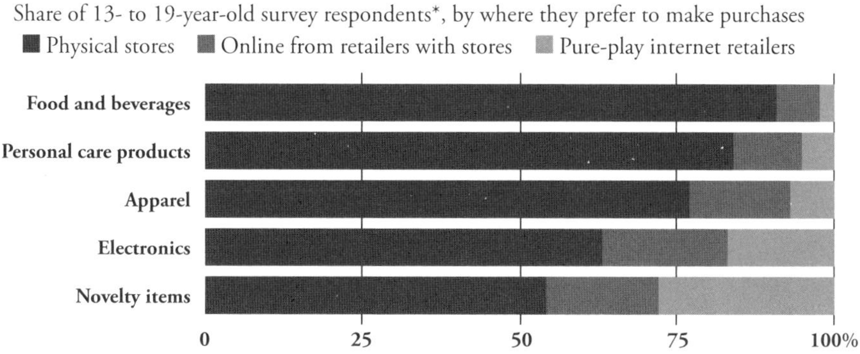
Share of 13- to 19-year-old survey respondents*, by where they prefer to make purchases
Physical stores
Online from retailers with stores
Pure-play internet retailers
Food and beverages
Personal care products
Apparel
Electronics
Novelty items
0
25
50
75
100%

Data: ICSC
* Survey of 1,002 13- to 19-year-olds in the U.S. conducted in May 2018 by Engine on behalf of ICSC
Source: Bloomberg[49]

For banks, this raises some fundamental questions. How are they reaching the Gen Z consumer? The *Economist* cites research by a consulting firm called Raddon that "85% of American millennials used mobile banking, and predicted that the share would be higher still for Gen Z. The main reason people choose a bank is convenience, the consultancy says. For older people that means a nearby branch; for younger ones it means an excellent app."[50]

The crux here is that this is the generation creating the future of finance. As already mentioned, John and Patrick Collison were nineteen and twenty-one when they started Stripe (in 2010), Vitalik Buterin was nineteen when he created the code that is becoming the backbone of the next-generation internet (Ethereum) and Ollie Purdue was twenty-one when he dropped out of university to launch a challenger bank in the United Kingdom (Loot).

Kids who can code are creating the next generation of financial services, and they do not like the last generation. This is because they have been polluted by the financial crisis, the rape of the environment by prior generations and the core issues of hate crimes. They hate hate crimes, climate damage and big banks.

49 Jordyn Holman, "Millennials Tried to Kill the American Mall, But Gen Z Might Save It," Bloomberg, 25 April 2019, https://www.bloomberg.com/news/articles/2019-04-25/are-u-s-malls-dead-not-if-gen-z-keeps-shopping-the-way-they-do.
50 *Economist*, "What bankers need to know."

Generation Z is not only putting a new spin on banking but also on consumerism. According to research, this generation will pay more for a product if the brand or retailer promotes meaningful social initiatives.

Figure 4.5 Ethical spending

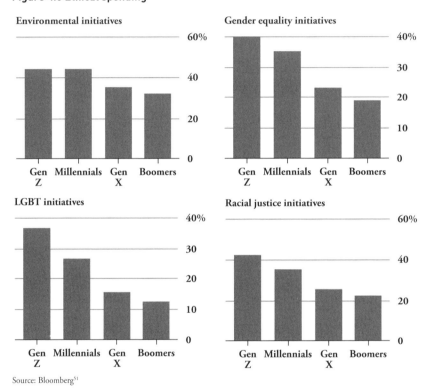

Source: Bloomberg[51]

They "demand more from financial institutions than older people do, and care more about values-based investing and corporate social responsibility. The young expect an answer to the question: 'Why are you in banking?', says Rick Spitler of Novantas, a financial consultancy. 'They think bankers should care about helping people to become wealthier, not just about their own bottom line.'"[52]

This message is not a positive one for banks that only have shareholder interests at heart. Equally, reaching Generation Z is much

51 Tiffany Kary, "Corporate America Can't Afford to Ignore Gen Z," *Business Insider*, 29 March 2019, https://www.bloomberg.com/news/articles/2019-03-29/how-gen-z-s-different-than-millennials-companies-try-asmr-memes.
52 *Economist*, "What bankers need to know."

harder than it used to be with previous generations because their major influence is social media.

Figure 4.6 How do you grab onto an audience that won't stay still?

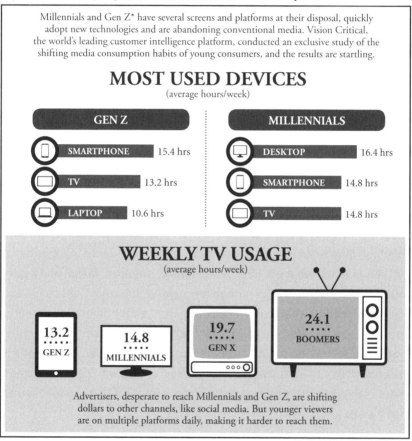

Source: *Vision Critical*

The conclusion is that Gen Z is going to be key to the talent war for coders and innovators so you cannot ignore them. The problem is that they can easily ignore you.

ff We started in earnest in 2010 with the concept of being truly customer obsessed and looking at everything through the customer's eyes first. 'What is their multiproduct experience like? What's my net promoter score around my product?' would have been the view. Today, the dialogue is very different. It is now about: 'What is the journey? How does this journey go across these products?' Even people inside of the product line are starting to ask about the relationship the customer could have between our different businesses. That wouldn't have entered the lexicon before. **JJ**

Bill Wallace, *Head of Digital for Consumer & Community Banking, JPMorgan Chase*

New Tech Is the Opportunity for Customer Focus

Technology is also now the enabler of reach or ignorance to these new generations of employee and customer. For example, we could talk about the difference in nuance between FinTech and TechFin. I claim that FinTech is doing what we have always done, cheaper, faster and better with technology. TechFin is reimagining everything with technology, and paying no heed to what was there before. It is a very different approach. One of the main differences in approach is that FinTech is taking old products and making them better with digital structures. TechFin offers the opportunity to start over, and serve customers with completely new services in completely new ways using technologies that are focused on their needs.

A good example of the latter is that Chinese internet giants like Alipay can offer loans for minutes and hours. The only reason we had annualised products, an annual insurance policy or a term-based loan was due to the fixed overhead of banks' physical structures. In a digital-first structure, there is no need to work on twelve-month cycles when you can work on twelve-hour cycles. That is the reason why Alibaba gives merchants loans for hours and minutes, rather than days and months. It is why some insurance start-ups offer insurance for minutes and hours.

Who needs to think months and years? For the traditional banks, this is a mindset shift that is hard to fathom. *How can you unthink everything that you have always thought?* It's a tough ask.

Whilst travelling the world, I find that most of the start-ups in the United States, Europe and developed economies are focused on FinTech. They are trying to take away redundancies and frictions of traditional banking. They may be neobanks, challenger banks, or API and Open Banking firms but their raison d'être is to remove old banking issues and do old-style banking, cheaper, faster and better with technology.

The TechFin firms ignore banking. They have no idea what a credit card or a mortgage is. They just start with the idea of technology and technology platforms. How can they connect you to money? What are you trying to do? How can they help you do that? Banks have had this conversation for years. No one wakes up thinking about money. They are thinking about what money can do. How can banks think past money and product, and focus on need and requirement? And if banks can shift their focus to the latter, how can they deliver that with today's technologies rather than with yesterday's finance?

These are the questions that many banks are grappling with, and have done for years. For decades, banks have talked about the fact that no one needs a mortgage as what people are actually trying to do is make a home. What bank understands the home-making requirement? What bank is delivering the need around that requirement, and not just focusing on the twenty-five-year, fixed-rate mortgage lock-in? What bank is truly thinking about customer need, rather than the product sale?

And there's the rub. If start-up firms can deliver against need and not sale, then there is their opportunity. They believe that they can truly disrupt large traditional banks by focusing on customer need, rather than the product sale.

> **❝** How can you maintain the best user experience?
> The users do not only include customers, but also the
> corporate customers and their personnel with different

positions in the enterprise. It's quite challenging. It is also true when we deal with the government because the government is also an institutional customer of a bank. Using Big Data intelligence, we can provide better services by treating different segments of customers with different services. In the digital world, how can we understand customer behaviours, their preferences, and deliver the right solution and right service at the right time? For example, mobile. Usually we only have transactions but now you know where the customer is, how they do the transaction, what the situation is, the climate, the timing. We know if they are interacting in the morning or in the afternoon on the subway, on a Monday or a Friday. It's different context and a different phenomenon to the customer. It's just many moments where they open to the bank many opportunities, but also challenges. We must compete not just as a bank, but as a FinTech company, as an internet company. It is all about the experience. **"**

Kunde Chen, *CIO, CMB*

BOTTOM LINE

Today's customer is harder to identify and reach than ever before because digital relationships are replacing physical interaction. This is why the customer should be at the heart of the transformation, as the customer is now in control. There is no point undertaking digital transformation if the focus is not entirely geared towards the customer need, experience and journey.

THE EMPLOYEE CHALLENGE

> **❝** There is no separate organisation for innovation. It is part of the entire organisation. What's innovation at Spotify or Facebook? It's a continuous process. If we believe that the real distinguishing factor lies in customer interaction, then we must constantly improve that. **❞**
>
> **Vincent van den Boogert**, *CEO, ING Netherlands*

It is easy to talk about the customer experience and digital relationships and forget that, when the rubber hits the road, it is usually because the customer has an issue and needs to call you. An app can serve most customer activity well. Checking balances, moving monies, making payments and even applying for loans and credit is all easily managed in the app. What happens if the balance is wrong, the payment does not go through or the loan application requires further explanation? This is when the human touch kicks in and can differentiate a truly digital organisation from one that just invested in digital to cut costs.

However, when the human touch is involved, you need to ensure that staff are happy. Happy staff make happy customers make happy business. How can you attract top talent, retain them and keep them happy? Well, the banks that are doing digital well have some secret sauce. It is called "let them join in". Let existing members of the bank be part of the future direction of the bank. Let them input, communicate, ideate and talk about their ideas for the future bank. After all, they often have better ideas than anyone divorced from customer contact in the management teams.

This is what sets apart the banks that are truly digital from the rest. Not only do their management and leadership have digital DNA, their people also are digital to the core. They don't just think that the bank has to adopt digital or do digital, they have to *be* digital as well. It is a different way of thinking and illustrated well by the few that are truly digital. These banks are on a continuous journey of developing digital services, replacing core systems, creating strong data analytics structures and converting the organisation to one that codes rather than transacts.

It is fascinating to talk with these banks as they do not talk like bankers, but more like Silicon Valley geeks. In fact, one was telling me a story about how they visited Silicon Valley before they embarked on their digital journey. They visited Facebook, Amazon, Google and Netflix and were impressed with the speed and structure of these firms. In particular, they were surprised to find people who used to work for a bank coding at Netflix. When they asked how this could be, the answer was quite amusing. Apparently, the Netflix executive said, "We hire the guys you fire and set them free."

I guess this is what a digital bank does if it takes digital to the core. The bank creates small teams and sets the people free. They are no longer part of a waterfall structure, where everyone has to sign everything off. They are instead moved into teams of fewer than ten people, the two-pizza microservices structure, and allowed to ideate, design, code and develop at will.

It is interesting to see this in action as developers, coders and designers are almost like a small team crafting an art. An artist cannot be constrained by structure. An artist would not allow their client to inspect their every brushstroke before being applied to the canvas. An artist would not test their music with the head of the music label before they started to try to play it.

Yet this is exactly how a traditional bank behaves with its development people. The bank wants them to test, show and explain everything and then get everything signed off before they will allow it into the bank. There is a great episode of the Andreessen Horowitz a16z podcast in which Adrian Cockcroft, the former head of cloud for Netflix, talks about microservices and being agile.[53] His key takeaway is that it is soul-

---

53 "a16z Podcast: All about Microservices," with Adrian Cockcroft, Frank Chen and Martin Casado, 1 September 2016, https://a16z.com/2016/09/01/microservices/.

destroying for people who code to work in a waterfall organisation, where everything has to be signed off from top-down.

A digital bank does not behave in this way. It sets its people free. It is really hard to do this in a company that traditionally has a strong command-and-control structure. Let the people go. Let them do their own thing. Set the people free. Equally, no bank can undertake digital transformation without scaring people. Set off the burning platform and compelling vision, and there will still be people afraid of losing their jobs.

Digital Banks Run with Digital Management

> We don't want to just be a bank or a digital bank, we want to become a digital company. How do you define and measure the transformation into a digital company? We focus on where the humans are interacting and the interaction platform, just like a digital advertising company or a Big Tech would look at those interactions. That's how we are looking at the human interaction level within the digital world because the Big Techs come at it from a view of high-frequency, low-value interactions. It tends to be that banking is coming at it from a low-frequency, high-value interaction view. We ultimately look at how people are interacting and how they are interacting with money and how money follows where people interact. It's not the manufacturing of a financial product that you sell but understanding where people are interacting. That's what the Big Techs have succeeded at doing, by looking at how people are interacting. Big Tech is influencing that interaction. We aren't creators of tech per se, but we understand a human interaction with technology and are building services and experiences around money."
>
> **Derek White**, *former Global Head of Customer Solutions, BBVA*

One of the notable differences between digital banks and traditional banks is that digital banks know exactly how every person is performing within the bank through digital management tools. A common theme among the banks successfully transforming is that the management and leadership teams have key metrics and measurements of their business available, in real time, all of the time, through data visualisation tools. These tools allow access to how a country, city, office, branch or individual is performing at any time from the macro view to the micro. They allow management to see how customers are behaving, their satisfaction levels, user experience, customer journey, product usage and more, all with a swipe. They allow management to see what works best where, which products gain the most traction, attribution and retention rates and more. They allow management to see when staff are being effective and ineffective, and when some may need training, redistribution or to be released. They may even allow analytics and projections of who might leave the organisation and when, based on employees' digital footprints through the organisation's workflows, and allow corrective decision interventions before staff get too low in morale.

Such tools are not simple or easy to build and deploy. It often takes years to get the data structures in place, and years more to get them to work well, but I have seen them in action and have been pretty impressed. In fact, what impresses the most is that the digital management dashboards allow immediate adjustment of business metrics for daily, weekly and monthly nuances. Such fine-tuning of the business in real time is key for a digital organisation to be effective.

Fast, real-time decision-making can only be supported by fast, real-time data. Providing key performance indicators from costs to income in simplified management dashboards is a key method of running a digital organisation. In particular, it means that parameters and alerts can be set within each area of the business to know when things are underperforming or outperforming and why. Basically, it creates easy management.

It reminds me of many years ago when I worked with a retailer to deploy an interactive system for looking at sales in store. The CEO of that particular firm turned to me and said that it was the best thing ever because he could call store managers first thing in the morning and ask them what had happened line by line with any specific issues that had occurred the day before. He liked the system as it meant he could breathe down the necks of his managers. Meanwhile his managers hated not knowing how he was getting this information so quickly.

Going back to why it is not easy to build and deploy such tools, it all comes down to enterprise data management and the efficiency of data structure, organisation and analytics. You can have the most amazing systems and visualisation tools in the world but, without good data, they are just going to be tools. Not useful tools. Just tools. The digital bank powered by strong data feeds into digital visualisation tools around digital services, digital marketing and digital connectivity that are the basics of strong digital banks. Digital analytics of that data to give 360-degree views around customer, employee, geography and organisation are then the keys to leverage that digital bank. This will get interesting as banks battle for better data, better data management and better data visualisation for management, leadership and day-to-day business.

Change Is the Only Constant

> **❝** We are very brave in trying to change the culture of the entire organisation, because some institutions believe they just need a layer of people to do digital. You leave the people who are not very interested in change alone, because they are just going to hold you back and then you re-architect the big piece that we want and we bring a lot of IT people in, the people who change the mindset. There are institutions that do that. We don't buy that philosophy. **❞**
> **Chng Sok Hui**, *CFO, DBS*

As banks embrace digital transformation, there is a high level of discomfort among bank staff around the change. First, they hear almost every day that AI and machine learning will automate their jobs. They fear the future. They fear losing their jobs. How can you reassure them that they can participate in the change without being a turkey voting for Christmas?

Second, they can see the bank turning into something different. The people walking around no longer wear suits and ties. Beards and jeans are being allowed in the office on weekdays, not just Fridays. A spirit of openness and communication is being evoked, which means that the snotty little graduate trainee is now allowed to talk back to his manager. Who allowed that? They need reassurance that this is a good thing that they can be a part of, and not some alien world forced on them.

Third, they joined the bank to have a job for life and felt comforted to be told what to do. The bank was all about command and control, hierarchy and order. You knew your place. Suddenly, that is all being removed. There is no job for life. Automation is taking that away. There is no command and control. It is all about coach and counsel. These days, the cleaners are just as important as the CEO, or so you are told. They need reassurance that the change in attitude is supportive and directed, not something that is weird and tortuous.

Fourth, the company is changing beyond recognition. Restructure after restructure is being implemented as the bank tries to move away from product focus to customer focus. The only constant is change. Objectives, focus, bonuses and work groups change almost by the month, and for many it is difficult to keep up with where they are meant to be going. They need strong communication and direction from the transformation team to bring everyone along without losing the many. There are many other things happening in this process but, as you can see, a lot of fear, uncertainty and doubt (FUD) is created as digital transformation happens. How can you overcome the natural FUD that grows with change?

In this world, it is always worth returning to the simplicity of "who moved my cheese?". A bank has typically grown a culture of mice that expect to find the cheese outside their front door every morning. There was little change, and everything was predictable. Now, the culture has to be to find the cheese—it moves every day—and create an organisation that is agile, nimble, flexible and constantly on the move. Change is the only constant, and nothing is completely predictable.

> **"**The last five years I've learnt several things. I've learnt that you can have comfort, discomfort and terror. I've been in quite a lot of discomfort but, at some point, I think that's okay. Initially I was probably seen as an executive that was daring. I did things and I thought that when it was difficult, I would manage. At some point, I wasn't sure if we could really handle it. That was critical for me. You have to learn how to live with comfort, discomfort, terror, but also how to be brave and stupid. We didn't know where we were sometimes. We didn't know if we were on the brave side or on the stupid side. It was discomfort but, because we explained and gave context to a lot of things, I think we managed.**"**
>
> **Vincent van den Boogert**, *CEO, ING Netherlands*

There Are Always Questions about the Future

There are always questions about the future because we don't know what will happen. What will happen when Amazon opens a bank? Will regulators create new rules about data sharing? How will quantum computing change the game? Are distributed ledgers and decentralised computing going to disintermediate us? Will I keep my job? What will machine learning do to my department? Should I fear for my team as they are doing things that seem fairly mundane? Look at what XYZ Bank just did, will we do that?

Quite often, the questions we ask about the future are ones of fear. We fear the fact that someone will move our cheese. Will Europe stay together? What will happen after Trump? Could there be a World War III? We fear that we might wake up and find that the world is nothing like it was yesterday. Yesterday, all our troubles seemed so far away. Our concerns are wrapped up in local, national and international affairs. Every now and then, we get hit by a black swan. An unforeseen event. Something that blows away the very fabric of our society, country or institution. Who knew that Lehmans would go under? Who knew that Trump would be elected president? Who knew that Boris would be negotiating a Brexit?

I have got bills to pay and jobs to be done. We need to move, sell the house, organise everything. How will the future look? Why is everything so uncertain? The thing is that many of our thoughts about the future are based on being grown up. We are mature. We have responsibilities, dependents, colleagues and careers. We need to be serious and focus. This is why we do not like change. For instance, a new manager has just taken over. Who is she? What is she like? Will I like her? Will I get on with her? What if I don't? What will I do? Where do I go?

We weren't like this when we were younger. When we had fewer responsibilities, were free and were just looking after ourselves and no one else. We were excited back then. Excited about everything. Particularly excited about change. I can't wait to see what happens next. Will I succeed? Will I get this job? Look, there's an audition on the 9th, I'm going for it! Let's take that risk.

It all boils down to risk. The older we get, the fewer risks we want to take. The younger we are, the more risks we are willing to take. This is why, when we talk about the future, we find that the older we are, the more we fear the future. The older we are, the more the future implies change and risk. The younger we are, the more we want the future to be about taking risk and change. The future is all about risk and change. The only constant is change, and the only thing we can change in the future is the change we make for ourselves.

Give People a Chance

> ❝ We are going through a cycle with the leadership team and getting to the place where they feel really comfortable with an empowered product owner owning the road map. That's probably the hardest thing

remaining for us to get over, which is organise the resource around the product area and let them go to town. Of course, you've got to put the right oversight, metrics, measures, things you want to watch for in place. You also need to be aware that the people sitting around the table with you aren't representative of the customer base we are trying to serve. We call them HIPPOs – highly important people's opinions—and HIPPOs don't always matter. They have insight, and we shouldn't discount that, but this goes back to the design-thinking strategy. Bring the customer base we are trying to serve into the organisation, get their input and listen to their needs. Also being aware that customers aren't always great at knowing what they want and don't want until you put it out on the market. **JJ**

Bill Wallace, *Head of Digital for Consumer & Community Banking, JPMorgan Chase*

One of the key attributes in transforming a bank is accepting that there will be redundancies from the old industrial organisation as it converts to digital. Even so, whenever possible, the transforming banks generally support people to change careers. There may be significant headcount reductions, if the bank is a heavily branch-oriented organisation, but banks do recognise that these people have invested years in the bank, have years of experience, have strong knowledge of the bank's culture and operations and want to keep and encourage their people, not just lay them off.

This is because the digital transformation programme is not about getting rid of staff, it is more about improving the customer experience, and doing this means bringing all the people with you. Creating happy customers requires happy people and how can you have happy people if they are being made redundant every day? How can you create a motivated work environment if there is blood on the floor?

These are challenging questions, but the consistent theme of banks transforming is that they do not get rid of staff, they reskill them. For example, staff in one bank were encouraged to visit the innovation lab. Once they arrived at the lab, they got to see all of the new ideas being developed, as well as being given the opportunity to reskill. If they took that chance, they were then offered a range of opportunities from learning to code in Python to being trained how to respond to customers on Facebook and Twitter. If they took that opportunity, then they had to commit as much as two hours a day for some courses. This demonstrates that the bank is keen to allow people to change career direction and support that change, and not just lay people off because they are surplus to requirement.

Now this is not easy, as I have seen some pretty dramatic changes in the last few years. For instance, Barclays reduced staff by a third between 2016 and 2018, as have many other banks. To put that in context, the equivalent of a football stadium full of people has been taken out of the business. Who are these people? I think that former CEO of Deutsche Bank John Cryan hit the nail on the head. Talking at a conference where I was also a keynote speaker, he said:

> "In our bank, we have people doing work like robots. Tomorrow, we will have robots behaving like people. It doesn't matter if we, as a bank, will participate in these changes or not, it is going to happen and if you spend a lot of time basically being an abacus, then your job will disappear."

This means that the people leaving the bank are those who cannot or will not reskill but, almost consistently, the banks that are succeeding in digital transformation are those that have motivated and supported their people to reskill. It does not mean that these banks are charitable institutions, keeping everyone around even if they are not needed, but they are banks making hard choices, supporting people to reskill when possible, and showing the door to those who cannot.

Bring One, Bring All

> ❝Today, we talk about so many jobs becoming redundant.
> I say, 'You work for an organisation that believes in training
> each and every one of the employees to be more skilled in
> this digital world.' Some will find it too stressful and maybe
> plan an alternative path, but our promise is that you can be
> part of a 26,000-person start-up. ❞
> **Chng Sok Hui**, *CFO, DBS*

As I have said a couple of times, one of the biggest issues companies
face with transformation—digital or otherwise—is bringing the people
with them. Some would say that anyone who does not join the journey
can leave, but that is quite a tough stance. "If you don't get with the
programme, you're out" is not a great way to manage. Specifically, being
hard-nosed and letting good people go leaves a bad taste in the mouth of
the people who are left. I actually worked for a company once that was in
crisis mode and heading towards bankruptcy. Their way of dealing with
it was to lay off groups of people every six months. The day I remember
well was when my colleagues were fired but I was not. We were all called
into the head office and called in one by one and given an envelope. The
issue was that if you got the fat envelope, you were out; if you got the thin
envelope, you were still in. It left everyone feeling that it was a horrible
way to deal with humans.

Interestingly, most of the banks engaged in digital transformation
that I have met are trying to bring everyone with them, with no
conscious fire-and-move-on focus. Instead, they focus on reskilling
people and giving them the opportunity to get a new career within the
bank. An example that illustrates this approach well is a story that
one of the managers recounted: "My son is fifteen years old and I've
talked to him about a career. In my life, I've had three major moments
where my career changed course, happening about once every decade.
However, I believe that his career and work life will change every two

or three years. You constantly have to reskill where change is the only constant."

The thing is that it is hard to reskill if you are made redundant and have no access to such resources. If the bank gives you the life skills to change path however, that is a different story. And that is what most digitally transforming banks are doing. They are teaching middle managers to code, they are taking branch tellers and giving them coaching in dealing with customer services through digital media and they are offering staff members aged fifty and above a chance to learn design.

The other issue is the frozen middle, the middle management of the bank, which fears change the most and resists it the hardest. Many middle managers believe that digital will make their jobs redundant; will remove their power base, which took them years to gain; will force them to change role and do something that they are not comfortable doing; will make their department defunct in the future; and so on.

How do you deal with these people? How do you bring them along? In asking that question, I discovered the interesting answer that you engage with them and let them determine the future. You get them to participate. There is nothing more fearsome than someone dictating your future and telling you what to do. However, if you engage them, keep doors open and let them tell you what they think, it is very different.

It goes back to the old message that people who work in banks, or in any other business for that matter, are humans. They have brains. They can think. They just need to be engaged. However, if you determine that Joe will be moved to account management from branch management, Mary will be asked to shed twenty of her team for the good of the bank and Chris can be given a fat envelope, you know what will happen.

And Make Sure that They Are Synchronised
based on input from Marko Wenthin, co-founder of Solaris and CEO of Penta

❝ People sometimes think that empowerment means total freedom. They think it's a trade-off between empowerment and alignment, but agile doesn't mean letting go. Alignment enables empowerment, because if you don't have alignment, you don't have empowerment. You have anarchy. It can only be fostered by strict discipline. That's why we are strict on practices such as how you do testing, how you do context delivery, what the rules are in order to bring something to production. This is something different to having hierarchy, where people formally approve and there are handovers. We are very strict on some practices, some disciplines, some controls but, at the same time, we give a lot of responsibility to the organisation in order to speed up delivery. Everything eventually is about handovers and speed of delivery. That's our competition. **"**

Vincent van den Boogert, *CEO, ING Netherlands*

It is only if you are able to bring business, operations and IT together that you will be able to answer to the challenges ahead in a timely fashion. This is hard to achieve in a traditional organisation because the organisational structure is just not prepared to cope with the demands of an ever-changing world. The traditional organisational chart with vertical reporting lines into line managers is all very well, but it prevents such an organisation from working quickly, agilely and coping with market requirements.

In a traditional organisation, you have business departments, such as sales, marketing and customer support, standing next to typical banking departments, such as compliance, legal and risk management. Yet another pillar would be the technology group providing IT development, IT management and operations. Then you have your financial management departments, such as accounting, regulatory reporting and so on. There are obviously many more but these are the main parts of a bank.

Various approaches are then used to get all of these parts to work together. There is always the aim that these groups work towards a team spirit in order to achieve the best results. There is matrix management and regular cross-functional team meetings. However, the problems arise when the objectives of one team conflict with those of another. If the sales team has needs to achieve that override the aims of the legal team, then human nature kicks in. The better a team functions, the more the people identify themselves with their group and their peers. That is not a bad thing but, as a side-effect, you get competition. Anybody who is not in your inner circle becomes a threat, and the words "we" and "them" get embedded in the way people communicate and work, even if they are all part of one and the same company. Instead of all working for the same side, there are internal company struggles, which mean that the greater good of a company becomes the secondary, if not a tertiary, goal. The end result being that the company slows down in every aspect of its business.

In particular, engineers are different from marketeers are different from lawyers/compliance people are different from operations staff and so on. If they all play in their own field, then the dynamics become dangerous for the company, and the larger a firm gets, the bigger the impact. This is why start-ups with ten people get much more done quicker than a larger organisation with a hundred people. It is speed boats versus container ships.

How can a larger or growing company embrace these challenges? Well, digitally transforming banks turn this into a strength. Rather than separating functions, they integrate them. Compliance and financial people sit alongside marketing and sales people, who sit alongside design and development people, all in small microservices two-pizza teams. The barriers between functions break down as the teams are now all-for-one and one-for-all. The organisation flattens and needs a new management operation to deal with such a structure.

The best way to then think about how you manage such a structure is to liken it to a synchronised swimming team. In synchronised swimming, you want to achieve choreography that ensures everybody moves in perfect synchronisation with everyone else. You would get this in a traditional organisation because everybody in one department is from a similar background in both education and outlook. This changes, however, in an agile, flattened structure as skills and experiences are far more mixed in the corporate melting pot. Now it needs coordination, and so every team needs to know its part in the choreography of the company. Overall, it changes the dynamics to one where many cogs make the engine work, but each cog is managed in its own right. As a result, all of the teams and all of the players in the team will want to achieve the same goals for the team and for the company, not just for their department and their function. What good is it to have the best-performing sales team if products cannot be delivered or the best developers' team if the products created cannot be sold or are sanctioned by the legal department?

In a synchronised swimming team, you bring together people who are different and have different skill sets, but the sum of those differences brought towards a common goal makes a great team. The common goal being to win the tournament. In digitally transforming banks, they bring the specialists of their field of business—legal, product, IT development, sales, operations—into many smaller clusters and coordinate them based on a very narrow focus for each cluster. In this way, they create their own, agile structure within the larger organisation, with a full set of skills and full ownership for their domain.

Naturally, they will form a real team to achieve the success of their operation and the company. The product owner makes a brilliant lead, keeping operations and IT development in the position to provide the right things (products); the central swimmers (sales and marketing) transform the right things into successful outcomes (goals); while the outer legal or compliance colleagues stop all of them from getting into trouble. In this case, the management becomes the coach on the sideline, keeping the market and the respective unit responses sharp and coordinated. They are the synchronisers of the synchronised swimming team.

Overall, it means that the old, hierarchical, monolithic bank based on command and control changes into a fresh, flat, microservices team-based bank based on coach and counsel. It is a very different company.

Synchronise through Fast and Regular Communication

> ❝I can recall, in my previous bank, taking nine months to get nine signatures on a piece of paper in order to go in and invest in something. Here, we had a stand-up meeting with the CEO in a room for forty minutes. The request was for a sizable investment. Done. Get on with it. ❞
>
> **John Laurens**, *Group Head, Global Transaction Services, DBS*

A further aspect of the digital bank's design for coach-counsel microservices structures is that they have reviews all the time. Not formal reviews, but fast meetings with the businesspeople, designers, developers and even audit and compliance all around the table. These are quick, frequent and informal, unlike in the old industrial organisation, which has long, annual and formal meetings. This is the spirit of being agile.

It reminded me of a company I visited in the 1990s and all of their meetings took place standing up. When I asked why, they told me that when people are sitting down, they talk for longer. So stand-up meetings were the way to go. These were very different to what meetings were usually like, where there would be a formal agenda and formal chair, an assistant to document the meeting and all parties invited to have their say during the meeting. I remember going to a meeting in the 1990s about a tradeshow that was coming up, and we spent two hours discussing the bag that would be given away. Should it be black or brown? Real or faux leather? What logo and writing should we put on it? It was so boring.

Fast-moving digital banks do not do things this way. Digital banks focus on quick and regular communication. It is similar to the movement away from formal letters to email to chatroom. Communication gets faster and faster and moves from offline to online to real time.

Often, in the old world, email was used as a way to cover yourself. You copied in anyone and everyone who you thought needed to see it in order to make sure you had covered yourself. This email trail would pick up like a snowball, getting longer and longer and bigger and bigger and harder and harder to digest. Emails are unnatural, which is why some firms enforced a discipline to only send an email with a title. No content. Just a title. That was their way of fast communicating. Today, in this world of Slack, Twitter, WeChat and WhatsApp, we talk non-stop. We chat. We do not send limitless garbage that needs to be printed out to work out what is being discussed. We just talk non-stop.

The twenty-first-century ways of communicating are making a fantastic difference to office life. Equally, so is the hot-desk policy. Work from home or work in the office. Work wherever you want. Just keep in touch. One bank that was moving from analogue to digital really struggled with this concept. The idea of hot desks instead of formal offices was a huge cultural shift. What? I don't have a desk? Where will I sit?

The bank got over this obstacle by making an analogy that compared the office to home. Home is the building, it is not a room. The bank is the place and the culture, not a desk. This means that you identify with the place, not the rooms in the place. Finally, the bank moved to hot-desk working, and it has worked well to this day. However, the banks successfully transforming to be digital do more than that. They regularly brainstorm and whiteboard. They have spontaneous meetings and idea generation. They do not have to gather all of the people and get all of the agenda locked down. It is all fast and in real time.

This is a critical factor in today's modern company. Everyone has an open door for communication, digitally and physically. There are no formalities, except for sign-off of critical moments, but the build-up to any formal sign-off is formed from hundreds of reviews and thousands of chats. What a great way to work and it is not specific to digital banking. It is specific to digital transformation. The office of 2020 is very different from the office of 2000 or 1980. It is fast and agile.

> ❝ In 2011, we would have had three major releases a year and that would have dictated the cycle. It created a culture of trying to get everything into the next release, which led to imperfect journeys for customers. When you are constantly

releasing, which we are today, you are in a
mode where you can introduce incremental changes
fast. That's a whole different way of working. **"**
Bill Wallace, *Head of Digital for Consumer & Community Banking,*
JPMorgan Chase

"It is another big cultural change. The comfort with
pilots, test and learn. Put it out there at small scale
and see what happens. That has been a big change.
Before, we had these big launches of things but
now we are able to learn a lot quicker, a lot better
and create this constant feedback network. **"**
Jason Alexander, *Head of Digital Platforms for Consumer &*
Community Banking, JPMorgan Chase

And Be Decisive

Another big difference in truly digital banks is fast-cycle decision-making and processing. This was brought home to me by two comments. One was from the CEO of a start-up that works with Alipay. The start-up began initial consultation about the service in spring 2016, signed contracts in June and went live in October. A four-month development cycle from contract to production was quite something. The start-up CEO made the observation that this is the usual time that it takes him to arrange a meeting with a senior bank person!

The second comment that illustrated the difference is the partnership between a traditional bank and a FinTech start-up. The CEO of the start-up told me about the painful onboarding process to work with the bank. Lawyers and compliance people were crawling out of the woodwork to get in on the act of vetting the CEO and performing the due diligence on the company. Then the auditors and accountants jumped on board before the procurement and purchasing people had even offered the start-up a form to fill in to start doing business. It was painful.

In a truly digital bank, the process is fast and easy. How can it be fast and easy, and how can a digital bank be so open and easy to access? It goes back to all of my other points about the digital banking culture. The culture is a flat organisation with fast and open communications. It is a company in which getting from first contact to CEO can be escalated and prioritised as needed, with meetings held fast and decisions made in real time. These banks believe in fail fast and are not stuck in lengthy cascading structures of hierarchies.

The phrase "fail fast" is unusual in the banking sector. You hear it a lot in digital companies—innovate, experiment, fail, pivot, reboot and so on—but it is not a discussion that you hear often in most banks, until now. Banks generally use regulations as an excuse not to do things and often avoid failure due to their fear of regulations. What happens in digital banks is that they embrace innovation and failure, and include the regulator in all of the dialogue. Rather than being scared of regulations, they create them. It is an attitude of "do things and ask forgiveness afterwards" rather than *not* doing things because you think you might make someone cross.

At this point, many ask, how can you allow failure in a bank? The answer is to make sure that you can test and develop in a secure and limited way before expanding further. This goes back to the snowball comment that I made earlier. Start small and let the idea roll until it becomes big. You do not deploy things that are untested across the bank. Instead, start small, test, fail, pivot, deploy, retest, fail, pivot, deploy, retest and repeat until the thing works and is proven, and can then be deployed across the bank. These are neither pilots nor projects, but continuums of development that eventually get you to mainstream and real time.

Truly digital banks have fast-cycle processes with real-time decisions and open access, and really know how to get things done. These banks can go from contract to operations within a few months. That is nothing like old banks that would probably go from contract to due diligence in a year. Move fast, act fast, think fast. Do nothing slow.

Thawing the Frozen Middle

> **"**Ten years from now, I can see a small number of winners, more Americans and Chinese than others. Those guys will rule the world of banking or at least will be setting the standard. The biggest challenge a bank or any company is facing is to get a sense of urgency that is big enough for them to move. In the banking world, there is traditionally no sense of urgency. In general, people are not used to working with a sense of urgency. Frankly, the majority of banks are still living in a very comfortable world, even though return on equity is being halved. We still see many people not fully realising what is happening and not counting in the same way as people in the industry are.**"**
>
> **Benoît Legrand**, *Chief Innovation Officer, ING Group*

As can be seen, converting from analogue to digital is hard and involves core systems change, strong leadership, organisational change management and nerves of steel. So how do you deal with the swathe of resistance that generally sits across the middle of the organisation? The middle management. The managers most worried about change as they may lose their jobs and/or power, which have taken years to generate.

Maile Carnegie, head of digital at ANZ, articulates this issue well:

"Increasingly, most businesses are getting to a point where there are people in their organisation who are no longer experts in a craft, and who have graduated from doing to managing and basically bossing other people around and shuffling PowerPoints. That frozen middle will resist change like death. It exposes that they have no skills any more. Figuring out how to deal with the frozen middle, once you have the boss' support, is the big thing. If they're not going to become craftsmen and learn anymore, they need to move on."[54]

---

54 Nadia Cameron, "Tackle the 'frozen middle' of your organisation or face irrelevancy," CMO, 24 May 2017, https://www.cmo.com.au/article/619739/anz-digital-chief-tackle-frozen-middle-your-organisation-face-irrelevancy/.

This is so true. It reminds me of when I was dealing with software for capital markets some years ago. The software could automate corporate actions, paying dividends, mergers, acquisitions, equity buy-backs and suchlike. However, the salespeople were frustrated that the target decision-maker for the software was the COO who, more often than not, would not sign off on such software because it would mean losing a lot of the people who made up his empire. Now that is another issue: empire building. If a person has climbed up the organisation and got to the point where they are managing one, two or three hundred people or more, the idea of cutting through that mass of minions is often a political one, and hard for the person to take when they are loyal to their people and, equally, it shows how powerful they are. The frozen middle. The managers frozen between climbing higher, keeping their power base or losing face and being exposed for their true skills, or lack thereof.

The constructive advice from talking to transforming banks is that if the leadership team of a bank or any other institution wants to really make digital transformation happen, the first thing that has to be done is unfreeze the middle. That is what walking the walk is all about. It is going round the organisation, explaining the digital transformation that is happening and seeing if people can follow the lead. It is not just presenting the change, but looking over shoulders and pushing the change through the frozen middle that is resisting it.

The Art of the Corporate War

One of the greatest challenges in digital transformation is the cultural change, which has to be led with passion and commitment from the top-down. That means a board mandate, and the chair and CEO being fully on board. What happens if you have the wrong CEO, however? What if the CEO does not get it?

Many financial firms may be constrained in embarking on digital change by the thinking of their CEO. They know that digital is important so they bring in people like me to show that they care. Then they do not do anything about it because they are "proud of their heritage", "want to keep their customers on side" and believe that their differentiation "is their history".

That does not work in the digital age. Yes, there is a place and role for banks in the digital age, but you have to work out what that place is and what that role is. If you are not 1000 per cent clear on that strategic focus and if you have not defined 1000 per cent who your customers are and why, then I doubt you will be around in a decade as there are hundreds of bigger tech and financial giants that are absolutely clear about their strategy and customer focus. If you have an organisation with a CEO paying lip service to change, you should change the CEO.

Now that is not easy and can only be done by a chairman and board. Take a look at HSBC, where John Flint was forced to resign as CEO after just eighteen months in August 2019; or John Cryan at Deutsche Bank, who was dismissed as CEO in April 2018; or Antony Jenkins at Barclays, who was fired in July 2015. A CEO can be changed, and often must be changed in order to deal with crisis. You cannot break the old way of doing things without banging a few heads together and ruffling feathers. In fact, my favourite quote about change is: *"If you're flying over the target and getting no flak, then you're flying over the wrong place."* You have to break the shackles of the past to affect change.

What about the C-team? And the level that reports to the C-team? What about them? Often in any large corporation, the C-team is like the Knights of the Round Table, with many of those at the table wanting to kill the king or queen to get their crown. It means being a discreet backstabber rather than an out-and-out murderer. This is the home ground of office politicians and their political games.

The major focus of people should be on their customer, whether that customer be internal or external, and yet often the focus is on how to get on to the next rung of the office ladder. A good illustration of this is when I joined a company and we had a meeting of managers off-site for the annual kick-off meeting. The top two hundred people in the firm assembled and, in the evening, were whisked off by buses to a superb dinner. Getting on to one of the buses, I sat with a colleague who exclaimed, "Oh look, here comes Richard Cranium,[55] he won't stay on this bus."

Sure enough, Richard walked up and down the bus, smiling, shaking everyone's hand and giving a few high fives, and then he got off.

"How did you know that he wouldn't stay on the bus?" I asked. "Because there's no one important on this bus," my colleague replied.

Two years later, Richard became the right-hand man of the CEO and I had left. But then, I never could tolerate office politics.

The challenge for the CEO and chair when engaging in digital transformation is to recognise that there are layers working against them. Not just the middle management who worry about losing their little empires, but the knights around the table who have spent years working the party line to get to be at that table and now the last thing they want to happen is to lose their prerogative ... or their bonus, for that matter.

What tends to happen in such situations is that the CEO, who is often new to the role, engages in a mass cull. Wipe out the immediate layer below and remove the threat. Set an example to strike fear into those who oppose the new way of doing things, and ensure that those who now rise to the table are loyal to the new way of thinking.

That sounds ruthless, but think how often it happens. And it really strikes at the heart of Machiavelli and Sun Tzu: to change the organisation, you have to change the management first.

Niccolò Machiavelli
"Never was anything great achieved without danger."

"The first method for estimating the intelligence of a ruler is to look at the people they have around them."

"I'm not interested in preserving the status quo; I want to overthrow it."

"Never attempt to win by force what can be won by deception."

Sun Tzu
"If you know the enemy and know yourself, you need not fear the results of a hundred battles."

---

55 Richard Cranium stands for "dick head" in English slang.

"If ignorant both of your enemy and yourself, you are certain to be in peril."

"The general who advances without coveting fame and retreats without fearing disgrace, whose only thought is to protect his country and do good service for his sovereign, is the jewel of the kingdom."

"He will win whose army is animated by the same spirit throughout all its ranks."

The War for Talent

> ❝ How do you hire good digital natives and people who understand technology? We used to have this old-fashioned way of interviewing, which was kind of a little bit dull. Now, we have Hack-to-Hire. We created an online competition. You sign up for the competition and the people who are top are invited to spend a weekend hacking with us. On the Sunday evening, the winners get job offers. So, they walk out with an offer. It's closed within a weekend. The first time we ran this, we had 12,000 applicants and they all came and did this hacker coding test. We invited the top 200 into the hackathon, and since then we've run several of these across Asia. We've hired hundreds of people through this method now. ❞
>
> **Dave Gledhill**, *former CIO, DBS*

One of the biggest challenges in digital transformation is attracting technology talent into the bank. The challenge of finding top coders is a big one as there are an awful lot of other firms out there to join. You could join a hot FinTech unicorn like Monzo, SoFi, Stripe, Ant Financial or Ping An or you could join one of the ponies (firms below a valuation of $100 million) or centaurs (firms valued at $100 million to $1 billion) out there. Equally, there are many others that could attract such talent and are fighting for the same people, from technology unicorns to technology titans. So why would you join a boring old bank when Amazon and Tencent are calling?

First and foremost, not everyone can join a technology titan like Amazon for a number of reasons, with location being a key one. If you are joining a Netflix or a Facebook, then you are West Coast bound to Silicon Valley where the average house price is $1.4 million. Not everyone wants to be based there, and many cannot afford to be there if they are just starting out on a coding career.

Second, for every unicorn a thousand ponies die. There are thousands of start-up firms out there with great ideas, but their burn rate is high and capital can often be hard to maintain operations. Even unicorns die, so you are taking a big bet if you join a start-up.

Third, many are motivated by doing something that can make an immediate difference to their friends and family. If you are involved in a start-up, it may be years before you see users using your code. If you join a technology titan or big bank, you will see the difference it makes to your friends and family within a few days. The satisfaction of seeing that is huge.

Fourth, it may well be that you want to change the world and what's the best way to do that? Attacking from the outside, with something unproven, unstarted, unused and unknown, or from the inside, with something being used by millions and trusted by all?

Finally, a banking career is attractive because the big banks are hiring, big time. There may be a hangover from the global financial crisis and the anger of the 99 per cent, but if you are able to code and code well, a job with a bank is a good job.

Interestingly, when you look on the internet, there are other reasons why you might join a bank to code. For example, on the question-and-answer site Quora, someone asked the question: why would software engineers work in finance instead of tech? The first and main answer was because that is where the money is. Other answers stated that it is because banks are tech companies and they may be right on that point.

In an *American Banker* article, the first paragraph makes this point:

"Goldman Sachs CEO Lloyd Blankfein calls the investment bank a tech company — and roughly 25% of its 33,000 employees are engineers. JPMorgan employs 50,000 technology workers (including a former Google artificial intelligence executive), which is nearly double the total number of employees at Facebook."[56]

The article goes on to say that the main motivation of developers joining a firm is to *solve interesting problems*, which goes to the heart of the point of making a difference for friends and family. Developers are drawn to companies that have Big Data to analyse using data analytics. It is all about the point that data is air, not oil, and banks have a lot of data. Real data. Data accumulated over decades. A developer is driven by taking good data and making it into good service. Therefore, a bank looking to get good talent really needs to focus on what problems they can solve with their data, and how to motivate developers to understand their data needs.

Banks need good coders as a priority, but also need to recognise that their cultural needs are different. In particular, they need a sense of purpose and belonging, and banks will struggle if they treat these individuals as peripheral and not core to the business.

When Code Is Art, How Do You Attract Great Artists?

> ❝If you are a new A* engineer, you might gravitate towards a start-up. If you've been through that cycle, you often find you do a whole bunch of work and no one actually got to use it because the start-up failed. Engineers really want to do stuff that their mother, father, siblings and buddies are going to use. That is part of that. You want to make an impact. The other part has been universally consistent in all of my career. When I interview people and ask: why are you interested in changing jobs? The answer is nearly always "I want to come to a place where I can make a difference. I love challenging problems.

56 Guarav Verma, "How banks can win the struggle for tech talent," *American Banker*, 5 September 2018, https://www.americanbanker.com/opinion/how-banks-can-win-the-struggle-for-tech-talent.

I'm a problem solver." I hear that all that time. When you are touching thirty-three million people's lives every day, that's making a difference. When you are working in a very cool start-up, it might be fun. You might have a really good time and yes, you have the potential of changing people's lives, depending on what the topic is, but you've got to have customers to have that impact. That's one of the values that we bring. In addition, if you work with smart people and in an environment with cloud-based technology and all of the latest things like AI and ML, you've got to have data. We have that data. Thirty-three million sets of it. **"**

Bill Wallace, *Head of Digital for Consumer & Community Banking, JPMorgan Chase*

Talking with one former Big Tech developer who had been headhunted by a big bank to be a gamechanger (GC) provides interesting insights. He had been gifted the ability to do almost whatever he wanted when it came to innovation, change, ideas and so on. He had taken that message to heart big time—go big or go home—and had started to restructure much of the stodgy old banking culture. That was when the CEO called him into his office for a chat.

CEO: I hear you've got some great ideas but my team is complaining. Care to share?

GC: Sure, you hired me to turn this big bank into a Big Tech Bank. That's what I'm doing.

CEO: But this idea of integrating developers with risk managers, treasury and compliance people. You cannot be serious?

GC: I'm totally serious. Your boring old bankers should learn Python. Everything is code. All of your people should be able to code.

CEO: You cannot be serious?

GC: I just said I was. You told me that technology is the future of the bank, the bank has to be digital and you're backing me all the way. If you believe that, then this is the way to go.

CEO: But why should bankers learn to code?

GC: I'll ask you in a different way. Why do you think Stripe is worth $35 billion [as of September 2019]?

CEO: I don't know. You tell me.

GC: It's just seven lines of code ... but it's beautiful code.

CEO: I don't get it.

GC: Well, the reason why FinTech is such a hot space is that you've got all these young engineers who can see how to do what you do with code. So, they're writing beautiful code. Adyen is also great code. It's an art.

CEO: Code is art?

GC: Of course, it is.

CEO: So, what does that mean?

GC: It means that if your code is clunky-bumpy-chunky-wunky, no one will use it. Engineers are designing the new world of trade and they look at code, and ask if they can write something as good as that. If not, they will use it and they will look for the best version of it. Then they stumble on one or two companies that are offering code, like Stripe and Adyen, and because they are engineers, they will strip it down and realise that it is beautiful code. It's art. Anything else just does not cut the mustard ...

CEO: So, what should we do?

GC: Well, you told me to come in here and stir up the shack, so that's what I'm doing. All of your guys see product, process, service and suchlike from a banker's view. It's all about the regulation, risk and compliance of those structures. Whereas what they should be seeing now is how to code those products, processes and services so that the regulation, risk and compliance are in the code, but the customer doesn't see that. It should just be simple, easy, beautiful and artistic.

CEO: And that's what you think these upstarts like Stripe and Adyen do?

GC: You've got it, you've got it. YOU'VE GOT IT!!!

CEO: No, I don't get it. What I get is that you're saying we should be coders first and bankers second?

GC: Well, kind of.

CEO: But we're a bank. We're bankers first and code comes way down the list.

GC: But how will you ever create great art?

CEO: We're not artists. We're risk managers.

GC: You don't get it, do you?

CEO: I don't think I do. Now, have a good day. Miss Simmonds will deal with your severance package.

The conclusion is that the FinTech community are like the internet commerce world of Amazons, Facebooks and Ubers, who all see code as art. The more intuitive, simple and beautiful the way the code is presented, the more likely it is to be used. However, bankers begin with banking products and banking mentality. They see the banking process first and then ask the coders to code the banking processes. This is one of the major reasons why banks struggle with attracting talent and transforming to digital. It is not just a technology game, but also a cultural one.

BOTTOM LINE

Banks have to rebalance the organisation to move from analogue to digital. This means shedding a lot of the analogue workforce, or preferably retraining and reskilling that workforce to be more digital. The biggest shift is in the structure of the bank itself, flattening the organisation and empowering small micro teams in a synchronised structure of management that has little hierarchy. That cultural shift is a huge challenge as there will be major resistance from middle management. The answer is to bring middle management in first to lead the change and not tell them how they have to change. In the meantime, the bank also has to get new blood from the talent pool that may hope to work for an Apple, Amazon or Stripe. To do this, the bank must treat developers like rock stars, and not just as ancillary to the main function of banking.

THE PARTNERING CHALLENGE

Partnering is never easy. This was illustrated by a presentation given by the CDO of a major European bank. Here's what he said:

1) "The bank does not have a monopoly on good ideas."

Whenever a new tech comes round, the bank thinks that it has to do it. It sees something like Face ID and says, "Wow, yes, that is good. Let's build one." Um, but Apple has built a very good one with APIs. We don't need to build it. "Yes we do, because it has to be secure." But Apple's Face ID is secure. "Ah, but we cannot give them our data. We need to keep the data." Under PSD2, you don't. And so it goes on. Banks see a lot of good ideas around the world but are convinced that they have to build a version of it themselves because no one else can do it as well or as securely as they can.

2) "Big Tech giants can iterate really quickly."

GAFA and their Chinese counterparts Baidu, Alibaba and Tencent (BAT) are fast, nimble, agile and quick. They each have a fantastic microservices-structured LEAN organisation that jumps at the request of anyone. Not a bank. The CDO recounted the story of a corporate client that processes billions of dollars with the bank and its CEO demanded that he had an iPad app that could sign off a $10-billion loan within a week of their meeting. Um, a multibillion-dollar corporate loan app in a week? You must be joking. Sure, GAFA and BAT can do that, but a bank? So, the bank fudged it and built a fast app that was specific to that particular corporate's CEO and CFO's sign-off structure. Banks must be nimble if they are to keep up with their customers' expectations, and corporate customers are as demanding as, if not more than, retail customers.

3) "Quick decisions matter."

This statement reminded me of the comment made by the CEO of a start-up that partners with Alipay in Finland. He said that they talked with Alipay in April, signed the contract in June and were live by October or "about the same time it takes to get a meeting with an SVP or CxO of a bank". Banks are slow to decide anything but, as the CDO pointed out, most corporates are too. Everyone has a voice and a black ball so anyone can sink an idea before it has even started. That cultural barrier has to be broken down if banks are to become more agile, like FinTechs.

4) "We should definitely do that."

Whenever the CDO showed the management team something new and interesting, like telling Alexa to shift money from his deposit account to his savings account as a concept, the team would say, "We should definitely do that". Then when the question "who should definitely do that?" was asked, vacant, glazed-over looks appeared on all of the team's faces. "Ah, not me" would be the refrain. Even if demonstrating something with a clear owner, like using AI to determine credit risk, the chief risk officer (CRO) and the senior vice president (SVP) of lending would look over the heads of the presentation team and say, "We should definitely do that." Then point at each other.

5) "We have to get out from behind our desks."

Most bankers are only comfortable when they stay within their comfort zone, behind the desk. They can watch and control everything, but do nothing. When ideas come along, they want those ideas brought to them, in their office, rather than going and seeking them out. Changing the cultural mindset to be hungry for ideas, rather than waiting to be fed them, is a key part of getting change to work. So true!

> **❝** Our approach to FinTechs is that we are willing to build, buy and partner with almost any of them. We study them. I've got a team of people in Silicon Valley who are connected

in that community. They like to deal with us, because of our scale, and we like to deal with them at a certain stage of maturity. They don't have to be super large. They just have to have enough robustness that they are going to have staying power. We bring something to the party for them – customers, scale and how to scale – we have a lot of expertise in dealing with scaling a business. In return, I find they've been so focused on a particular customer pain point that their user insight is extremely valuable and powerful. **”**

Bill Wallace, *Head of Digital for Consumer & Community Banking, JPMorgan Chase*

Platform, Marketplace, Ecosystem—Buzzword Bingo!

When discussing partnerships, many people arbitrarily throw around terms like "platforms", "marketplaces" and "ecosystems". People use them interchangeably, and I sometimes wonder whether they really understand what they are talking about. Many of them may well do, but these terms are often thrown into a conversation like a buzzword bingo game. Add AI, blockchain and Open Banking and you have got the win! Just in case, let us define these terms a little more before I talk about partnerships on platforms, marketplaces and ecosystems.

Probably the most important starting point is the platform. A platform allows anyone to develop and deploy code that can then be integrated and used by others, and is generally seen as the owner of the marketplace. In the case of the internet, which is the world's largest platform, there is no owner. Then there are other platforms that offer opportunity. Apple owns the App Store, which is a platform; Alibaba and Amazon each offer a platform; Facebook is not really a platform, although it has attributes of one. The reason why I make this distinction is that Facebook's business model is based on advertising while Apple, Alibaba and Amazon are commerce-based. A platform should really offer the opportunity for developers to make money. Sure, you can make money from ads, but downloads and purchases are better because you have to pay for them, which is when banks and FinTechs get interested.

The marketplace refers to all of the companies that have turned up on the platform to offer their services. Stripe, Adyen, Square, iZettle, eToro, PayPal, Plaid, Finicity and more are all API FinTech firms that play on platforms, mainly on the internet but some can be found on the App Store and elsewhere. They are all stallholders on the platform's marketplace vying for business, and you find them via Google, their websites, an advert on Facebook or a download from Apple.

The ecosystem is then the partners in the marketplace who work with each other to leverage business for each other. The Stripe market stall gets far more business as it is known to work with key players like Indiegogo, Lyft, Square and more; Adyen's success is based on big names like Uber, Tiffany & Co. and Spotify; and so on. Each time these stallholders get a big name, they get more revenue as the big name generates transactions, and it also lowers costs as the big name does the plug-and-play drop of the code into its apps and online services. The key aim for any stallholder is, therefore, to get traction in the marketplace by demonstrating that it is more attractive than the next stall, just as you find in any marketplace.

Given the definitions above, where does a bank fit in? Banks talk about owning platforms, but they don't own any; they talk about marketplaces, but find it hard to work out where they fit into the marketplace; they believe that they manage an ecosystem, or even own one, when they are just a part of one. In fact, what they will actually become are curators of ecosystems. A curator looks at all of the stallholders in the marketplace and curates the best of them to deliver the best customer experience for its clients. This is a key factor: identifying where others develop better code, better capabilities and better competencies, creating partnerships with them to bring that code, capability and competency to the banking customer and delivering a better experience than the bank could offer directly itself.

The reason why the bank should do this is because its customers do not have the time or necessarily the ability to perform due diligence on a financial marketplace stallholder. Their focus is on other marketplaces, such as retail, manufacturing, energy, transportation and so on. This is why the best organisations to vet the stallholders in financial marketplaces are banks. However, in order to be an effective curator of the ecosystem, the first thing a bank needs to do is work out which stalls they want to offer themselves to and which platforms to focus on. After all, banks can also be stallholders of apps, APIs and analytics in the open marketplace.

How then can a bank make its stall better than other banks and FinTech firms? It may be a cleverer strategy to try not to be better than other banks and FinTech firms on those platforms, but partner with them instead, as already mentioned. At this point, the bank needs to build an ecosystem of win-win partnerships. Partners who can all work together on the platform's marketplace to get business in a mutually beneficial way.

> **"** We have three main objectives of why we want to look at ecosystems as a new way of banking. The first is really to acquire customers where we weren't before. 'Not everyone will come to a bank for banking' is the thesis. We have to be where the customer is. We would think about acquiring customers where customers are through chat, messaging, social and other properties, and making that experience seamless and invisible. The second big objective for us is around getting non-traditional data for credit underwriting. It's something that we think can only be enabled if you partner. For us it means we have a much better data underwriting for customers that we couldn't have previously lent to, that's another big space, where the only logical way for this space to make sense is via ecosystem partnerships. Finally, it's really enhancing and improving our product offering. If non-banks are getting into financial services, you have to somehow make it a much more level playing field and be open to the fact that banks need to get into

non-banking spaces and businesses. Not for the pure sake of doing those businesses because, as a bank, we will always be at the core of banking. But to be able to stitch up consumer journeys earlier in the value chain or in the customer journey will allow us a better fighting chance with some of these TechFins and FinTechs that are encroaching from the commerce, advertising and social space. It's allowed us to think of opportunities for us to create offerings that are not purely financial services related. **"**

Gene Wong, *Head of Ecosystems, DBS*

Partnering in the Ecosystem Is Not Easy

Talking of partnering, I was assigned the role of negotiating a contract with a partner of a large technology firm some years ago. The partner specialised in the insurance markets and we ended up in a war over the contract wording. For quite a while, it was "if you do this, then we do that" and "if you do that, then we do this". There was a sense of mistrust upfront so why were we doing the deal? The partner felt that the deal would give them access to a vast swathe of insurance customers in our large technology firm. Little did they know that most of those insurance customers regarded us as hardware merchants and not solutions providers, which is what the software firm offered. For us, we were trying to do a deal with a solutions firm to reposition the company as not just being a provider of hardware. Suffice to say, the partnership fizzled out rapidly and we never agreed a contract.

A while later, I was involved in the negotiations of another major partnership in the area of customer relationship management (CRM). The firm was called Siebel. We had already signed a contract to be its partner and were now working out how to get our sales teams to engage with its product specialists and technicians. It was difficult because our sales teams had little idea of what CRM was or how to sell it while its product specialists had little interest in dealing with salespeople who had no interest in their product. Equally, there were two or three bigger name technology partners that received all of their attention, as we were viewed as a second-tier company partner. Suffice to say, this partnership also fizzled out slowly and we never sold anything.

Now, you may be thinking that I appear to be one of the worst people to be put in charge of partnerships, and you might be right, but I have learnt a lot from these failures. As banks try to develop more and more partnerships with FinTech start-ups, I wonder if banks really understand how these relationships work. In particular, will the FinTech upstarts really respect and trust the banks to do the right thing?

It is not an easy thing to do. Partnerships, that is. Relationships are tough to start, hard to maintain and easy to break. The average U.S. marriage lasts eight years while the average American stays with the same bank twice that length of time. That is because a marriage is a relationship while banking is just a utility.

How will banks work as curators of FinTech start-ups through an ecosystem of partnerships? How will a bank deal with the situation where a competitor offers the partner more revenue and sales and so their partnership loses its focus, as evidenced by my CRM example above? Similarly, if you are trying to partner but one side feels weaker than the other, then the relationship will flounder through mistrust, as shown by my contract negotiation above. For a partnership to really work, it has to be a marriage of equals, with equal opportunity and benefits for both sides. If either side is on the back foot or treated as second fiddle, it is not going to work.

There are many management guru books out there about building successful partnerships, not to mention lots of Harvard and similar papers and columns, but you can scrap all of the academia and theory. The reality is that even if the partnership is created as a marriage of allies, do the thousands of managers and staff who have to implement the marriage within the bank feel the same way? Many times, partnerships are scuppered not because the intentions were unhonourable, but because the reality is that aligning two distinctly different organisations of thousands of people to work together in harmony just does not hold true.

If banks do want to fulfil this role of curation and partnerships in an ecosystem, they may well do themselves a favour by approaching people within the IT industry. Many of these people have decades of experience of doing these ecosystem relationships and marriages, so it would do banks no harm to hire a group of system integrators from the technology world to become their leads in developing banks as value integrators in the financial world.

> **ff** [On curation] my analogy is if you think about how the internet led to the streaming industry. What came before Netflix and Spotify was Napster, BitTorrent, etc. What was there before is the equivalent of full decentralisation. It's anarchy. People can go there, but it's the Wild West. You don't know what you're getting. It's a mess. Pay Netflix or Spotify a few dollars a month and I get great content, right? I want to go there because there is some level of curation and quality. There's no original content but I can trust Netflix and Spotify to bring quality. This is analogous to how banks should be thinking about their position in a fully decentralised world. **JJ**
>
> **Gene Wong**, *Head of Ecosystems, DBS*

Eyes Wide Open

> **ff** You either take a stake in some FinTechs or, at some point, you work together. My vision is that everything goes with API not long from now. It's much easier to onboard new APIs and offboard old ones that are no longer needed. For example, if we invite two or three FinTech start-ups to cooperate and we have 80,000 customers each, then we see which is the best over a period of months. Then the other ones need to come out. **JJ**
>
> **Vincent van den Boogert**, *CEO, ING Netherlands*

I recently met a head of innovation at a major bank, who left her position rather abruptly. She and her innovation team had been brainstorming and came up with a lot of areas in which the bank could improve delivery through partnership. They then created a road map of companies that they wanted to deal with. The finesse had been a facilitated ideation process which, at the end of the ideation process, came up with five concrete proposals for the future and a list of eight partners to sign up to do this. She then went to see a C-level decision-maker to get his view on her recommendations and road map. The meeting did not go well.

"You can't do that because the regulator won't allow it," he said. Even though no one had spoken to the regulator.

"That won't work because we tried it before and it failed," he said. Even though it had been years since they had last tried it and technology had moved on since then.

"That's a good idea, but I think we should try it once proven," he said. Even though the bank would have to try it to prove it. After all, that is the nature of *innovation*.

Then, to top it all off, he recommended that there should be a sign-off process for anything going through the innovation programme. When she asked him what the sign-off process was, he expounded the idea that compliance and risk must be involved, along with the product managers and technology team. That was when she lost the will to live and left the bank.

Unfortunately, these sorts of meetings are far too frequent within traditional institutions, and it demonstrates a closed mindset created by years of avoiding change. The more you can place barriers in the way of change, the less you have to change. And even if one person in the chain can open their mind, there are still a dozen more who can shut it down. The organisation either waits you out or wears you out.

This is why the bright young things are starting their own companies and have vision, agility, focus and execution. The bright young things are changing things because they can. They do not work like the traditional firms because they are open to new ideas, embrace new things, demand that change happens and work with zeal. Then the big old firm with its big old budget and its big mass of customers reaches out its hand to say, "Hello pardner, let's partner." And the bright young thing, with its rose-coloured spectacles and a bit wet behind the ears, shakes the hand and says, "Sure thing."

No wonder co-creation and bank-to-start-up partnerships are hard things to manage. In fact, someone recently said to me that their start-up had tried to forge a partnership with a bank but the bank had kept stalling. Teams and teams and reams and reams of people from the bank had crawled all over the start-up, assessing its business ideas, code, structure and developments. They had visit after visit, meeting after meeting, call after call, and yet nothing ever got signed, no money exchanged, no results delivered. Eventually the start-up got fed up and told the bank to go where the sun don't shine.

The bank surely did go but, in the process, it assigned a team of people to develop and deliver something that looked mysteriously similar to what the start-up was doing. Of course, there was a non-disclosure agreement and suchlike, but how can you prove that the bank stole an idea if its version of the idea is not exactly the same?

"You can't do that, because the ethics wouldn't allow it," the start-up says.

"We just did and you can't do a thing about it," the bank says back.

Just a word of warning for those in the co-creation and partnering world. Keep your eyes wide open.

How It Feels to Be a FinTech Partnering with a Bank
based on input from Philippe Geilis, CEO and co-founder of Kantox

The CEO of a successful FinTech company shared his experiences of working with banks with me. Here are a few of his insights, which should be useful for a start-up trying to work with a bank and, equally, for any bank trying to work with a start-up.

"We really like their technology and the unique value they bring to clients. Nevertheless, they recently stole two good clients from us, so we will not disclose any more information and there's no way that we will partner with them."

These are the words from the head of Corporate FX at a German bank about its small FinTech partner. The partner had been introduced to him by someone else from the same bank in order to have a discussion about a technology partnership, and this is how the discussion ended. This is also how many traditional bankers think, and how challenging partnering with any bank can be.

It is because banking is one of the most risk-averse industries of all. It is not only due to their clients' risk in relation to credit, loans, derivatives and so on—which is most banks' core business and the main reason why they are heavily regulated—but about how individual bankers approach risk as a career breaker or enabler.

When you start working for a bank, you almost never build anything from scratch. Rather, you are inheriting a franchise and a portfolio of clients or products, which generate a certain amount of business and revenue. Your role probably includes generating some revenue growth but, first and foremost, it is to protect and maintain that portfolio. In the old banking world, this franchise was quite stable. You lost some clients to other banks but also gained some clients from them. All in all, market shares were quite stable.

In recent years, the playing field has changed dramatically. Interest rates are close to zero, which is having a significant impact on the bank's business model. Thousands of well-funded FinTech companies have appeared and technology giants have also shown a real appetite for FinTech.

Banks know how to compete with banks as they have the same structure, culture and behaviours. Competing with nimble, very fast-moving competitors starts to scare them.

Inside banks, innovation teams are, at best, an entry door to the bank and the matchmakers to the different business lines. Beyond that, they have little influence. They are often incentivised to launch the pilot projects, but not necessarily to make sure they succeed.

One of the key lessons learnt by many of the small FinTechs trying to work with the banks is that navigating banks is very complex. There are many people there whose jobs are basically to spend time speaking with FinTechs about innovation, and not much else. Their timelines are also ten times longer than those of FinTech companies. Discussions can last forever and may go nowhere if you end up discovering that you are speaking with the wrong people. If you are a third party trying to work with a bank, the first thing you must do is identify the relevant business line and ensure that you are dealing with someone who holds some kind of internal power or influence. Then, you have to go upwards in the hierarchy to make sure you move forward.

"Are you ISO 27001 certified? This is very important for us as we only work with vendors that are ISO compliant." This is the sort of question a FinTech firm may encounter after a few months of discussion. It arises to sober the relationship and makes it clear that there are often new and completely unexpected requirements to consider. Why weren't these ISO certification requirements mentioned earlier in the discussions? The reality is that the people from the business line you are negotiating with were not aware of the IT or compliance requirements. They basically discovered them at the same time as the prospective partner, and so aligning all interests early on is key to creating a successful partnership when looking from the outside-in.

Banks are all still silo-structured. You need to secure the green light from each silo to get a deal done.

Inside banks, there is also no single decision-maker. No one can decide by themselves to move the partnership forward. You need to convince multiple stakeholders that the partnership makes sense, that it will create significant extra value for both parties and that the risk of cannibalisation is low. Once that is done, you then need to convince their compliance department, IT team and legal. This is the "tick-the-box" moment. You need to fit the bank's processes and requirements almost perfectly, and must maintain a high degree of flexibility to adapt to them, because the bank will not adapt to you, the third party.

Start-ups may be nimble and flexible by design but, nevertheless, meeting all the requirements is challenging and time-consuming. It is a fine balance between the start-up's willingness to adapt to partnership requirements and its ability to walk away from the deal.

"We like your technology but we believe it's a bit expensive so we will think about it and come back to you."

These are the words of a bank that is no longer interested in partnering. In fact, in this instance, that particular bank announced an almost exact copy of the start-up's core product a few months later. It was so obvious what the bank had done because the description of its new facility was exactly the same as the production description on the start-up's website. Months later however, the bank had no product on the market and was invisible when it came to pitching for new clients. The lesson here? Speaking about innovation is easy, executing it is somewhat harder. Interestingly, the start-up learnt later that the person in charge of that particular bank's function had been under pressure from the management to deliver more innovation to the bank's clients so he had taken a shortcut and just announced that the bank was going to do what the start-up had already done. However, due to internal resources, nothing could actually be delivered.

When discussing partnerships with banks, FinTech firms and start-ups are always trying to find the right balance between disclosing enough information to make their technology appealing and not saying too much and giving everything away. Equally, most start-ups have vision *and* execution *and* speed. This makes all the difference, and that is why most start-ups should never really fear competition from the banks. Banks take too long to respond.

In summary, here are a few takeaway lessons for any start-up considering partnering with a bank:

- Do not look for partnerships: instead engage with banks that are approaching you proactively.

- Do not spend too much time with innovation teams: instead navigate ASAP to the business line that makes sense for your proposition.
- Check the bank's partnership record and its appetite. Many banks can build teams that will spend years discussing partnerships without reaching any business outcome.
- Understand fast how the bank perceives you. Does it see you as a business enabler, as a revenue generator, as a way to boost loyalty, as a way to upsell, as a way to better engage clients or as a way to provide an improved user experience versus being a potential business cannibaliser?
- Be very clear on what you are keen to do and what you will not accept. For example, be clear if you will white-label, be a vendor to banks or only accept co-branding.
- Engage at the highest level possible with people that have influence inside the bank.
- Secure a project manager inside the bank to lead the process. This makes all the difference in reducing friction and improving coordination between business lines, IT, compliance and legal. If one is not allocated, put pressure on the bank to appoint a technology-savvy project manager, as proof of its motivation to partner with you.
- Be patient. Banks are slow to move, particularly at the beginning. Realistically, you should consider allowing at least twelve months from the moment you engage to the moment you have a partnership agreement signed.

Clash of Clans or New Bank versus Old Bank?

In a final aspect of discussing partnering, there is always the opportunity to acquire the start-up rather than partner with it. This is also a route fraught with friction. For example, I was talking with some friends at Fidor, one of the most innovative banks in Europe. Fidor was acquired in 2016 by French banking group BPCE and I heard no more about it until two years later when Fidor asked to divorce BPCE. It came as no surprise to me but, then again, I was more surprised that a traditional large old bank had acquired the then most innovative bank in FinTech in the first place.

If you are not aware, BPCE is the merger of two large, old French banks that date back two hundred years. At the time of the Fidor acquisition, the press release stated: "the planned acquisition of Fidor is fully in line with Groupe BPCE's strategic plan *Another Way to Grow* and will contribute to the acceleration of the rollout of the group's digital strategy."

François Pérol, then chairman of the Groupe BPCE management board said:

> "This operation constitutes a key step in the acceleration of the digital transformation of our group. It further demonstrates our commitment to innovation, to develop a customer-centric approach enabled by a digital banking technology and to be more involved in the digital and mobile banking field. We are very proud and happy to welcome Fidor's teams, community and clients within Groupe BPCE."

So what happened? Why didn't it work out? First, there is the question of governance. According to sources familiar with the development, BPCE never integrated Fidor into its thoughts on digital. This might be attributed to BPCE's CDO, who acted as the chairman of the board. He had only recently joined the bank, coming from SNCF, France's national state-owned railway company. He joined after the Fidor deal had taken place. It was not his deal. He inherited it.

This is where internal politics started to destroy everything. I understand that the new chairman of the Fidor board found it difficult to work out how to sell the deal to the provincial bankers, bearing in mind that BPCE is formed of many small banks. Equally, the new leader was not a banker. As mentioned, he came from trains and it would be a hard task to talk digital and digital banking among all of those offline bankers protecting their little kingdoms in the French provinces. Specifically, coming from outside, he had no "political network" within the bank, no experience in digital banking and no understanding of regulations such as PSD2.

On top of this, a romantic affair was taking place between two members of the C-suite, and this led to more political infighting. As these individuals had been responsible for the Fidor deal, the heads of local banks started a campaign against them and, because of their involvement with Fidor, the hate campaign targeted that deal too, as accepted collateral damage within their internal politics. All that is public information as Groupe BPCE internal leaks fuelled French media with all kinds of confidential details. Sounds like a very French Netflix series, but it isn't. It is real life.

It is also easy to assume that there must have been a clash of cultures between a German-born bank and a French-centric bank. The language barrier is one obvious challenge. More important, there was more than likely a clash of cultures between a new, innovative, FinTech start-up and an old, risk-averse, incumbent bank. For example, Fidor is one of the leading and most experienced financial services operations when it comes to cryptocurrencies. You would imagine that there must have been discussions on that area during the acquisition phase, but it turns out that BPCE was not that interested after all, as there was no further involvement in crypto after 2016.

Some positives have come out of the acquisition. The consumer banking business increased threefold and business banking fourfold over the two years of acquisition. The balance sheet has been completely cleaned up for Fidor, thanks to the support of Paris. That will clearly have a positive effect as any new investor will get a super clean operation, with a balance sheet of around €1.5 billion.

What can FinTechs learn from this? Well, it illustrates the challenge of FinTech partnering. Many banks are trying to innovate, become digital and be more hipster and less control freak. They are trying to work with young start-ups and move away from being old fuddy-duddies. This is not as easy as it may look when the young start-up fundamentally challenges the old ways of thinking. Equally, the old ways of thinking are so ingrained culturally that any change to that thinking creates a political backlash that is hard to temper. In these situations, whether it be an old bank acquiring a new bank or an old bank working with start-ups, you need strong leadership to bring everyone along. It just won't happen otherwise.

> **❝** Every domain and every product group is constructing APIs to support their functionality. That's actually a mandate. The initial view is internal, but the value we get by reducing dependency inside allows the speed of innovation and the clock speed for everybody else. My team will go to people and coach them in terms of what they need to do in APIs, what's coming, what makes sense, what's changing in the market and manage the API portal for them, developer.chase.com, which we use for both inside and outside developers. The aim is to create ubiquity of form and function through the API portal, covering experience APIs, product APIs, feature APIs, platform APIs and so on. **❞**
>
> **Jason Alexander**, *Head of Digital Platforms for Consumer & Community Banking, JPMorgan Chase*

BOTTOM LINE

Banks are more than aware that they need to change and adapt to the demands of the digital world, but many have not effected the internal changes required before engaging with the external world. This is most clearly seen in the areas of partnering with start-ups. Most banks would rather do it themselves than partner. Even if they have changed that attitude, their internal organisation is not ready to partner in many instances. Even if that changes, the partnership model is not an easy one as there are two different players' interests on the table, and both players have to be evenly matched and serviced. The partnering in the ecosystem aspect of digital transformation is probably harder than the cultural change requirements, and should come last on the bank's transformation agenda after those internal changes have taken place.

IS DIGITAL TRANSFORMATION WORTH IT?

Two of the banks furthest along in their digital transformation journey are BBVA (started in 1999) and DBS (began in 2009). They both started early, with leaderships team that are committed and driving down this road with results. Results in terms of awards and recognition within the technology community, but what about in the investment community? Perhaps not. I recently noticed a headline in the *Economist:*

> "BBVA, a Spanish bank, reinvents itself as a digital business: It wants to be as nimble as a FinTech start-up; shareholders are having to be patient."

The point of the article was that for all of the bank's changes, it has underperformed in the market compared to its peers. The same is true of many of the banks engaged in digital transformation. This is because it is hard to correlate digital change with investment performance in the short term. It is also a point that I raised with some of the banks interviewed for this book.

DBS came back to me with an interesting response, claiming to be the first bank in the world to demonstrate the link between digitisation and shareholder value creation. First, DBS CEO Piyush Gupta talked through the bank's digital strategy and journey. The strategy begins with four core capabilities:

ACQUIRE
- Increase customer acquisition through wider distribution
- Lower acquisition cost

TRANSACT
- Eliminate paper
- Create instant fulfilment
- Decrease cost

ENGAGE
- Drive "sticky" customer behaviours
- Cross-sell through contextual marketing
- Increase income per customer

ECOSYSTEMS
- Pipes to platforms
- Data
- Be insights-driven

The bank recognised that capabilities were not enough. It had to change the culture too. Thus, a vision was put into play: making banking joyful. In order to do this, the bank recognised that it had to put digital to the core of the company and act like a 26,000-person start-up. This was delivered by focusing on customer journeys and, in those customer journeys, making the bank invisible. In other words, take all the friction out of every customer interaction and experience with finance.

This meant moving from legacy systems to open APIs in a microservices architecture living in the cloud, moving from a waterfall management team to agile and moving from projects to platforms. For me, DBS has done something upfront that many other banks are yet to implement. The bank recognised that to change the culture and the focus of 26,000 employees meant changing the measures and rewards to reflect digital.

Figure 5.1 How DBS measures successful change

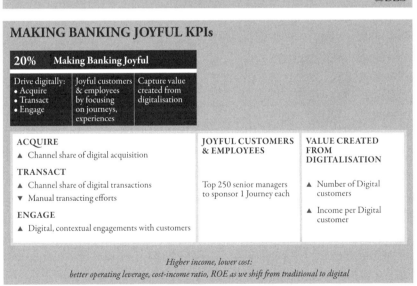

Changing the culture is the most critical part of any digital transformation, and those who treat digital as a project to delegate will never get there. The fact that DBS built digital into the corporate fabric was evidenced by the *Euromoney* award given to DBS in 2016 when the bank was named the World's Best Digital Bank.[57] When presenting the award, Clive Horwood, the editor of *Euromoney*, said: "It is demonstrably the case that digital innovation pervades every part of DBS, from consumer to corporate, SMEs to transaction banking and even the DBS Foundation."

The bank is also delivering results that shareholders can recognise. For example, 38 per cent of DBS's 2015 revenues of S$10.8 billion were derived from digital platforms, rising to 44 per cent in 2017 (S$11.6 billion) and 60 per cent by 2019.

Figure 5.2 Figures for the main retail consumer and SME services (Singapore, Hong Kong)

Consumer and SME (Singapore, Hong Kong)
Pre-empt Disruptors

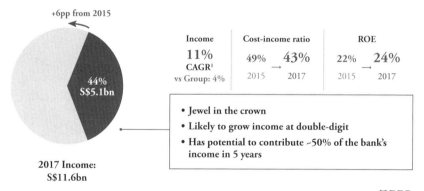

+6pp from 2015

Income	Cost-income ratio	ROE
11% CAGR[1] vs Group: 4%	49% → **43%** 2015 2017	22% → **24%** 2015 2017

44%
S$5.1bn

- Jewel in the crown
- Likely to grow income at double-digit
- Has potential to contribute ~50% of the bank's income in 5 years

2017 Income:
S$11.6bn

2017 figures annualised based on 1H17, where applicable [1]
2015-2017

✕DBS

Of those 2017 figures, what is really telling is that the compound annual growth rate (CAGR) and ROE figures are for digital users versus the traditional physical services (branch, call centre and offline).

---

57 The bank went on to win the award again in 2018 and was named the World's Best Bank by *Euromoney* in 2019.

Figure 5.3 2017 Income

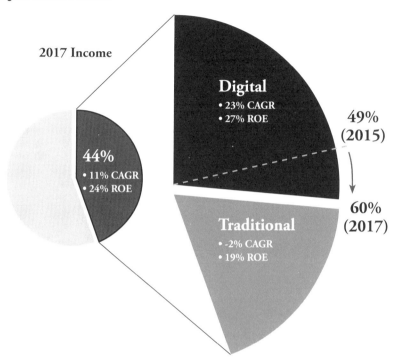

2017 figures annualised based on 1H17, where applicable; CAGR refers to 2015-2017 income

There are clear differences between customers who use traditional offline services (T) and those who use digital online services (D).

Figure 5.4 Profitability of digital customers

2017 profit and loss (S$bn)	Total	T	D	Digital is material
Customers (m)	5.9	3.6	2.3	39% of customers contribute 60% of income and 68% of profit before allowances
Income	5.1	2.0	3.1	
Costs	2.2	1.1	1.1	
Profit before allowances	2.9	0.9	2.0	
Key indicators				**Digital is more valuable**
Income per customer (S$,000)	0.9	0.6	1.3	2X income per customer
Cost-income ratio (%)	43	55	34	20pp lower CIR
Return on equity (%)	24	19	27	9pp higher ROE

In fact, DBS is finding that as digital customers grow, they are delivering far higher profitability. In 2017, 39 per cent of customers were delivering 68 per cent of profits.

Figure 5.5 Digital share of customers, income and profit before allowances

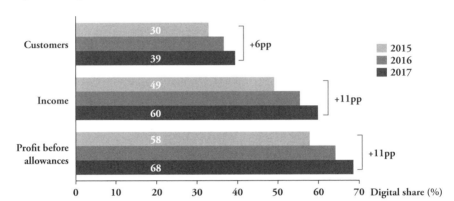

This is because digital customers:
- have lower customer acquisition costs
- use lower cost-to-serve channels
- have higher income per customer year-on-year
- have consistently faster growth in income per customer

Then there is the bank's investment in growth markets of digibank, currently running in India and Indonesia. This is all about reaching high-value customers in scale markets by offering an entire bank in a smartphone, and it is all delivered by curating a marketplace of partners through APIs (ring any bells?).

Gupta summarised everything by stating that:
- The strategy leveraging Asia's megatrends has paid off with diversified growth and higher returns.
- Digitalisation creates opportunity to pre-empt disruptors, disrupt incumbents and improve business profitability.
- DBS's digital transformation is pervasive, encompassing technology,

Figure 5.6 The DBS ecosystem

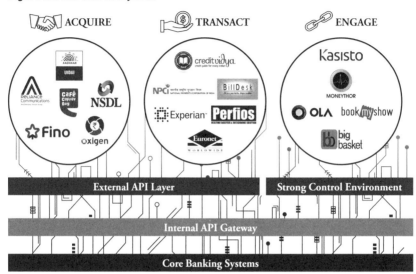

customer journey and a start-up culture. This is difficult to replicate and creates competitive advantage.

- The bank has established a management and measurement system to drive this transformation, and a robust methodology to track financials.
- Early results are encouraging. Digitalisation has accelerated income growth and lowered structural costs, boosting operating leverage. The opportunity space is significant.

CHINA MERCHANTS BANK

❝ We have 1,830 branches and over 136 million retail customers. As far back as 1993, we realised that we had too few physical outlets to compete with large state-owned banks. Therefore, we chose the strategy of developing e-banking to expand our business. CMB, in the early stage of development, selected technology as its differentiated competitiveness, and CMB was the pioneer in issuing debit cards in China. Then, in 1996, it completed the retail e-banking service system of online banking and telephone centre. In the 1990s, we based more operations online, instead of putting emphasis on establishing outlets. Customers mainly get the services from CMB through electronic channels, after they open accounts. Right now, in terms of the market share online, we account for about 11 per cent of the total market share in China and, in the Visa network, we are ranked fourth among all the international banks worldwide in terms of cross-border credit card transactions. We can see that our volume of transactions is getting higher and higher as time passes. The ranking of market share of CMB in the digital world is significantly higher than that in the physical world, which reflects the value created by technology.

ff We launched the 'Mobile Priority' in 2015 so as to transfer all kinds of banking services to the apps as much as possible. Today, the monthly active users (MAU) of CMB apps has exceeded 81 million, which is second only to the Industrial and Commercial Bank of China (ICBC). Ninety per cent of transactions between our customers and CMB, more than 70 per cent of our wealth management product sales and over 50 per cent of consumer finance activities are conducted by our apps.

ff Second, we advocate 'Building platform internally, expanding scene externally and managing traffic', so as to promote the transformation of the business model. The apps can connect various digitised external service scenes and further expand the scope of CMB services, such as taking the subway and bus, ordering food, booking movie tickets, utilising government services, etc., through our apps. Nowadays, 26 per cent of traffic of the CMB app serving debit card customers and 46 per cent of the flow of the CMB Life App for credit card customers come from these non-financial service scenarios.

❝In the last three years, the absolute number of retail customers arriving at physical branches of CMB has decreased by over 10 per cent every year. CMB restored the interface of customer contact through the implementation of mobile priority strategy. Nowadays, customers of CMB can view about 1.6 billion pages via our mobile banking, which helps us accumulate a lot of customer behaviour data. CMB set up more than 3,000 labels for customers and over 220 personalised recommendation models by integrating customer account transactions and customer information. Every day, we provide customers with more than 200 million personalised advertisements via mobile banking, with a response rate of 1.04 per cent, equivalent to creating two million sales opportunities for us, whereas this number was 0.24 per cent three years ago.❞

Min Hua, *Head of Strategy, CMB*

BBVA

❝One example is the percentage of our sales across the globe that happened digitally. This started at 8 per cent in January 2016, rising to 41 per cent in units in December 2018. In Spain it's higher, and in Turkey it's higher still, but the important thing here is it's not going to stop growing. It's going to keep growing. It's going to cross 40 per cent, 50 per cent, 60 per cent, 70 per cent and may eventually have an asymptotic behaviour, but it is growing. We know these facts because we have all these dashboards. Dashboards that represent different representations of data from digital sales to sales by product and by country. I can see, for example, that Turkey started with 20 per cent of digital sales three years ago and, as of December 2018, it's at 48 per cent. In 2017, our core revenues were growing at 8.8 per cent and costs were growing at 0.9 per cent; in 2018, the revenues are growing at 10.4 per cent and the expenses at 2.5 per cent. That's a widening mark when it comes to total revenue minus operating expenses because revenue starts at a higher total figure—and I believe this will continue to widen, this difference between cost and revenue, because of digital. In other words, the 41 per cent of digital sales will become 75 per cent over time and the question is: what does that do to our revenue growth?

It increases the revenue growth. What does that do to our operating expense? It reduces our operating expense. The investor community is starting to see the value of that. Another dimension of digital engagement is a reduction in customer attrition. The percentage of customers that leave the bank in a twelve-month period is going down. Take Spain. Customer attrition in Spain dropped from 9.2 per cent to 7.1 per cent between January 2016 and December 2018. That's a 200 basis points reduction in attrition in the last three years. **"**

Carlos Torres Vila, *Group Executive Chairman, BBVA*

WHAT HAPPENS IF BANKS DO NOT TRANSFORM?

Throughout this book, my contention has been that banks will not survive in the long term if they do not adapt and change. That is obvious. It is Darwin's Law for the survival of the fittest. So how come some species die, even though they tried to adapt and change? It is because they changed the wrong things. That is the central tenet of *Doing Digital*: many banks are changing but they are changing the wrong things. They may be spending millions or billions, bringing in armies of consultants, hiring crazy hipsters and giving the CIO a blank cheque, but none of this is going to mean a jot if they are changing the wrong things.

The belief in this is critical, as it is core to the survival of the bank. If you are changing the wrong things, then even if you adapt, you will not survive. If you are changing the systems but not the organisational structure, you will not survive. If you are investing in systems but not changing the core systems structure, you will not survive. If you are adding technology but purely for lower cost rather than better user experience, you will not survive. This paragraph could go on for much longer but you get the idea.

Throughout the book, I have finished sections with a bottom line, and the bottom line here is that if you are not treating digital as a transformational project of bank structure and culture but, instead, treat it as a project or a channel, then you will not survive. It will not happen tomorrow or next week, but maybe in a few years or even in a decade or two. As Roy Charles Amara, past president of the Institute for the Future, said: "We overestimate the effect of a technology in the short run and underestimate the effect in the long run."

We are at an impasse where the rise of new structures using open technologies, Cloud Computing, AI, machine learning, distributed ledger technology and more, all wrapped up in the internet and mobile network, means that industries are being ripped apart, reimagined and rebuilt. This has happened quickly for some industries—entertainment, music, technology and travel—but has been at a much slower pace for others— banking, finance, pharmaceuticals and government. The industries that are seeing slower change are far more regulated. Nevertheless, it is happening whether we like it or not.

The fact is that any organisation trying to evolve its old way of doing things from industrial to digital without fundamental rethinking will fail. This is the underlying premise of all of my writing. As we go through the digital revolution, we must radically rethink and reinvent. If we do not, we may adapt and change but we will have adapted and changed too little. We will not have thought big. "Go big or go home" so the saying goes but, in the case of digital, "Go big or just go".

Therefore, in this final chapter, it is hoped that you have been convinced that digital is more than just a project or function, and that it requires fundamental structural change. In making that structural change, there are a few areas left to mop up, such as what to do with branches and how fast this change must happen.

Digital Does Not Happen in a Day

Digital does not happen in a day. It takes time. It creeps up behind you, slowly but surely, and then hits you on the head. Equally, it does not happen equally. I travel a lot and, on those travels, it is fairly obvious that the world is not homogeneous. Whilst the Chinese leapfrog the West and move to mobile banking, Europeans are seeing a surge of new banks trying to challenge the old whilst the United States has megabanks like JPMorgan Chase and Bank of America investing $10 to $11 billion a year *each* in digital transformation. Africa is seeing the rise of financial inclusion, doubling from 23 per cent to 43 per cent since 2011, India is going cashless fast and many South American nations are leveraging their gross domestic product (GDP) through FinTech innovations. The world is changing quickly, but it is not changing at the same pace and, in all the commentary about change, it is often overlooked by commentators who seem to treat the world as homogeneous.

For example, many talk about the redundancy of bank branches and yet branch networks are growing in some countries for good reason, as in they did not have any before. In other countries, branches play an important role not just for banking, but for community relationships and trading structures, so it makes sense for them to remain. Equally, we talk about being able to do everything in an app, which is certainly true in China with Tencent and Alibaba, but try doing everything in an app in Europe or the United States. Sure, I can order books and download films from Amazon but can I check my balance while doing this? Not yet. It would be interesting to see what will happen with Open Banking and open APIs if Amazon and other providers could do it. Now if I could get to the checkout and see all of my balances on all of my cards and in my accounts, and then just swipe the one I wanted to pay with, that would be extremely useful.

Nevertheless, all of this takes time—digital is not built in a day—and we are taking our time to build the new digital world. Although it takes time, as it is built, it is truly transformational.

When Does Digitalisation Stop?

I am sometimes asked, when will we know that we have done digital? This question is quite vexing, as it shows a lack of understanding of what is happening. We live in a digital revolution that is as big as the Industrial Revolution, but on steroids. The inventions of electricity, the telephone, automobiles and more shook the Victorians to their core, but that is nothing compared to what we are going through today. We are in a situation in which things that took decades to develop during the Industrial Revolution are happening in months in this digital revolution.

Just as in the Industrial Revolution, would you have ever asked, when will we know that we have done industry? There is never an end to industrialisation. It continues to this day. This is the same with digital. We will never finish digital. We are on a journey that is a continuum of change. Twenty years ago, we were all dealing with Y2K; ten years ago, we were all talking about Big Data and cloud; today, we talk a lot about machine learning and blockchain; ten years from now, we will all be talking about quantum computing.

Technology and industry never stop. They keep progressing and changing. That is why digital will never stop. It will just keep developing and changing. Change is the only constant. Keeping up with change is our challenge, and change is happening faster every day. Therefore, as we embark on digital transformation—a reimagining of our industrial-era structures to digital—the process will never stop. It will just be constant change.

If we are on a journey of digital transformation that never ends but demands constant change, why didn't we think along these lines earlier? How did we allow our core systems to become so embedded in the bank that they sit in the bank's heart, like a heart of stone? Firmly cemented in place and hardly beating, these old systems have never changed. They have just been added on to and, in the process, become feet of clay. If digital demands constant change on a journey to a destination that is unclear, why did we allow ourselves to be cemented into roots of stone?

Banks Still Need to Provide Physical Access

One of the perennial questions as we digitalise is what will happen to physical assets, like branches. The role of the branch is one of the biggest and most contentious issues in almost every bank. It strikes to the heart of what the role of physical assets is in a digital bank model. In designing a digital bank and engaging in digital transformation, the real question should be: if we were starting again, with a digital structure and digital core, what role would buildings and humans play?

Unfortunately, most banks have the buildings and humans already in play, so this question does not work so easily and is why we talk incessantly about the role of bank branches and the potential for a branchless future. So what is the outlook for the future? There is always a role for a branch in banking, but not the branch as we know it. The old branch was all about transactions: pay in, pay out, cash a cheque, deposit some coins and so on. All of that is going or has gone. However, there are four elements to a branch.

One, it supports a community, and specifically the business community in the area. Businesses have different needs from consumers, and do often need access to a human. People forget that. Two, money is not the same as a Facebook update. If you lose a post saying what a nice time you are having, it is not the same as losing a deposit of $10,000. In fact, I often state that if you woke up today and found that your bank app confirms the balance you expected, you would be happy. However, how would you feel if the balance were $10,000 short of what you expected? Would you just sit there and ignore it? Of course not. You would call the bank or go to the nearest branch to eyeball someone. This is because money is different. It is far more emotional than other parts of our lives because it is *the* controlling factor in our lives.

Three, a lot of people forget what it is like to get your first job, first car and first home. These are big moments in a young person's life and to imagine that they would all be dealt with through an app is a little bit strange. A great example was given by Deutsche Bank, which opened an amazing branch in Berlin for its high net worth clients. Along with the mandatory café and shop areas, the bank designed two rooms nicknamed the "iPod room" and the "Senator room". The iPod room was designed for its young customers and was all white plastic and hip; the Senator room was for its wealthy clients and was all oak and red leather, like a library. When the branch opened, the staff were therefore surprised when all of the young customers wanted meetings in the Senator room while the older customers wanted to meet in the iPod room. Think about it. Old people want to be young and hip again while young people feel that money is a serious and important topic and so demanded a serious and important room to talk about it in.

Four, building on the last point, money is serious, critical and central to most people's lives, and needs a human interface. Of course, you can build the human interfaces into a Skype call, and we will, but removing the humanity and the human physical access from a service so fundamental to our lives is stupid. It demeans the role of the bank and banking, and is undermining the role this service has in people's lives.

All in all, you can see why some people think that branches are not necessary, but it is clear that most banks and I would argue that they *are* necessary. Not for their old role of transactions or for the role of advice, although that is still quite important, but mostly for their core role of trust. Roberto Ferrari, formerly of digital bank start-up CheBanca! in Italy, articulated it well. When visiting his branch in Milan, I asked him why the bank had branches. He told me that it was for three reasons. The first two were customer services and for trust, but the most important reason he identified was for marketing. His branch network was for marketing purposes. Where the bank had a physical presence, it received two-and-a-half times more deposits and assets than where it did not. In other words, the bank that has a branch has far more chance of getting people's trust and money than ones that do not.

This is also well illustrated by Metro Bank, the first new retail bank in Britain since 1840. It has been followed by many other challengers, but it is one of the few challenger banks with branches. Launched in 2010 with its first store in Holborn, London, it now has almost seventy branches across the United Kingdom. It is also in profit, announcing growth of 23 per cent in account numbers between 2018 and 2019, bringing the total number of customer accounts to 1.8 million, up from 1.1 million in 2017. Surely, that is a testament to the branch, or rather *store,* strategy.

Another example that shows the importance of branches are Larry Page and Sergey Brin, the founders of Google. Back in the 1990s, they had a meeting with a major investor when they first set up the company. The meeting went so well that they walked out with a cheque for $100,000. As they left the meeting, the first bank branch they encountered was one of Wells Fargo's, and they immediately went in to deposit the cheque. That is the reason why Wells Fargo was and still is the bank behind Google. Now there is a good reason for having a branch if I ever heard one, although who uses cheques these days?

This Bank Branch Is Dead

Although there may be good reasons for keeping some branches, most will disappear. Physicality comes at a high cost. This is why most developed economies are shrinking their branch networks by up to 80 per cent. Four out of five traditional bank branches may no longer be needed, but this is a controversial subject. For example, Lloyds Banking Group made record profits in the first quarter of 2018 but also announced the continuation of its branch closures. In response, Mike Cherry, chairman of the Federation of Small Businesses (FSB), said:

> "When a town loses a bank branch it hurts vulnerable consumers, high street footfall and small business revenues. We've seen challenger banks who are expanding their branch networks also report strong results, so we know it's an approach that works from a commercial perspective. If a small firm can't deposit and withdraw cash easily it has to store more on site, making it a target for theft. Equally, many small business owners have working relationships with branch staff that go back years. That's not something that can be replaced by an app."[58]

Banking is emotional and psychological. Access to a physical store gives people reassurance and comfort, but is it worth it? When banks are driven by numbers, can they afford such a luxurious overhead? According to most banks, no. In fact, the United Kingdom's total branch network has decreased by half since 2007.

---

58 James Sillars, "Lloyds urged to rethink branch closures as profits surge," Sky News, 25 April 2018, https://news.sky.com/story/lloyds-faces-call-to-rethink-branch-closures-as-profits-surge-11345789.

Figure 5.7 The decline of bank branches in the United Kingdom

Lender	Branches in 2007	Branches in January 2019	% change
Co-operative Bank	355	68	-81%
HSBC	1,501	626	-58%
Clydesdale/Yorkshire	330	159	-52%
Santander	1,286	614	-52%
RBS (incl Natwest)	2,278	797	-65%
Lloyds Banking Group (Halifax, HBOS, BOS)	3,042	1700	-44%
Barclays	1,810	1054	-42%
Nationwide Building Society	681	676	-1%
Total	11,283	5694	-50%

Source: *Guardian*

According to the European Banking Federation, there were almost 240,000 bank branches across Europe in 2009. Today, there are 183,000, down more than 20 per cent in the last decade.[59] The United States is later to the challenge, but it also shut down branches, with under 80,000 today, down 5 per cent since 2009.[60] This definitely has had an impact. A 2014 study estimated that when branches close, new small-business lending falls by 13 per cent in the surrounding area.[61] In low-income neighbourhoods, such lending contracts by nearly 40 per cent. That is the issue: closing branches makes a financial desert of the surrounding area.

All is not lost though as, since the financial crisis hit, most banks in Europe and the United States have focused on wiping out cost overheads by switching customers from physical to digital. This is the primary focus of many banks' digital strategies: to switch customers from bank service to self-service. It is a cost-reduction focus, rather than a customer focus. It shouldn't really be the case. The strategy should be to switch customers from poor branch experiences to superb digital experiences, but that is another matter.

59 "Bank branches and staff numbers continue to shrink across the EU," Finextra, 11 September 2018, https://www.finextra.com/newsarticle/32636/bank-branches-and-staff-numbers-continue-to-shrink-across-the-eu.
60 "Number of FDIC-insured commercial bank branches in the United States from 2000 to 2017," Statista, https://www.statista.com/statistics/193041/number-of-fdic-insured-us-commercial-bank-branches/.
61 "The closing of American bank branches," *Economist*, 27 July 2017, https://www.economist.com/finance-and-economics/2017/07/27/the-closing-of-american-bank-branches.

The net result is that we will move to a less-branch future, but never a branchless future. Humans need access to humans, and they always will when it comes to our deepest and most emotional areas of our lives: relationships and money. That is why some banks, like Bank of America, are opening new branches. Dean Athanasia, president of Bank of America's Consumer Banking and Small Business Operations, said that the bank is opening five hundred new branches, an increase of over 10 per cent of its existing network, "for our clients, not for us."[62] The new branches focus on providing as many meeting spots as possible for clients to talk to staff about mortgages, retirement, savings, small-business loans and other products. They have little to do with transactions, deposits or cash. The rider on this is the closing sentence, however: "apps now handle the deposit-taking volume of 1,200 financial centres". When mobile apps replace 1,200 branches, you know that you have something surplus to requirement.

The Branch of the Future Is NOT about Advice

As demonstrated by Bank of America and other banks that are opening more branches, the branch has a strong role for customer engagement. This will last well into the future, but not as a service centre or a place for advice. The branch is far more of a marketing investment to secure the bank brand. This is because money is emotional. It is not a rational thing. If you have your most valued items in the trust of a third party that has zero physical representation, it is difficult for many to handle.

This is reinforced by a study from McKinsey, whose research proposes that branches need to turn smart and that most customers still prefer an in-branch experience.[63] A key chart towards the end of the McKinsey report shows that the smarter the branch becomes with technology, the lower the cost and the more the revenue.

62 Laura J. Keller, "Bank of America to Open 500 U.S. Branches," Bloomberg, 26 February 2018, https://www.bloomberg.com/news/articles/2018-02-26/bank-of-america-to-open-500-u-s-branches-push-into-ohio-retail.
63 Klaus Dallerup, Sheinal Jayantilal, Georgi Konov, Hans-Martin Stockmeier and Akos Legradi, "A bank branch for the digital age," McKinsey & Company, July 2018, https://www.mckinsey.com/industries/financial-services/our-insights/a-bank-branch-for-the-digital-age.

Figure 5.8 Digital channels are on the rise, but a significant percentage of customers still prefer branches for at least some banking needs.

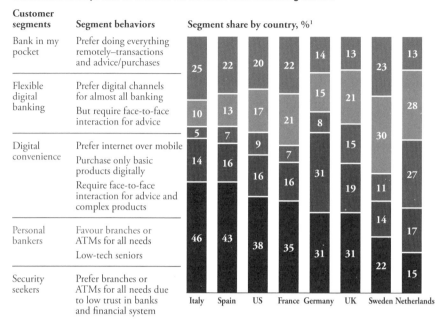

Customer segments	Segment behaviors	Segment share by country, %[1]
Bank in my pocket	Prefer doing everything remotely–transactions and advice/purchases	
Flexible digital banking	Prefer digital channels for almost all banking	
	But require face-to-face interaction for advice	
Digital convenience	Prefer internet over mobile	
	Purchase only basic products digitally	
	Require face-to-face interaction for advice and complex products	
Personal bankers	Favour branches or ATMs for all needs	
	Low-tech seniors	
Security seekers	Prefer branches or ATMs for all needs due to low trust in banks and financial system	

[1] Figures may not sum to 100%, because of rounding.
Source: McKinsey 2016 Retail Banking Multichannel Survey; Finalta Digital and Multichannel Survey

Figure 5.9 The impact of smart branches can be seen across a range of metrics.

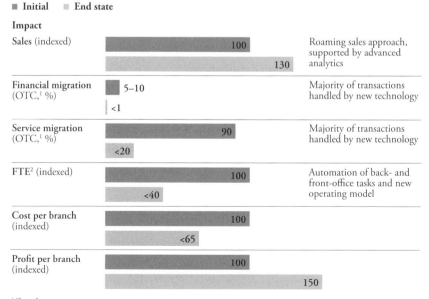

■ Initial ▦ End state

Impact

Sales (indexed)	100 / 130	Roaming sales approach, supported by advanced analytics
Financial migration (OTC,[1] %)	5–10 / <1	Majority of transactions handled by new technology
Service migration (OTC,[1] %)	90 / <20	Majority of transactions handled by new technology
FTE[2] (indexed)	100 / <40	Automation of back- and front-office tasks and new operating model
Cost per branch (indexed)	100 / <65	
Profit per branch (indexed)	100 / 150	

[1] Over the counter
[2] Full-time equivalent

This is the key as it reinforces so many other discussions about technology. As we automate everything, and software eats the world, the more that human activities are augmented with intelligence, the more the service improves. Robots and algorithms do not get rid of all of the physical assets and human beings; instead, they make the physical engagement more compelling and intelligent.

Ten years ago, I saw a prototype of the branch of the future where facial recognition was used as I entered the branch so that a robot could greet me: "Hello Chris, I believe you're here to talk about a mortgage today. Please go to Room #3." When I met the mortgage advisor, she had no questions to ask about me or my financial history and required no form filling. It had already been done. Now, this is the real issue here. Banks are updating branches for the digital age without thinking about what the digital-age branch should look like. Branches are getting facelifts and staff are given iPads, but why is the customer coming to the branch? It is not for advice or services, which is what most bankers think it is for. It is for understanding, empathy and a feeling of worth. Yes, they may want a mortgage—most bankers claim that it will be the big-ticket items that branches will exist for in the future, because customers require advice—but the customer can just as easily find a mortgage online. If the customer does come into the branch for a mortgage, the customer is not looking for advice, but for understanding. How long does this mortgage last? What happens if I want to break out of this mortgage early on? Can I move this mortgage on to the next house, and is that free?

In fact, most customers want the bank to advise them on all of the things that the bank currently does not. I always remember my first mortgage from a bank. The branch manager invited me in, and we had a great dialogue. I felt reassured that this was the right thing to do and signed the forms. What I did not realise was that the branch manager had sold me mortgage protection insurance that I did not need, and that if I repaid the mortgage within the first five years, there would be significant early redemption charges amounting to thousands of pounds.

It is this culture of hiding the things that make the bank's profit but punishes the customer that has to change. If banks can transform into trusted advisors in branches, and break out of their mentality of making profits from hidden fees, then there is every chance that the future branch as a marketing investment will work.

If Banks Provide No Advice, What Do They Provide?

For many years, banks have talked about moving away from transactions and towards advice. They claim that the branch is for advice, that they will become trusted advisors and that they see the value-add of banking because the information analysis around customer data enables them to offer advice. This is not true, however, when banks are not trusted for advice. There have been many banking scandals around the world that show that banks cannot be trusted as they focus on sales, revenues and profit at the customer's expense.

The issue is that retail banks shifted fundamentally from being a local community service focused on helping people to manage their money safely as an advisor to a firm focused on pushing people into debt to get the maximum returns on their interest on credit. That is the issue banks are trying to turn around in this age of new competition and digitalisation, but is it too late? Can banks really turn around and say "Trust me as an advisor" when, for the last fifty years, they have tilted to the other end of the spectrum, "Don't trust me, I'm just a sales machine".

What do banks offer if they do not offer advice? What is a bank for? If they do not offer advice, why do they have branches? If a bank does not offer advice, then the bank becomes fairly redundant, to be honest. A bank without advisory services is a pure store of value and a transaction machine. The transactions can be done by anyone these days, and the store of value offered by any regulated service from exchanges to challengers to start-ups.

There is far more at stake here than just being told by the regulator that giving people sales incentives, commissions and bonuses for sales of banking products is no longer tenable. In fact, banks are fundamentally seeing their foundations eroded through toxic bad practices, poor leadership, digital technology changes, fierce new competition and regulatory encouragement for change. These are tough times that we live in and, if you are a bank, show even more fundamentally why radical transformation is required, and not just evolutionary change.

Banks Also Need to Consider Their Brands

Why are most bank brands just acronyms? Maybe it is because no one wants to say that they bank with John Pierpont Morgan Chase when it is much easier to say JPMC. Here are just a few: HSBC, SCB, OCBC, DBS, ICICI, ICBC, ANZ, BOA, BBVA, RBS, BNP, ING, TSB, DNB, AIB ... the list goes on and on. In fact, banking is one of the only industries with large-scale acronym mania.

There is only one acronym in the automobile industry: BMW; in technology, there are IBM, HP and SAP; in retail, you get CVS, H&M and IKEA; but in banking, nearly everything is an acronym. The main reason for this is that banking is very business-oriented. When you are dealing with commerce and trade, people do not mind abbreviating the company name to a few letters, but when you are a retailer, you need a cool name like Apple, Nike, Samsung, Amazon or Disney. Interestingly, most of the challenger banks do not use acronyms in their names either: bunq, Che, Monzo, Hello, Atom, Starling, Soon, Tandem and Tide, to name just a few.

The above is yet another reason why start-ups regularly ask the question—who wants to deal with a big, corporate faceless bank?—because that is how most traditional banks appear. An industry that has corridors of people wearing suits and ties, with stringent rules and massive atrium-styled receptions. The image is all about being big and corporate. It is meant to promote stability as a big, corporate organisation, where staff are given uniforms to sit in the front desks. It is not necessarily what customers want. In fact, it is another sign of the cultural change of finance that millennials want their banking to be boring, but fun. How can this be achieved? Hire Will.i.am (Atom Bank) or Snoop Dogg (Klarna)?

It is a tough call, but the banks that are digitally transforming are heavily focusing on their branding. For example, one of the stars featured in *Digital Bank* was mBank, Poland, and its transformation. When the new bank was launched, it threw away the old bank. It completely rebranded overnight from BRE Bank, a name that had been around since the 1980s, to mBank. Overnight, all of the branches rebranded and all of the bank's physical and digital marketing materials did too.

Retail banks may think that this is not that important, but the one thing you really need to do as you relaunch the bank for the digital age is ask: does our brand work? Do people like walking into a firm whose name means nothing? Do you need to rethink your logo, colours and name to make this new digital bank work?

Will Bank Brands Survive in this Digital World?

Another debate about brand loyalty in a mobile world is the way in which banking has evolved with technology. It began with dealing with a branch; then a branch and a call centre; then it was a branch, a call centre and online; now, it's a branch, a call centre, online and mobile. How do you provide a consistent experience?

Some people refer to branch, call centre, online, mobile and digital as channels but, if you do, it means that you consider these things to be adding to the bank's old structure, rather than redesigning the structure to be digital. Digital should be at the core. An enterprise digital data structure that offers access for all devices and methods and ways of access. Any form factor accessing the digital core would then get the same experience, whether that be a customer support representative in a branch or customers themselves using a mobile app. More important, as we move to the Internet of Things, all of the customers' things would get consistent access to the digital core. That is the key point: a consistent online-to-offline (O2O) experience.

Then the question is how to build relevance across that experience so that the customer comes to the bank first and not to someone else like Amazon or Apple. This means that banks must not be dumb pipes but smart plumbing, providing all of the underlying digital structure and data analytics to be relevant whenever the customer needs to transact, store or exchange value. This is where PSD2, open APIs and Open Banking can really make a difference, by adding data enrichment to every transaction. Data enrichment through APIs to add more depth of knowledge about every digital activity of the customer can create more relevance, and turn the bank from a dumb pipe with dumb data into smart plumbing with data intelligence.

Now this is all well and good, but what does data intelligence really mean and can banks seriously expect to be as intelligent about customers' digital lifestyles as Amazon or Alibaba? Well, if they are not, they lose relevance. After all, if you are not needed in the process of transacting, storing and exchanging value, then why does the customer need you?

It is all about building relevance, that is, the four future roles of a bank. The future bank will offer:

- a data store and enrichment service, which is achieved by being
- a curator of apps, APIs and analytics from best-of-breed trusted third parties across the network, which, when combined, allow the bank to be relevant as
- a manager of life experiences and as a
- real-time financial provider of loans, savings and insurance measured in seconds, not days or years

I have touched on each of these areas in this book but to summarise here:

A data store and enrichment service is all about locking data that has value. If Facebook deleted my account tomorrow, I would lose over a decade of memories. Most of what I have on Facebook, however, is not that important, except for the photos. Nevertheless, I have backed up those photos on a hard drive, but what if that hard drive was corrupted? Okay, I have them backed up on Google too, but what if Google were to lose my photos? What guarantee do I have with Facebook, Google or anyone? And how valuable are those fifteen years of digital photographs? A bank can secure those digital assets. Not just my photos, but any digital asset: intellectual property, contracts, media, ideas and more.

A curator of apps, APIs and analytics is the rebundling of FinTech. This is unsurprising as most consumers cannot be bothered to change their bank, let alone research the thousands of FinTech firms doing one thing brilliantly. However, if their bank partnered and collaborated with a few of the thousands of FinTech firms doing one thing brilliantly, and integrated them all into an amazing customer experience, then that would be good. Specifically, consumers cannot be expected to do the due diligence on the trust of a FinTech start-up firm, but a bank can and should.

A manager of life experiences is a world of opportunity. Instead of focusing on just processing financial transactions, look at the bigger picture and focus on supporting the customer's financial life. Everyone has big events like moving house, having children, getting divorced, losing a job and suchlike. Manage the whole of these events by partnering with the marketplace of activities that need to be integrated for these lifestyle events. Bring the client the removal firm, decorators, gardeners, designers and insurance for their home move, not just the mortgage. Bring them the counsellors, recruitment firms, job opportunities, payments protection and career planning when they lose their job, don't just process the redundancy cheque.

A real-time financial provider provides everything in the here and now, not sometime in the future. Instead of having annualised auto insurance or term-based products or loans and mortgages on a set timer, finance becomes embedded in real-time things. A $50 loan at 08:00 in the morning, which is repaid at 14:00 for a fee of $0.05. Auto insurance for each journey, and not for a year. A pension where the contribution amounts can vary daily, rather than a flat monthly payment on a term policy. Everything becomes dynamically priced in real time and the idea of "term" products disappears. The focus is to take a bank's traditional role of trust, as a secure store of value, into a new structure for these days of digital insecurity.

Fast Follower Strategies Fail

> **ff** Previously, we thought about banking as high touch, driven by relationship managers. Now, we think about banking as being able to reach anyone anywhere. It helps us because it's low cost, it gives us greater scale and access. Big Tech were able to take advantage of the fact that you don't need to have visible presence, you can digitally market it to anyone. You don't need high touch by relationship managers, because businesses will scale via high-frequency, low-value transactions that are highly engaging. You don't need standardised products. You need customised and personalised products. That can only be enabled by data. All these companies that are coming from the other side, they are already set up in a way that would completely leapfrog how a bank is doing digital banking. Where we're seeing it as a threat to banks is apparent. **JJ**
>
> **Gene Wong**, *Head of Ecosystems, DBS*

For many years, banks have believed in a fast follower strategy. Don't be the first to market something. Wait until something is proven and then follow it fast. Copy it and that will suffice. It used to be that a bank could adapt and change when it saw things working. It had the luxury of time. Regulatory and capital requirements meant that new competition was slow to make an impact and, if it did, the bank could just copy what the competition was doing. That strategy used to work. It doesn't anymore.

Today, regulatory and capital requirements have been lowered so that almost anyone can launch a bank. This means that the things new competitors are doing are much harder to copy because they are nimble and quick, with new systems and supreme customer focus. This cannot be copied fast as a follower if you have old structures, fragmented systems and legacy thinking.

The difference with UK challenger banks like Monzo, Starling, Tandem and others is that they began in today's world. Their core systems and their data are designed to be leveraged. They can provide proactive and personalised service through algorithms. The good old bank has its core system designed to be a historical snapshot of transactions. It was built for debits and credits in branches in the 1970s. As a result, the bank can provide zero analysis or personalisation around that data and gives no knowledge of the customer's financial lifestyle as a result. That is why challenger banks are getting the lifestyle-banking customer while old banks get the basic utility transactions.

The old bank needs to think about how to create a data structure that can be proactive, personalised and rich with informational analytics. There is no way that the old bank can ever achieve that with a core system designed for branch operations. The systems were designed for an offline world of the 1970s, which means that it is impossible to follow new challengers with their real-time analytics with such outdated back-office structures. In fact, it leads to slow following. The traditional bank has to restructure and rationalise its old systems structures, refresh them and renew them, and then add the analytics and personalised capabilities to its apps and services. That will take about five years, if luck is on its side. This is not being a fast follower. It is actually a bank stuck in last-century thinking with last-century leadership. This is why a fast follower strategy leads to final failure, as the bank is not fit to compete with the Big Tech and FinTech firms that really get the data.

The world of the future will be dominated by firms that can analyse and leverage data for customer intelligent marketing and service. Any bank that has customer data in a static, fragmented, silo structure will fail in that world.

Compliance Will Kill the Bank

One banker told me that he is not worried about Amazon, Google or Alibaba; he is not concerned about FinTech start-ups like Revolut or Monzo; he does not care about Open Banking and software; and as for machine learning, AI and the like, forget it. The only thing that concerns him is compliance. He did not mean in the regulatory sense, just compliance in general.

A large, global bank has to deal with 185 regulatory changes per day, or one change every twelve minutes,[64] and a typical bank faces five times more regulations than a technology firm. Regulatory compliance is a big overhead. According to some banks, one in three people is checking what the others are doing, but if a bank could automate compliance, wouldn't it make a big difference? If a bank could use AI to manage that requirement, wouldn't that make a difference? If a bank could get rid of the human checkers and have the whole thing run by software, wouldn't that make a difference?

"Yes, yes, yes," he told me. "But it's too late."

"It's too late?" I responded. "What do you mean? It's never too late."

"Yes, it's too late," he told me. "By the time we develop the software structures to automate compliance, we'll be out of business."

Admittedly, there is a whole raft of regulations that banks need to deal with. Unfortunately, in Europe and the United States, banks also have the view that if the regulator does not allow it, then they will not do it. Challengers have a different view: do it and then ask for forgiveness. Traditional firms are conditioned to not try out anything without asking for permission first.

This means that most traditional banks take each and every regulation and try to implement it in its entirety. This is why many traditional banks end up absorbing thousands of words of regulatory text and then employ thousands of people to implement it. They end up with a raft of people

---

64 Chris Skinner, "Bank regulations change every 12 minutes," Finanser (blog), 30 January 2017, https://thefinanser.com/2017/01/bank-regulations-change-every-12-minutes.html/.

working on regulatory implementation and then another raft of people checking that the first set of people, and their working counterparts, are adhering to the interpretation of that regulation.

That is why banks have one in every three people working on compliance, and why there is such an overhead in banks of checkers checking the checkers checking the workers who are being checked again. Compliance. It might not kill the bank, but it sure does give it a headache.

A Saving Grace?

After all this debate, there is one thing that might be the saving grace for a bank that has yet to digitally transform (or does not want to): the regulator.

Banks sit at the heart of economies and commerce, and governments work with banks to ensure financial health, wealth and certainty. When that cooperation fails, you have crisis. Governments are now struggling with the internet age, and how to regulate a network that does not recognise country borders or boundaries. The internet is global. It has no home in any country and, for this reason, is hard to regulate and is getting harder every day.

Who governs the internet? The internet? No, the government of the internet is the government. When things go wrong, you need to have a supervisory authority to sort it out. This is why, for all the power that the internet places in our hands, there will still be an authority over it all. We will always have governments, courts, rules and structures. The challenge in today's connected world, however, is that the internet does not recognise borders. The internet does not recognise countries, governments or structures. The internet is a global network without borders.

This is a friction that regularly occurs in debates about the future world. How do you regulate a world without borders? What is the law when the transacting counterparties are without law? Having had this debate for a decade about bitcoin, my answer is that the law wins and governments rule. Unless you believe that the owners of the platforms rule. Do Jeff Bezos, Mark Zuckerberg, Pony Ma and Jack Ma run the world now?

> ❝ Management. The word is there for regular companies. At Alibaba we treat it more like governing an economy, as we have to manage so many companies dependent upon us as partners. ❞
>
> **Jack Ma**, *co-founder and former chairman of Alibaba*

Are the Big Tech giants the new global governors or are the governments of the world going to manage the network?

BOTTOM LINE

The banks engaged in digital transformation are demonstrating that it is worthwhile, but their results are yet to show notable breakthroughs. This is because the journey that they have embarked on is yet to finish. On top of this, investors in financial institutions judge such institutions in a very different way from FinTech start-ups and technology unicorns. Banks are judged on their real returns on equity and investment, not on the hope of building and creating new markets. As a result, the jury is still out on whether digital transformation succeeds in the short term as the banks I studied, like BBVA and DBS, have similar valuations to their peer groups (take a look at the appendix for the results of these banks compared to their peers). In the long term, it is believed that this will change, as everyone states that banks must transform or die, but there is still time to change in the short term.

CONCLUSIONS

In concluding *Doing Digital*, it is difficult to pin down any winning formula for digital transformation. After all, every bank is different. There are commonalities in the experiences of all five banks I interviewed in-depth, as well as many others that I have talked to around the world, but there is no silver bullet, magic mushroom or fairy dust that you can pick up and drop to make this change work. You just need to absorb the themes: a board mandate, a burning platform, a compelling vision, a committed leadership, an engaged middle management, a change of systems and structures and so on.

Equally, it is obvious that changing a bank built over centuries, with billions invested in its structures and operations, and millions of customers, is a mammoth exercise. It begins with leadership and a board mandate, but then rolls through cultural change, organisational change and technology change.

What is clear from my research and interviews is that, in order to make these changes happen, there are four distinct phases:

- What to do
- How to do it
- Do it
- Do it better

The lessons from leaders that have been covered in the majority of this book are not distinct to one phase, but run across all four. The most critical lessons include:

- **Board mandate:** ensure that the CEO and chair have the support to focus on digital transformation as the number one priority
- **Leadership is committed:** if a bank is going to do digital transformation, the executive team must lead the change throughout the whole organisation and not just delegate change down the management chain
- **Lead by values:** have clear principles and be outcome-focused
- **Customer-focused:** digital banks have customer-obsessed principles
- **Strategic planning:** work out the bank's core competencies and strategy for change
- **Communicate:** create an urgency for change through a burning platform and ensure that there is a compelling vision to show people where to go
- **Change the people:** reskill and retrain
- **Organise for agile:** flatten the organisation and build real-time communications that are fast and decisive
- **Technology is business:** digital banks do not see IT as a separate function; they see business and technology as fully integrated; there is no segregation
- **Behave like Big Tech:** learn from the technology titans and emulate what they do
- **Monitor:** real-time measurements using balanced scorecards drive the organisation
- **Data is differentiation:** data is the air that allows any digital corporation to succeed or fail
- **User experience is key:** design is internalised and part of every internal discussion
- **Build a digital core:** cloud-based and enterprise-wide
- **Be open:** a bank can no longer work on its own, but needs others in the platform marketplace

- **Partnering is not easy:** the bank needs a whole new set of skills to deal with technology partnerships
- **Co-create:** with partners, and with customers too
- **There will be pain:** no one likes change, so help them
- **Change is the only constant**

If I am honest, when I set out to write this book, I wanted to list these lessons as a step-by-step guide, like an ABC of how to do transformation. It was only as I interviewed these banks in-depth that I realised that there are no fixed steps that you can follow. Every bank is different. The only thing you can learn from these leaders are the things that they found useful, and that is what has been listed here.

Having said that, five general steps that overarch all of these did become apparent to me when talking with banks about digital transformation. These five steps are as follows:

Lesson #1: Sort out the basics

The first lesson is to get your house in order before you start. Get the basics done and take baby steps towards change, by standardising operations and optimising processes. You cannot run a marathon on day one. To start, you just need to take those first steps, then start running a mile or two and, eventually, you will get to that 26.2-mile marker. Just don't try to get there on day one.

Lesson #2: Lipstick is expensive

We often talk about "lipstick on the pig". Adding nice front-end apps to rotten back-end systems is never going to work and can often be an expensive mistake. If you do not tackle the big issues and simply roll out the easy-to-do stuff, you may find yourself in a bigger mess than when you started.

Lesson #3: People with different skill sets solve different problems

You need diversity in the organisation to go digital. If you have a homogeneous group of people, they will never address the needs of change in the right way because they will only look at it in one way. You need people who can see all of the angles, and not just one.

Lesson #4: Invest in your people

The biggest mistake a bank can make is to discard employees because their jobs have gone. Find them new jobs. Upskill and reskill them. Sometimes, bank leadership teams believe that it is good to downsize the workforce. Often though, that workforce can be good at something else and it takes a lot longer to find a new employee who fits in than reskill an old employee who already gets it.

Lesson #5: Keep your eye on the customer

You may believe that you are doing digital well, but the customer knows best. As digital is all about the customer, keep that focus front and centre. Ensure customer feedback is engaged by everyone in the organisation. There is nothing like hearing direct feedback from users and their user experience to keep you on the edge of your seat.

I hope you enjoyed reading *Doing Digital*, and found it useful. I look forward to discussing these lessons and learnings with all of you in more depth in the years to come. Good luck with your change programme and, if you ever need help, you know who to call.

> **"** If we transform, we might survive,
> but without transformation we might die. **"**
>
> **Min Hua**, *Head of Strategy, CMB*

APPENDIX: THE FIVE BANKS SELECTED

As mentioned at the beginning of this book, I wrote down a list of banks that appeared to be doing digital transformation well. The list consisted of large banks that will be familiar to all. I then narrowed down the list based on my own instincts regarding bank encounters, the media coverage of each bank's digital efforts, the awards each bank has won for its digital banking and more. The list was not long.

One of my criteria was that the banks had to be of a decent size, with regional or global coverage or in a market with scale, as in China and the United States. At the time of writing, JPMorgan Chase is the largest bank in the world, with a market capitalisation of $390 billion (12 January 2018). China Merchants Bank is the tenth largest ($123 billion), ING is twenty-fifth ($79 billion), BBVA is thirty-sixth ($61 billion) and DBS is forty-fourth ($55 billion). In other words, of the 30,000 or more financial institutions around the world, I chose some of the largest.[65]

Equally, there were other factors in my consideration. BBVA had a figurehead for many years who demanded digital transformation in the form of now retired CEO and Chairman Francisco González. González began life as a programmer and "got digital" therefore. The bank was one of the first to talk about the threat of the Big Tech giants, invest and acquire FinTech start-ups and transform internal operations to the cloud. BBVA gets it.

---

65 Figures are taken from the 2018 list of the world's largest banks, as compiled by Relbanks. See https://www.relbanks.com/worlds-top-banks/market-cap.

CMB is one of the largest retail banks in China, and yet only launched in the late 1980s. It is new to the market, when compared with the state-owned banks, and yet has rocketed into the major league using technology as its focus. It began as a bank built for the internet age, talked about being a digital bank and is now a FinTech bank. Its whole modus operandi is focused on engaging with customers through technology. No wonder this bank gets so many awards for its digital operations and services.

DBS garners headlines worldwide as the best digital bank in the world. Some are cynical about this, especially those who use the bank in Singapore. They claim that the reason why the bank is regarded as such is because the bank has good marketing. The reality is that I picked DBS because of these headlines but was surprised and gratified to learn that it not only talks digital but walks it too. Every single person I met at the bank—that number being more than any other bank I spoke with—talked the digital talk about customer journeys, agile, digital being in the DNA and more. This was exceptional and makes me think that the cynics out there might want to rethink their stand.

ING's wake-up call was with ING Direct. A bank that expanded from being a large Dutch retail bank to a global brand through start-up operations that were digital from day one. These learnings fed back into the bank and throughout the organisation, and it has been working on innovation with technology for over a decade.

Finally, JPMorgan Chase has regularly made announcements of digital achievements and investments. These cover everything from blockchain and cryptocurrencies to AI and cloud. A fifth of its workforce are technologists and, since Jamie Dimon noted in his shareholder's newsletter that Silicon Valley was coming to eat the bank's lunch back in 2015, they have been consistently transforming the bank to align with the digital world.

In conclusion, these five banks demonstrate digital well. However, I am neither condoning and endorsing them for their digital efforts nor am I saying that they are the best or the only banks doing digital. What I will say is that these five banks take digital transformation seriously, are investing and demanding to be digital, have leaderships that walk the walk as well as talk the talk and are making change happen. For these reasons, they are leaders that we can learn from.

In this final section of the book, I will leave you with facts, figures and further background, garnered from the banks' annual reports between 2013 and 2018. I believe that the statements and commentary in these reports provide a useful summary of what doing digital really means. In addition, it adds a final reality check to show that even when a bank invests billions in being digital, it is still not an easy task.

CHART

This chart below shows the performance of the five banks selected against relevant peer group banks during the period 2013 to 2018 as they went through their digital transformation processes. It is interesting to note that none of the banks' metrics makes them stand out specifically against their peer group members, which implies digital transformation does little for the share price. That is true, using traditional financial metrics. However, as discussed in this book and by these banks, perhaps we need to look at non-traditional metrics, such as how these banks are deepening digital relationships for retention of customers and service at lower cost with broader reach.

JPMorgan Chase							
	2013	2014	2015	2016	2017	2018	
ROE	9%	10%	11%	10%	10%	13%	Return on common Equity
#EMP	251,000	241,000	234,000	243,000	252,000	256,000	
CIR	72.37%	64.42%	63.09%	58.69%	59.10%	58.14%	Cost: total noninterest expense. Income: total net revenue
SP DEV	44.85	51.66	58.21	61.60	88.51	108.79	* Source: https://www.macrotrends.net/stocks/charts/JPM/jpmorgan-chase/stock-price-history

Wells Fargo							
	2013	2014	2015	2016	2017	2018	
ROE	13.87%	13.41%	12.60%	11.49%	11.35%	11.53%	Return on average common shareholders' equity
#EMP	264,900	264,500	264,700	269,100	262,700	258,700	
CIR	55.46%	55.49%	55.51%	55.62%	59.84%	55.54%	Cost: noninterest expense. Income: noninterest income + interest income
SP DEV	34.10	43.92	49.06	45.17	52.26	53.98	Source: https://www.macrotrends.net/stocks/charts/WFC/wells-fargo/stock-price-history

Bank of America							
	2013	2014	2015	2016	2017	2018	
ROE	4.62%	2.01%	6.28%	6.69%	6.72%	11.04%	Return on average common shareholders' equity
#EMP	242,000	224,000	213,000	208,000	209,000	204,000	
CIR	77.83%	88.08%	69.45%	65.81%	62.67%	58.50%	Cost: total noninterest expense. Income: noninterest income + interest income
SP DEV	12.54	15.29	15.68	14.80	24.06	29.37	* Source: https://www.macrotrends.net/stocks/charts/BAC/bank-of-america/stock-price-history

CitiBank							
	2013	2014	2015	2016	2017	2018	
ROE	7.00%	3.40%	8.10%	6.60%	-3.90%	9.40%	Return on average common shareholders' equity
#EMP	251,000	241,000	231,000	219,000	209,000	204,000	
CIR	63.09%	71.29%	57.12%	59.27%	57.72%	57.43%	Cost: operating expenses. Income: noninterest income + interest income
SP DEV	45.59	47.46	50.46	44.19	63.38	68.17	* Source: https://www.macrotrends.net/stocks/charts/C/citigroup/stock-price-history

BBVA							
	2013	2014	2015	2016	2017	2018	
ROE	N/A	N/A	N/A	0.073	0.074	0.115	
#EMP	109,305	108,770	137,968	134,792	131,856	125,567	
CIR	0.523	0.513	0.52	0.519	0.495	0.493	
SP DEV	8.95	7.85	6.74	6.41	7.11	4.64	

BNP Paribas							
	2013	2014	2015	2016	2017	2018	
ROE	6.1%	7.7%	8.3%	9.3%	8.9%	8.2%	
#EMP	184,545	187,903	189,077	192,419	196,128	202,624	
CIR	67.6%	67.7%	68.1%	67.7%	64.6%	65.4%	
SP DEV	47.2	52.72	54.11	51.08	63.38	59.56	

Barclays

	2013	2014	2015	2016	2017	2018	
ROE	9%	10.3%	11.4%	12.4%	13.3%	/	
#EMP	139,600	132,300	129,400	119,300	79,900	83,500	
CIR	71%	70%	84%	76%	73%	/	
SP DEV	3.04	2.31	2.53	1.66	2.3	2.11	

ING

	2013	2014	2015	2016	2017	2018	
ROE	9%	9.9%	10.80%	11.60%	13.3%	11.50%	
#EMP	64,373	55,945	52,720	51,943	51,504	52,233	
CIR	56.6%	57.9%	55.3%	54.2%	55.5%	54.8%	
SP DEV	8.24	10.6	13.62	10.43	13.81	13.65	

China Merchants Bank

	2013	2014	2015	2016	2017	2018	
ROE	22.22%	19.28%	17.09%	16.27%	16.54%	16.57%	* ROAE (return on average equity)
#EMP	68,078	75,109	76,192	70,461	72,530	74,590	* Employees including dispatched employees
CIR	34.23%	30.42%	27.55%	27.60%	30.21%	35.05%	
SP DEV	16.52	19.46	18.3	18	30.55	29.15	* HKD (Hong Kong Dollar)

DBS

	2013	2014	2015	2016	2017	2018	
ROE	10.4%	10.9%	11.2%	10.1%	9.7%	12.1%	
#EMP	/	21,000	22,000	22,000	24,000	26,000	
CIR	44%	45%	45%	43%	43%	44%	
SP DEV	16.19	17.62	19.14	15.44	20.8	26.36	

UOB							
	2013	2014	2015	2016	2017	2018	
ROE	12.30%	12.30%	11%	10.20%	10.20%	11.30%	
#EMP			24,092	24,781	25,137	26,153	
CIR	43.10%	40.60%	43%	44%	43.70%	43.90%	
SP DEV	20.51	22.27	21.85	18.61	23.24	26.19	
OCBC							
	2013	2014	2015	2016	2017	2018	
ROE	11.60%	13.20%	12.30%	10.00%	11%	11.50%	
#EMP	25,000	>29,000	29,000	29,792		29,706	
CIR	42%	39.10%	42%	44.60%	42.40%	43.45%	
SP DEV	10	9.6	9.85	8.6	10.68	12.05	* S$ (Singapore Dollar)

BBVA

❝ Knowing how to give customers advice, to provide them the services they want, anytime and wherever they are: this is the key to differentiation. ❞
Francisco González, *CEO, BBVA, 1999*

Francisco González became CEO of BBVA in 1999. In 1999, the digital world travelled at 56 kilobits per second (Kbps) whereas, currently, home connection speeds can reach 300,000 Kbps. The launch of the iPhone—considered the first smartphone, a device that would revolutionise communications—was still eight years away. The democratisation of the internet was still merely a vision, with home penetration reaching only 4.6 per cent of the globe, according to the World Bank.

Given these statistics about the state of technology back then, González's speech at BBVA's 1999 Annual General Meeting in Bilbao has proven to be nothing less than visionary. Here it is:

We are in times of profound—extremely profound—change. The technological revolution undoubtedly advances at different paces in different sectors. But the financial sector has been the most impacted by this transformation, and it is also the sector that has the most to gain, if it can plan ahead and make timely decisions.

This is the very nature of the financial business, which is based on enormous numbers of transactions, drawn from a wealth—a real wealth—of complex data about millions of customers. In this changing world where boundaries are blurring and barriers are disappearing, banking can position itself to offer a wider range of products and services by using its large customer base and its reputation for quality and trust.

Knowing how to give customers advice, to provide them the services they want, anytime and wherever they are: this is the key to differentiation.

Managing such a complex process of transformation, defining and implementing appropriate strategies in a dramatically changing world is, of course, not a simple task.

The scale and capacity of technology is available to many. But it will only be those banks with teams of people who understand this change—who define and implement appropriate strategies in order to be prepared, to move forward, to plan ahead at the right time—it will be these banks that will be successful, that will be the prominent industry leaders of the 21st century.

And the best way to achieve this is to be a major proponent for this change. To lead the charge. To understand, support, and put ourselves at the forefront of change. This is BBVA's resolve. A competitive position vis-à-vis traditional banks, vis-à-vis the so-called startups.

This is what I would like to express: I insist that at BBVA we are going to lead this change. I know we can because, as I said before, we are starting from a privileged position. Because the endeavor is clear; the project we've set ourselves is well defined. It entails knowing how to connect the present with the future, the physical networks with the virtual, and technology with people, and it is therefore people who will be, as they already are, the key to BBVA's success.

González's vision was not just that of a banker who graduated with a degree in Economics and Business, but also the vision of an IBM 1401 programmer. In 1964, BBVA's future executive chairman set out on a career in information technology: "This job made it abundantly clear to me that technology is not merely thrilling in and of itself, but also because of its enormous potential to impact lives on a social and economic level," he stated. Banking, as González imagined it, began to take shape when he realised that tabulators would be replaced by computers. His passion for technology has been one of the keys to BBVA's vision.

Twenty years after he made that speech, his vision lives on in the new management team led by Carlos Torres Vila.

The results of the bank's efforts are intriguing and do not show, necessarily, that the bank is achieving the returns expected. However, in my opinion, it is doing the right things for the future.

On the next page are extracts related to digital transformation from BBVA's annual reports (2013 to 2018).

Figure 7.1 Following up with a remote interview with Carlos Torres Vila, chairman of BBVA

2013

In 2013 we continued to make progress in our transformation. *(Note: BBVA was talking digital transformation back in 2013, before most other banks even knew what digital was.)* BBVA is reinventing itself, building on the three pillars of our strategy: Principles, People and Innovation, and underpinned by a diversified business model, with growth potential and prudent management. It is changing from an analog bank to a 21st-century digital knowledge services company.

As of today, the new entrants are more flexible and efficient; but banks have a significant advantage: a vast amount of information originated by their activity. The great challenge is to turn this information into knowledge and give customers what they demand. Digital customers want to operate in real time from any mobile device and access new contents and products seamlessly across the various channels. This requires Big/Smart Data technologies and large processing capabilities.

To tackle all these demands, banks need to design new platforms, built and developed under today's new paradigms, such as the one we have already built at BBVA. In 2013 these platforms enabled us to launch new digital products, such as BBVA Wallet and Wizzo and develop new ones, currently in the pilot stage, with a planned 2014 launch date.

2014

For BBVA it was a productive year because we achieved good earnings, took important decisions that improve the Group's growth potential and made notable progress in our digital transformation strategy to become the best Bank in the world.

After completing the initial construction stage of the new, highly innovative and world-class technological platform which we initiated eight years ago, we are now working hard on the next stage, creating new distribution models, processes and products and a new organization, while we explore new digital businesses. To accelerate the process, in 2014 we created the Digital Banking area, made up of more than 3,000 people from the Group's different geographical areas and to which we are adding external talent from top-level digital companies.

Apart from transforming our business internally, in 2014 we have followed very closely the emergence and development of new digital businesses, in some cases as investors and in others as new owners.

This balanced and diversified model is based on sound franchises, with a sufficiently large customer base and leadership positions in our core markets (Spain, Mexico, South America, the Sunbelt region in the United States and Turkey), as well as three global franchises: Digital Banking, Corporate & Investment Banking (CIB) (wholesale business) and Lines of Business (LoBs), a unit that includes the global activities of Consumer Finance, Asset Management and Insurance.

Transforming from and for customers

BBVA has been working for a number of years on the transformation of its business model to a more digital model, based on technology and innovation as key levers. The aim is to offer the best experience for our customers, generating a significant improvement in productivity, efficiency, profitability and value creation for the Group's shareholders.

The market has already recognized this transforming effort of recent years. The British magazine *Euromoney* has awarded one of its global Euromoney Awards for Excellence 2014 to BBVA's digital project to head up the financial industry of the 21st century, as the best transformation by a global financial institution last year. The jury highlighted BBVA's achievements in transforming the business, based on a profound strategic review of the Bank to address the new challenges in the industry. BBVA considers that there are five basic elements for tackling this transformation process. Transforming processes and adapting the product offering BBVA is transforming its processes so they are more responsive and adapting its product offering to new customer needs. The Bank has launched a number of digital products and services and is working on new developments that continue with the Group's digital strategy. The following are some of the initiatives worth highlighting: BBVA Wallet, an application launched in 2013, which in 2014 received some major updates. Mid-way through the year, BBVA announced the commercial launch of a Near-Field Communication (NFC) payment solution, which uses the Visa cloud-based specification. The new system allows BBVA customers with Android NFC-equipped terminals to make purchases by simply downloading the updated BBVA Wallet app.

Currently it is the most used and popular mobile banking payment app in Spain, with more than 400,000 downloads, according to data as of the close of 2014. Thanks to this success, it has already been launched in Mexico and its launch in the United States is planned for 2015. This app has received a prize at the Contactless & Mobile Awards 2014, which recognize the most important innovations in Europe in applying contactless technology in the market. In this case, the award highlights the efforts "the Company is making to bring mobile payments to the mass market".

Boosting the development of new digital businesses

In addition, the Bank aims to promote the development of external initiatives in order to be at the cutting-edge of transformation in the financial industry and understand the changes in the digital world in real time.

- First, through BBVA Ventures, the Bank invests in disruptive startups in the area of innovation and financial services. In 2014, BBVA has announced investments in Taulia, DocuSign and Personal Capital. And already in January 2015, in Coinbase, the leader platform to carry out transactions with the virtual currency Bitcoin.

- Second, by acquiring digital companies from which it can learn and that reinforce the Group's digital transformation strategy. The acquisition of Madiva Soluciones, a Spanish startup specialized in Big Data and Cloud Computing services, together with the aforementioned acquisition of Simple are an example of this kind of operations that BBVA aims to carry out.

2015

BBVA has been aware for some years that transformation involves adapting banking services to people's real lives. Consumers today rate convenience very highly, i.e. being able to make informed and well-advised decisions through face-to-face, remote (by phone or email) or digital channels, depending on their needs. This is demonstrated by the major investment in innovation and technology that BBVA has been making over recent years, with an annual average of around €800m since 2011.

Increase in the digital customer base

BBVA is continuing to expand the number of customers who interact with the Bank through digital channels. As of December 31, 2015, the Group had 14.8 million digital customers, that means a penetration of 33% and 19% up on last year, of whom 8.5 million are in mobile banking (up 45% on 2014). BBVA's app has had more than 4.2 million downloads and BBVA Wallet, the card management app, 2.3 million. The BBVA Contigo customized remote account management service has more than 600,000 customers in Spain. In short, the functionalities developed through digital transformation make financial transactions more agile and simple, while also changing traditional banking concepts.

Transformation at the branch offices

BBVA's branch network has taken a leading role in the Bank's growth and transformation. It aims to adapt to the profile of customers by using a mix that combines face-to-face, remote or digital service in a 360° model. Beginning in November 2015, the managers of BBVA Contigo in Spain have been working integrated into the branch network teams. Branches also assist customers who have any queries so they can learn about the tools that will make their transactions easier.

In Mexico, the branch office rehabilitation and upgrading project, which has reached 1,400 branch offices in 2015, becomes a reality with the Bancomer Tower. The change in the comprehensive business model drives technological innovation with a view to improving customer experience.

Today, flexibility and convenience make mobile banking and the Internet the most highly rated channels among BBVA customers. But customers do not have to choose between self-service and the face-to-face channel: they can select face-to-face, remote or digital banking according to their needs at any given time. The new distribution model boosted by digital transformation means that activity in the branch, as measured by the number of transactions, continues to decline.

Engineering

The Bank has created the Engineering area that not only manages technology operations but develops software and processes for customer solutions with a global approach. With the focus on digital transformation, in 2015 it structured its activity around the following lines of action:

- Developing the Group's technological architectures toward more standardized models, boosting the adoption of Cloud Computing (a paradigm that allows us to offer computing services through a network, usually the Internet)

- Transforming the Technology production function by incorporating elements of new technologies.

- Optimizing processes in search of improved customer experience, efficiency and operational control.

- Guaranteeing integrated management of security, as well as control of operations and information security.

- Facilitating the integration of Garanti and CX.

2016

During 2016, the BBVA Group made great progress in its transformation Journey, strongly supported by the Group's Purpose and six Strategic Priorities. The Entity's new strategy has been bolstered with particular focus on digitalization and customer experience, simplifying the organizational structure and in 2017 redefining the Bank's new tagline: "Creating Opportunities". Digitalization is making an impact on the financial industry, since it can satisfy the new demands of customers in various ways.

Firstly, the entry of mobile devices has led to changes in the distribution model. Society as a whole is permanently connected, regardless of location. Mobile devices have become the main channel of contact. The number of mobile banking users worldwide has grown exponentially and customers are increasingly interacting through their mobile devices. Moreover, new developments in technology (Big Data, artificial intelligence, blockchain, the cloud, data processing, biometry, etc.) represent a major advance in customer experience. These technologies allow us to analyze automatically data and algorithms (risk profile, habits and preferences, financial needs and expectations, etc.), together with simple interactions and a fluid transition across channels and vendors. Likewise, they provide easy access to the best solutions available on the marketplace with the most beneficial conditions by default. Technological innovations reduce unit costs thanks to process automation and scalability. New technologies foster the democratization of financial services: the entire world will be able to gain access to better and more sophisticated services that were up to now only available for high-value segments. In this context, having access to a customer's relevant information with his/her consent has proven to be critical in providing automated and personalized advice. And to achieve this, it is essential to earn the customer's trust.

Additionally, new, specialized players are entering the financial industry and successfully tackling parts of the value chain (payments, financing, asset management, insurance, etc.). Their disruptive proposals are primarily based on improving customer experience and enhancing specialization in certain products. These players include FinTech companies and large digital corporations (Google, Amazon, etc.), which are now competing with banks in the new environment.

In conclusion, traditional banking should respond by becoming more competitive and providing value-added solutions, with greater focus on customer experience and the development of their digital offering.

2017

During 2017, the BBVA Group made significant progress on its **transformation** process, firmly underpinned by the Group's Purpose and six Strategic Priorities. The Bank's strategy has been strengthened with a particular focus on digitalization and customer experience under a new tagline: "Creating Opportunities", as well as the Values established to steer the behavior of the Organization as a whole. A necessary transformation process in order to adapt to the new environment in the financial industry described previously and preserve its leadership.

Within this context, the pace of **change** in the environment in which BBVA operates is accelerating: exponential growth in new technologies is providing customers with new products and services tailored to their evolving needs, at the same time as significant changes are taking place in the different sectors and companies, which is leading to a weakening of boundaries between sectors.

2018

Our business is changing both profoundly and quickly. These changes are exemplified by our increasing digitization. **In 2018, 41% of BBVA Group unit sales were made through digital channels**, compared to just 16% two years ago. In terms of value, digital sales account for 32% compared to 12% two years ago. This significant transformation is not only reflected at the Group level, but represents a trend that is repeated in each of the countries where we operate. The evidence shows that customers who use digital channels interact with us more frequently, and report greater satisfaction and loyalty to BBVA. **In 2018 we achieved a key milestone: our digital customer base surpassed the 50% threshold**, reaching 27 million. The bank's mobile customer base has increased by 29%, reaching 23 million mobile users, or 43% of total customers. Our goal is to have more than 50% our customers interacting with us through their smartphones in 2019.

Digital activity is outpacing growth in overall economic activity. Society is changing in line with the exponential growth in technology (internet, mobile devices, social networks, cloud, etc.). As a result, **digitalization** is therefore revolutionizing financial services worldwide. Consumers are altering their purchasing habits through use of digital technologies, which increase their ability to access financial products and services at any time and from anywhere. Greater availability of information is creating more demanding customers, who expect swift, easy and immediate responses to their needs. And digitalization is what enables the financial industry to meet these new customer demands.

Technology is the lever for change which allows the value proposition to be redefined to focus on customers' real needs. The use of **mobile devices** as the preferred and often only tool for customers' interactions with their financial institutions has changed the nature of this relationship and the way in which financial decisions are made. It is crucial to offer customers a simple, consistent and user-friendly experience, without jeopardizing security and making the most of technological resources.

Artificial intelligence (AI) and Big Data are two of the technologies that are currently driving the transformation of the financial industry. Their adoption by various entities translates into new services for clients that are more accessible and agile, and a transformation in internal processes. AI allows, among other things, offering personalized products and recommendations to customers and make decisions more intelligently. These technologies are not only in the hands of traditional companies but Fintech also makes use of them.

Data are the cornerstone of the digital economy. Financial institutions must make the most of the opportunities offered by technology and innovation, analyzing customer behavior, needs and expectations in order to offer them personalized and value-added services, and help them in making decisions. The development of algorithms based on Big Data can lead to the development of new advisory tools for managing personal finances and access to products which until recently were only available to high-value segments.

The **digital transformation** of the financial industry is boosting efficiency through automation of internal processes, with the use of new technologies to remain relevant in the new environment, such as blockchain and the cloud; data exploitation; and new business models (platforms). Participation in digital ecosystems through alliances and investments provides a way to learn and take advantage of the opportunities emerging in the digital world. The financial services market is also evolving with the arrival of **new players**: companies offering financial services to a specific segment or focused on a part of the value chain (payment, finance, etc.). These companies are digital natives, rely on data use and offer a good customer experience, sometimes exploiting a laxer regulatory framework than that for the banking sector.

CHINA MERCHANTS BANK

I selected China Merchants Bank on the basis that it consistently wins awards from publications that I work with, such as the Asian Banker, for being the best digital bank in Asia. Its internet and mobile-first strategies have shown the bank to be far ahead of many rivals, according to this research. In particular, CMB started as a technology-led bank in the 1980s, was one of the first to offer internet banking in China and describes itself today as a "FinTech bank".

Figure 7.2 With the executive team at CMB, Shenzhen, China

Here are a few highlights from its annual reports to give further background:

2013

During the reporting period, the Company aunched innovative products and services such as the M+ debit card, the WeChat Banking Platform, the mobile wallet and the comprehensive service solution for remuneration finance.

The Company attached high importance to the innovation and improvement of its e-channels, continually innovated the functions of online banking and direct banking as effective supplements to our physical channels, and proactively explored the development of mobile finance service.

The Company pioneered the mobile finance online portal in China, and proposed the concept of "one-stop open platform for mobile banking". As a result, the number of downloads made by mobile banking users and iPad banking users ranked at the forefront in the industry. In addition to the WeChat customer service introduced for its credit card users in March 2013, the Company launched the "WeChat Online Banking" service in July 2013, the first of its kind in the industry, which helped the Company maintain its leading position in customer experience.

Fourthly, by adhering to the "customer-centric" principle and stressing to improve its customers' internet banking experience, the Company upgraded and refined its products such as online banking and mobile banking so as to improve its customers' online banking experience.

The mobile user application was the first of its kind in the domestic credit card industry, which effectively met the customers' needs in this mobile Internet era and thus broadened the channels for soliciting customers and improved the efficiency of soliciting customers, thereby continuing to put more efforts into soliciting these valued customers, so as to optimise the structure of the customer base.

The Company attaches great importance to developing and improving e-banking channels such as online banking, mobile banking and direct banking, which are highly recognised by the society and have effectively relieved the pressure on outlets of the Company.

The Company's online banking business continued to grow rapidly in 2013; its users were increasing dramatically and the frequency they use online banking grew as well.

As for its retail online banking business, as at 31 December 2013, the number of active users of the retail online banking professional edition of the Company reached 15,828,700, and the relevant replacement ratio in respect of retail online banking was 89.36%.

The total cumulative number of retail online banking transactions was 947,742,300, up by 28.75% as compared with that in the previous year; and the accumulated transaction amount was RMB 19,540.044 billion, up by 28.59% as compared with that in the previous year.

Specifically, the accumulative number of online payment transactions was 694,654,300, up by 26.32% as compared with that in the previous year; and the accumulative amount of online banking transactions was RMB412.421 billion, up by 90.33% as compared with that in the previous year.

The personal mobile banking service of the Company continued to maintain rapid growth in 2013, and the Company's mobile banking service was awarded the "Best Mobile Banking Product in China" by The Asian Banker. Ahead of its peers, the Company introduced a brand new mobile banking product, 'WeChat Banking', which extends the convenience of Internet banking services to increasingly popular mobile applications used by a large number of customers, therefore establishing a multi-level and diversified intelligent customer service mode, providing a handy way for customers to use mobile banking service as well as promoting the innovation and rapid development of WeChat Banking.

Following the introduction of mobile banking apps for iPhones and Android smartphones as well as iPads, the Company also introduced Win8 banking service in December 2013 which received enthusiastic applause from our customers.

As at 31 December 2013, the aggregate number of mobile banking apps being downloaded had exceeded 22 million. The number of logins of mobile banking users reached 265,519,800 times, representing a year-on-year increase of 216.16%, and the number of mobile banking users, transactions and payments has been increasing dramatically with very active users. The total number of mobile banking contracts signed had reached 15,690,300, 62.34% higher than that of the previous year, of which the number of active customers had reached 5,440,100.

Cumulative transactions (excluding mobile payment) amounted to 51,356,000 transactions, up by 294.97% as compared with the previous year; and the accumulated transaction value reached RMB 1077.434 billion, up by 165.42% as compared with the previous year. The aggregate number of mobile payment amounted to 208 million transactions, up by 259.89% as compared with the previous year; and the accumulated transaction value was RMB 59.078 billion, up by 443.10% as compared with the previous year.

2014

In response to the changing environment, the Bank will take initiatives in continuous transformation in order to grow stronger and strive to become China's best commercial bank with a distinctive edge, an edge that helps the Bank to win customers' testimonials in market competition, to lead people's lifestyle in an era of technological innovation, to obtain employees' recognition in its continuous development, and to receive investors' and regulators' acknowledgement of its sound operation.

In 2015, the Company will, in adhering to the service concept of "customer-centricity" and the business philosophies of "Change as situation does" and "We are here, just for you", fully capitalise on the state-of-the-art internet technologies, especially the increasingly mature mobile internet technology, to launch innovative services and increase service channels, striving to provide better service experience to its customers and create greater value for its investors and our society.

Information communication, internet applications and other emerging technologies will inevitably encourage banks to offer more quality services through platform construction, data exploitation and liquidity operation.

2015

During the reporting period, the Company continued to implement mobile Internet transformation for its credit card business by rolling out CMB Life 5.0 and pioneering with the user-oriented platform system, thereby achieving a successful transformation from a payment tool to an open platform with over 20 million subscribers. During the year, the bank:

- optimised its service channels primarily consisting of the smart "WeChat/Weibo customer service" platform, which brought into reality the "Internet+"-based integrated multi-channel services and improved customer's experience and enhanced its service value.

- improved and launched the "online application + offline verification" project across the Bank to boost the cross-sales across the retail system of the Bank.

- received the "Best Mobile Banking Technology Achievement Award" and "Most Innovative Mobile Internet Financial Products" award for its CMB Life App.

- continued to build the multi-level and multi-dimensional credit card product system by rolling out co-branded credit cards such as mobile Internet-based Hearthstone, Menghuanxiyou and Momo, as well as Diamond Credit Card tailored for high-end customers and All-Currencies MasterCard tailored for customers who have overseas spending needs, with a view to actively secure high-value customers through product innovation.

In 2015, the Bank, adhering to the customer-centric service concept of "We are here, just for you", vigorously promoted the deployment and innovation of Internet finance by utilising mobile Internet concept and focusing on diverse cross-industry cooperation, and diligently studied and explored new business models in payment and settlement, consumer finance, mobile banking, direct banking and credit verification service.

As for improving customer experience, the Bank proactively made innovations based on the perspectives of Internet, mobile handsets and scenarios and launched various new functions including "visual counters" and "cash withdrawal via face-scanning", thus offering more convenient and efficient services to its customers.

Our open mobile finance platform has served a sizable number of users, the APPs of Mobile Banking and CMB Life (掌上生活) were both upgraded to the next generation, and the registered members and transaction volume of Small Business E Home continued to surge.

During the reporting period, the Company continued to establish the "light" operation platform to develop its mobile phone-based retail business, thereby effectively raising the e-bank channel replacement ratio. As at the end of the reporting period, the overall counter replacement ratio in respect of retail e-banking channels reached 97.32%, representing an increase of 1.94 percentage points over the previous year. Visual electronic counters played a remarkable role in replacement of processing non-cash transactions at outlets, with the replacement ratio of non-cash transactions reaching 20.48%.

2016

The Company highly valued infrastructure construction, and followed closely on the latest developments and innovative applications of new technologies with a continued investment in infrastructure in areas including mobile technology, Cloud Computing, Big Data and artificial intelligence.

While continuing to increase resource investment in retail business and maintaining reasonable outlet and staff allocation, we will also vigorously explore and promote financial technologies so as to overcome the limits of linear growth pattern and create a new business model for retail business of the commercial banks in a speedy manner.

Many innovative products and services of the Company, such as "All-in-one Card", a multi-function debit card, "All-in-one Net", a comprehensive online banking service platform, credit cards, the "Sunflower Wealth Management" services and private banking services, Mobile Banking and CMB Life App, global cash management, bills business, offshore finance and other transaction banking services, as well as asset management, asset custody, investment banking and other services, have been widely recognised by consumers in China.

Focusing on the strategy of "prioritising the development of mobile phone applications", we have launched Mobile Bank 5.0, first put Machine Gene Investment into operation, integrated the W+ platform, the smart marketing system and the personalised recommendation system for mobile phones, and preliminarily designed the branch "O2O" service processes focusing on mobile phone applications. As at the end of the reporting period, the total number of corporate online banking customers increased by 32.75% as compared with the end of the previous year.

In respect of retail finance, the Company adhered to the strategy of "prioritising the development of mobile phone applications" while constantly migrating its customer service interfaces to mobile phones and encouraging innovation in its mobile-based products and business models. During the reporting period, with the launch of "Mobile Banking 5.0" and "Machine Gene Investment", our mobile application CMB Life was continuously improved, aiming to provide personalized and intelligent customer service which enables more agreeable and friendly customer interaction with the biological identification technology.

The total number of registered users of our mobile user application "CMB life" topped 31.49 million, with 30.21 million active users each year.

We continued to innovate customer service models with mobile internet technologies. Relying on the online banking platform of the Company, the mobile cheque service extends and expands its application scenarios in corporate business and creates a new business ecosystem for payment and settlement through mobile payment. Such business developed rapidly in 2016 with 5.88 million effective transactions and accumulated transaction volume exceeding RMB 306.2 billion.

In 2016, the Company further enhanced the efficiency of its relationship managers and the customers' experience through further consolidating its mobile internet platform and setting up a PAD-based platform for retail loans, resulting in a rapid growth of its retail loan business.

The personal mobile banking business of the Company continued to maintain rapid growth in 2016 as mobile banking customers were increasingly active with an aggregate of 2.185 billion logins in the Bank's mobile banking application, making it the most dynamic e-channel for customers of the Company. As at 31 December 2016, the aggregate number of downloads of the Bank's mobile banking application reached 96,633,400 and the aggregate number of customers who downloaded the application reached 41,519,200, of which 25,779,200 users were active customers during the year.

Meanwhile, the number of mobile banking transactions and volume of mobile payments increased rapidly. In 2016, the total cumulative number of mobile banking transactions amounted to 4.569 billion, up by 80.95% as compared with the previous year; and the cumulative transaction amount reached RMB 14.17 trillion, up by 54.02% as compared with the previous year. Of which, the number of mobile banking transactions was 735 million, up by 37.38% as compared with the previous year; and the amount of mobile banking transactions was RMB 12.10 trillion, up by 51.25% as compared with the previous year; the number of mobile payment transactions was 3.834 billion, up by 92.66% as compared with the previous year; and the amount of mobile payment transactions was RMB 2.07 trillion, up by 72.50% as compared with the previous year.

During the reporting period, the Company proactively focused on mobile internet, vigorously built the light-operation platform designed to develop its mobile phone-based retail business, and successively launched the CMB APP5.0, with core concepts such as intellectualisation, integrated services and financial real-time interconnection, and launched new versions for four major channels of "Mine", "Reference", "Wealth Management", "Homepage", and also launched four new features of Machine Gene Investment, Revenue and Expenses Records (收支記錄), Income Report and Biometrics, and completed optimisation for 121 major items, thus starting a new era of intelligent finance management. In addition, the Company continued to improve the diversified multi-facet light-operation intelligent service model, optimise and upgrade its "WeChat Banking", and the number of users has currently reached 11.2166 million.

As for the retail online banking business, as at 31 December 2016, the number of active users of the retail online banking professional edition of the Company reached 19,710,400. In 2016, the total cumulative number of online retail finance transactions was 1.541 billion, representing an increase of 33.77% as compared with the previous year; the accumulated transaction amount reached RMB 31.14 trillion, representing an increase of 2.00% as compared with the previous year.

With respect to product R&D, the Company had software development centers in Shenzhen and Hangzhou, mainly focusing on self-development; the Company completed more than 4,000 projects during the year, including launching APP5.0 mobile banking, and the Company utilised the biometrics and Big Data technologies to bring new experiences of natural interaction and intelligent service between the Company and customers; the Company also launched an intelligent investment and advisory services "Machine Gene Investment", whose technology had a leading position in the industry. While in the credit card field, the Company launched products such as Apple Pay and others, and commenced to layout the NFC mobile payment.

2017

We were determined to seize the opportunities arising from the commercial applications of 5G technology, and to develop Internet supply chain financial services by way of embedding into the industry chain. The services of CMB will be available wherever the customers are.

By closely focusing on customer needs and in-depth integration of technologies and businesses, we used technology agility to drive business agility and created the best customer experience.

We know that technology is, after all, just tools and means, and that customers are the origin for all business philosophy. In the past, we competed with our competitors. In the future, we need to catch up with our customers. Therefore, during the strategic period of the new era, we further put forward the objective of "building the bank with best customer experience", regarded customer experience as our guiding star, and focused on enhancing customer experience as the principle of all works.

Centering on the theme of "enhancing customer experience", we are fully committed to the changes of financial technology from 2018 onwards.

In 2018, focusing on improving customer experience and leveraging the monthly number of active users of its two major APPs, namely CMB APP and CMB Life APP, the Company will remove obstacles and concentrate its effort on the innovation and operation of financial technology so as to strive for the "double agility" of business and technology.

"Qian Ying Zhan Yi" is a strategic brand of the Company to serve the emerging small- and medium-sized innovative technology enterprises. The Company continued to explore for target customers through a carefully-compiled list. During the reporting period, the Company continued to step up its effort to expand the customer base under "Qian Ying Zhan Yi", and to innovate finance products specific for technology enterprises by launching "Gao Xin Dai" and other products.

In December 2017, the Company successfully settled the world's first Blockchain-based cross-border interbank RMB clearing deal, through leveraging the industry's first open interbank clearing platform based on the Blockchain technology.

Online Corporate Banking: during the reporting period, the Company innovated and launched U-Bank X, the tenth generation online corporate banking platform, making full use of new technologies in the Fintech field to create open and intelligent Internet services, omni-channel and scenario-based payment and settlement products. In addition, the Company took the lead in the application of Blockchain technology to reshape global cash management, innovatively supported enterprises to build their industrial Internet ecosystem with Big Data, and launched various featured products and services including smart "Little U" robot, mobile payment and forward mobile check.

Corporate Mobile Banking APP: as at 31 December 2017, the number of the Company's enterprise mobile banking users reached 401,600, representing a growth of 73.85% as compared with the end of the previous year; the number of yearly active customers was 224,600; the number of transactions was 17.8950 million, a year-on-year growth of 204.17%; the amount of transactions reached RMB 1,051.968 billion, a year-on-year growth of 243.53%.

In 2017, in a market environment where complicated and volatile situations overlap with relentless challenges, the Company adhered to the development strategy of "Light-operation Bank", "focused on advantages and extended the depth", returned to the fundamentals of business and customers, increased its investment in Fintech, and maintained its development in mobile technology, Big Data, Artificial Intelligence and other fields of infrastructure.

The Company implemented the strategy of "mobile priority", recording more than 45 million active users per month of our retail APPs. The Company actively pushed forward the switching from bank cards to mobile APP for our retail services. Its mobile APPs introduced a new business mode of "outlet + APP + scenario", thereby establishing an integrated online and offline customer management mechanism. From offering customised services on the frontline to implementing automated and intelligent backstage operating procedures, CMB's mobile APPs further enhanced its customers' experience in our retail services. Striving to "become the top APP in consumer finance services", our mobile CMB Life APP continued to promote innovation in mobile consumer finance products, and enhanced the capability in data traffic operations and value output. By encouraging our customers to use our mobile APPs so as to increase the data traffic, the number of active users of our two major APPs reached 45.09 million per month. 40.35% of our cardholders have already switched to mobile banking, while 81% of transactions were carried out on our mobile platform.

On such basis, the Company built an intelligence-oriented marketing tool for active marketing and passive marketing, offering real-time recommendations to mobile customers and relationship managers. There were 97 recommendation tags in our mobile APP, offering 7,132 customised product portfolios and recommendations to 130 million persons per day on average.

During the reporting period, leveraging on its excellent services and innovations in Fintech, the Company received various awards for its credit card business, including the "Best Experience of Mobile Social Media", a technological innovation award awarded by *The Asian Banker* and the "Top Brand in China Brand Index–Credit Card Category" awarded by Chnbrand, a Chinese brand rating and brand advisory institution.

By focusing on mobile Fintech innovations, the Company took "building the best consumer finance APP" as its core objective and fully enhanced the operational capability of CMB Life APP.

Thanks to its continuous efforts to consolidate the "C+ Cash Settlement Solution" brand, the Company recorded 261,100 newly opened accounts and 810,800 newly issued "All-in-one Cards for Company (公司一卡通)". The annual amount of transactions through mobile checks amounted to RMB 1.05 trillion. The basic cash management business experienced a healthy growth.

CMB APP:

The personal mobile banking business of the Company maintained a rapid growth in 2017 with a more active mobile banking user population, and had amassed 3.228 billion logins to its mobile banking application during the reporting period, making it the most dynamic e-channel of the Company. As at 31 December 2017, the total number of CMB APP users in aggregate was 55,793,400, with 40,571,400 annual active users and 26,186,700 monthly active users, and an average monthly login of 12.77 per user, and a closer bond was forged between CMB APP and its users. Meanwhile, the CMB APP transaction volume has been increasing rapidly, with 1.032 billion APP transactions and a total transaction amount of RMB17.87 trillion in 2017, up by 40.41% and 47.69% respectively, as compared with the corresponding period of the previous year. Among all these transactions, a total of 26,457,600 transactions belong to wealth management transactions originated by 3,227,700 wealth management customers, representing a year-on-year increase of 132.32% and accounting for 61.70% of the Bank's total number of wealth management transactions and a total wealth management sales value of RMB4.43 trillion, representing a year-on-year increase of 90.13%, and comprised 43.17% of the overall Bank's wealth management sales. China Merchants Bank made great headways in its mobilisation, and CMB APP has become an important front of retail operations.

During the reporting period, the Company put the development mobile service as its priority and continued to create and upgrade the CMB APP-based mobile financial services platform by launching CMB APP 6.0 to achieve significant progress in intelligent wealth management, providing specialty customer products that include wealth management channels, smart service, "Flash Loan" and "Wealth Check-up", thus building up a smart personal financial assistant that fosters new breakthroughs in terms of smart service, connectivity and interaction, that would enhance core competencies in a more institutionalised retail regime.

In 2017, the Company had successfully launched the 6.0 version of its CMB Life APP to satisfy demands on the consumption value chain over all scenarios and entire life-cycle with the whole range of its e-series loan products, coupled with Fintech solutions such as the intelligent recommendation engine "e-Zhi Dai" to hasten advancement in mobile consumer financial products innovation, and to enhance traffic flow and value output in order to achieve inclusive and intelligent consumer financial products. During the reporting period, users operation on top of CMB Life APP had seen major upgrade through effective utilisation of Fintech to develop a credit card customers' operational regime that facilitates new financial services, ease of payment and effective risk control and service guideline. As at the end of the reporting period, the total number of users on the CMB Life APP platform reached 47.4379 million. Total number of active users comprises 45.0105 million per annum, and 27.3257 million per month.

Emphasising mobile priority and data priority, the Company released CMB APP 6.0, so as to consolidate an "outlet + APP + scenario" model, and to enrich the content within this life-cycle. Marketing-oriented transformation is realised in visual counters; the enterprise online banking service was upgraded as U-Bank X, to provide an open and intelligent online banking service.

2018

The Company will strive to combine "experience" with "technology", build a leading digitised innovative bank and an excellent wealth management bank, and form a new model for retail banking service in the Internet era.

As many a little makes a mickle, in 2018, the digital banking transformation moved forward in a progressive manner, from products to systems, and from businesses to organisational culture. We firmly adhered to the strategy of "mobile priority", and significantly improved the capabilities of platform empowerment, digital operation and providing digital services; we expedited the internal establishment and outward expansion of scenarios, and stepped up the construction of an ecological customer service system; we increased investment in technology infrastructure so as to promote business agility by means of technology agility.

Therefore, we will re-examine all aspects of the operation and management of the bank by focusing on customer experience and leveraging on Fintech, and fully commence the digital transformation.

In 2019, the Company will continue to use MAU as the North Star Metric and implement the "mobile priority" development strategy. By focusing on building the capability of acquiring mass customers at low cost and the capacity of digital operation, the Company will fully exploit the potential value of customers and technology, so as to forge the new growth engines for the future.

In order to adapt to the rapid development of technology-based finance, the Company took the initiative for its retail finance business to get out of the comfort zone of traditional business and formally moved towards the retail finance 3.0 Era, so as to embrace the evolution of service ecosystem through digital transformation of its operating organisations. In 2018, under the guidance of the "Mobile Priority" strategy and "MAU North Star Metric", the Company constantly empowered the retail finance by enhancing the functions of the digital platforms, which optimised the platform system, product system and service system towards a coverage of "full-customer, full-product and full-channel", further improved the customer classification operation based on the existing segmentation-based customer management and continually consolidated its retail customer foundation. While maintaining the systemic competitive edges of core retail businesses such as wealth management, private banking, credit card, retail loan, consumer finance and e-banking, the Company has vigorously marched towards the "APP Era".

The construction of the digital platform was gradually deepened. The two major APPs became the main platforms for customer operations. The percentage of debit card customers acquired through online channels reached 17.89%, while the percentage of credit card customers acquired through data reached 61.21%.

The number of customers of online bills discounted business reached 9,110, of which small and medium-sized enterprises accounted for 88.44%, and the digitalised inclusive finance services capability continued to improve.

There was steady progress in the development of the Company into the bank that offers the best customer experience. The two major retail APPs have established a quantifiable user experience monitoring system and a rigorous feedback mechanism. A dedicated user experience team and a corporate Fintech experience center have been established for the wholesale business line. The new outlet 3.0 was debuted to present new digital experience for customers.

Firstly, we will adhere to the target of transformation towards retail digitalisation to create a bank with the best customer experience. Our retail business will continue to be oriented by the monthly active users (MAU) in order to solve the two major problems of acquiring a large number of customers at low cost and developing our digitised operational capabilities. We will focus on improving operational capabilities and promote the formation of a virtuous cycle of business operation and customer acquisition.

By further promoting retail digital transformation, focusing on key areas, and strengthening scenario expansion, the Company will promote the rapid growth of MAU, strengthen its own customer acquisition capacity, and tamp solid foundation for the growth of retail non-interest income business.

During the reporting period, the Company continued to focus on upgrading mobile service capabilities with a customer-oriented vision, CMB Life APP as the platform and technology as impetus, while focusing on high-frequency daily consumption scenarios and creating quality life so as to lead the transformation of the credit card industry. As at the end of the reporting period, the total number of CMB Life APP users was 70,027,300, of which non-credit card users accounted for 24.38%.

As at the end of the reporting period, the Company gained a total of 122 million fans through third-party credit card channels (mainly from WeChat, Alipay service window and official QQ account).

The Company continued to develop our smart service portfolio: promoting an upgrade of AI technology-driven smart services, introducing a new interactive form and AI core; launching the service traffic oriented decision engine, speeding up the efficiency of two-way coordination between intelligent robots and service specialists; achieving an innovative full-service coverage from traditional channels, third-party service channels to emerging service channels through the application of a leading voiceprint recognition system, an audio Big Data analysis platform, intelligent service robots and smart speaker service admission, so as to accelerate the formation of the APP service ecological closed loop and improve the integrated online service experience.

DBS

DBS caught my attention with its regular awards for innovation as a digital bank. I also attended the launch of digibank, its digital-first bank without branches in Indonesia, and was impressed with the commitment and understanding of digital banking amongst the management team. However, I regularly get pushback from colleagues in Asia who claim that the bank is still very traditional and has not converted to be truly digital. I would accept this if it were not for the figures—its market share and brand has risen dramatically over the last decade—and the fact that the bank is succeeding on a number of different metrics.

After all, if JPMorgan Chase's investment analysts pick out DBS as a global digital bank leader, there must be something behind it.

"In our 2018 Stockpicker's Guide, we put forth a view that most regional banks were not prepared for the massive disruption that lies ahead in the bank industry. While we had been previously focused, however, on where regional banks stacked against mega banks, we have now expanded our scope to look at banks outside of the US. What we found was that although some investors may look at the very large technology spend at several US mega banks and feel comforted that these banks are staying ahead of the curve, we see disruption within the banking sector as actually playing out on a global stage, with a significant threat coming from mega banks overseas. Moreover, with the majority of US banks having outdated core systems that are 30+ years old, as well as having a "fast follower" or, even worse, "wait and see" mentality when it comes to technology, we view it as virtually impossible that most of these banks in the US stand a chance of remaining relevant in the decade ahead. To this end, within this report we take a deep look at how US banks stack up in the global landscape and identify the most disruptive banking technologies in retail and commercial, as well as countries that house the banks that are well ahead of the curve. To this end, our analysis led directly to DBS Bank in Singapore, one of the global digital leaders, which we believe provides a roadmap for regional banks ... as we look across the spectrum of bank technology leaders outside of the US, one bank that truly stands out is Singapore's largest bank, DBS Bank. With DBS having embarked on a digital transformation journey since 2009, the bank has transformed into not only a digital powerhouse in Asia but also arguably one of the world's top digital banks ... the conclusion of our analysis is that the reason many regional banks are at risk of falling behind the technology curve has less to do with the fact that they can't spend on par with the mega banks, but rather much more to do with a philosophy to respond to threats from disruption rather than drive it."

– Quote extracted from the JPMorgan Chase equities research paper titled "U.S. Mid- and Small-Cap Banks Worldwide Technology Report," December 2018.

Here are a few highlights from its annual reports to give further background:

2013
Technology has transformed the way we think about banking. As customer interaction shifts from physical branches to the online and mobile space, banks need to develop new ways of engaging customers. The engagement goes beyond products and services to relationships and insights.

Harnessing analytics and Big Data is key to building this engagement. DBS has been using voice analytics at our customer call centre to improve customer satisfaction. Customer touchpoints such as ATMs, which were merely output channels previously, are now a customer sensor point for us, delivering real-time information that we can use to form a better picture of our customers and their needs. We are tapping on IBM Watson to assist our wealth relationship managers to analyse large volumes of data, so as to provide better quality insights to our customers.

Recognising that new technologies have revolutionised the way people bank, we continued to innovate new ways of banking. Much progress has been made on this front. In Singapore, we launched DBS Home Connect, an app designed to make the home-buying process easier for our customers by providing them with all the essential information they require 24 x 7 via their mobile devices. In the corporate banking space, we pioneered the launch of a fully automated online account opening service for companies. In 2014, we announced an agreement with IBM in which we will deploy its Watson cognitive computing innovation to deliver a next-generation customer experience. We are also collaborating with research agency A*STAR to set up a joint lab to research emerging technologies for the benefit of customers.

Our efforts to be at the forefront of banking innovation have been recognised. In 2013, our mobile banking apps strategy was ranked #1 in the world by Swiss research firm MyPrivateBanking. We were named "Most Innovative Transaction Bank in Asia-Pacific" by The Banker magazine, and "Trailblazer of the Year in Asia-Pacific" by Banking & Payments Asia. To step up our game in the innovation space, we recently announced plans to invest SGD 200 million over the next three years to better harness digital technologies. This will enable us to access large retail banking markets and better integrate banking into our customers' lifestyle. A new digital banking organisation has been created to spearhead this transformation.

We enhanced our online infrastructure as part of efforts to make continuous improvements to customer experience and reach. DealOnline, our full-fledged online treasury platform, offers auto price streaming and auto-dealing in spot foreign exchange, swap, forward and non-deliverable forward contracts. The platform offers corporate and financial institution customers flexibility to conduct a range of banking activities and services with a secure login. In Singapore, 2,000 SMEs have also signed up.

Corporate customers are able to enquire, book their foreign exchange and manage their cash and trade transactions over a highly customisable dashboard, receive real-time updates via email and SMS on all banking activities and always stay informed. With the same platform, corporate customers can utilise their foreign currencies for either remittance or trade financing purposes. DealOnline also offers individual customers in Hong Kong a 24-hour foreign exchange pricing engine.

2014

DBS has been pursuing a strong innovation agenda, driven by a desire to shape the future of banking. We recognise that with changing customer behaviours, rising smart device and social media usage as well as the encroachment into the payments space by non-bank players, the way banking is done is fast changing. In 2014, we announced plans to invest SGD 200 million over three years to better harness digital technologies. This is on top of the SGD 1 billion we have invested in strategic technology initiatives.

Among our cutting-edge initiatives is a partnership with IBM that makes us among the first in the world to use artificial intelligence to provide contextualised and customised wealth advice to high net worth clients. This is currently being piloted in the bank for rollout in 2015. A partnership with Singapore research agency A*STAR to explore emerging technologies that will simplify the lives of customers is also progressing well.

In May 2014, we launched DBS PayLah!. This app allows our customers to transfer funds to others via their mobile phone with a few simple taps, just by knowing the payee's mobile number. Since its launch, we now have more than 200,000 registered users, helping to facilitate over 60,000 payment transactions every month.

To make it easy for owners of small and medium enterprises (SMEs) to open business accounts with the bank, we launched a first-of-its-kind capability that would allow them to do this online. This significantly cuts down the time needed to start a relationship with DBS. During the year, we also rolled out DBS BusinessClass, an app which offers start-ups and SMEs valuable resources, including a unique platform through which they can consult and connect with industry experts, investors and fellow entrepreneurs. Our mobile banking apps strategy was ranked #1 in the world by Swiss research firm MyPrivateBanking for the second year running.

Using technology to enhance the customer experience

The number of customers using our internet and mobile banking platforms increased to more than 2.7 million and 1 million respectively, with over 24 million internet and 11 million mobile transactions on average each month. Our digital channels are increasingly becoming the preferred channel for our customers to transact, engage and buy products and services from us, especially as we continue to advance the use of analytics to provide our customers with the most relevant offers at the most relevant time.

In Singapore, we launched an SMS banking service that allowed customers to carry out banking transactions such as checking account balances or paying credit card bills even if they did not have internet access. This freed up as much as 15,000 hours of automated teller machine (ATM) usage time every month for customers to perform other transactions on ATMs.

In addition, we rolled out mobile banking across China, Taiwan and India in Q4 2014, and are already seeing significant customer sign-ups and activity. In China, we were the first foreign bank to launch online unit trust trading services, with customers now able to subscribe for, redeem, switch and transact unit trusts online.

We also expanded our overseas remittance service that provides same-day fund transfers at low costs. Previously available for India and Indonesia, it now includes Hong Kong and the Philippines. With greater convenience and attractive fees, the number of remittances doubled over the previous year.

In Singapore and Taiwan, we have provided our relationship managers (RMs) with tablets that come with specially designed apps such as "Your Financial Profile". This has not only improved RM mobility, enabling our RMs to serve customers at the place of their choosing, it has also significantly improved the quality of our conversations with customers and the overall customer experience.

In Hong Kong, we launched a tablet version of "mobile loan centre" to provide customers with the flexibility to apply for a loan online, via mobile or tablet. The online loan centre was recognised as "Asia's Best Mobile Banking" service in the IDC Financial Insights Innovation Award 2014.

2015

New digital technologies (mobile, social, Big Data) are powerful tools available to banks today. But we are not enamoured with technology for its own sake. Instead, we are focused on how we can create joyful banking experiences for customers. To do this, we place ourselves in their shoes, focus on their needs and ensure we know what the real "customer job to be done" is. We look at their journey with us from beginning to end, and apply human-centred design to develop relevant solutions. We believe that embedding ourselves in the customer journey and embracing digital form a potent combination that will make banking increasingly simple and seamless.

Today, retail, wealth and corporate customers can open accounts with us through their mobile devices, anytime, anyplace. We are digitalising our customer onboarding processes to be simple and intuitive, by simplifying forms, pre-populating fields on behalf of customers, and automating the entire process so that starting a bank relationship can be done almost instantaneously.

The strategy is paying off and we are increasingly acquiring new customers digitally in SME, credit card and unsecured banking. Even in private banking, which is a high-touch business, the digital option has been well-received. In 2015, 16% of new wealth customers opened accounts with us digitally. 51% of SME customers in Singapore did the same through our Online Account Opening Service. Online account opening saves them significant time, with the process now taking 15 minutes compared to the industry average of one or two hours.

We are investing in capabilities to simplify day-to-day banking. We are redesigning our operations to drive straight-through processing and instant fulfilment for customers. This also results in lower costs for us. Simplifying day-to-day banking for customers is an ongoing journey, but we are already seeing success with some of our recent initiatives. For example, with DBS Remit, customers can instantly send funds across markets while on the go. This service has gained popularity and, today, over 90% of remittances are done digitally. With DBS PayLah!, customers are able to make payments to friends and merchants easily with a few simple clicks on the phone. Our digital services allow customers to get instant approval for credit cards or receive an unsecured loan approval on-the-spot. In a first-of-its-kind service, SME owners are also able to apply for up to 11 types of loan products with no signatures required. They track the application in real time and obtain instant notifications on the progress of their loan application.

We seek to seamlessly integrate banking into our customers' everyday lives so that banking becomes simpler, and they have more time to spend on people or things they care about. With the DBS HomeConnect app, we engage customers during their house hunting process, giving them information such as the last transacted price, rentals and the nearest amenities, on their phones. The app contains a loan calculator to help customers work out the financing required. They can also contact a DBS loan specialist via the app. SMEs in Singapore are able to access an online business community through our DBS BusinessClass app. The app connects them to 15,000 members and the brightest business minds in Asia. It also links them with tech start-ups to facilitate the adoption of new technologies to enhance productivity. We are currently regionalising the app to facilitate cross-border connections and support mass-scale virtual events.

As the pace of digital adaptation increases, we are sparing no effort to deliver world-class digital capabilities to our customers. We are upping the ante on not just the breadth of our digital offerings, but also on the holistic customers' experience as they use our platforms. For example, we are one of the first banks in the region to build in-house design and user experience capabilities, which we incorporate as an integral part of our digital offerings.

We continue to see strong growth in our online and mobile banking customers. In Singapore, we have the largest base of online banking customers with over 2.5 million iBanking users and 1.25 million mBanking users. Our mobile activity continued to lead the industry in Singapore and mobile accounted for over 60% of our daily logins of over 400,000. Close to 70% of financial transactions took place through digital channels, across the region. We launched digital account opening for new customers. This breakthrough initiative means new-to-bank customers can open accounts at their convenience, without having to visit a branch. We accelerated our digital acquisition initiative. In Singapore, almost 38% of credit card customers came through digitally, from 27% in the previous year. We also revamped our equity trading capabilities to deliver a more user-friendly trading experience for customers in Singapore and Hong Kong.

2016	
Figure 7.3 What makes DBS the World's Best Digital Bank?	
Reimagine Banking **World's Best Digital Bank**	**What makes DBS the World's Best Digital Bank?** **It starts with reimagining banking.** From Singapore's favourite mobile wallet to India's first paperless, branchless, signatureless mobile-only bank. A first-in-its-class social network for SMEs to hackathons across Asia and fintech internships in DBS These are just some of the reasons we have been recognised as the World's Best Digital Bank. Our digital transformation pervades every part of the bank. We are driven by one relentless purpose, which is to live and breathe innovation to Make Banking Joyful.

Since 2009, DBS has executed well against strategy, doubling both top-line and bottom line. Many of our regional priorities including becoming a leading regional wealth and transaction banking player, as well as growing outside Singapore, remain relevant and continue to have a lot of headroom. At the same time, we have also been making progress in driving a digital agenda. Our vision in the next phase of growth is to "Make Banking Joyful". We seek to act like a 22,000-person start-up, able to respond and innovate quickly to deliver simple, fast and contextual banking in the digital age.

To be truly digital involves a complete transformation of the bank. This goes beyond customer interfaces, such as digital apps or mobile/Internet banking on the front end. Much of the heavy lifting is at the back end, where the bank has spent the past few years re-architecting our technology infrastructure. Today, we have a common platform of services and APIs which enables us to integrate best-in-breed technologies, allowing us to move faster on the front end. As we move forward, we aim to adopt the practices of global technology companies known for their ability to constantly experiment, automatically scale and rapidly bring new features to market. Like them, the bank is embracing microservices and cloud technology.

Having invested time and resources in digitalising the bank, we have seen visible results in a number of areas:

- **Expanded customer reach and acquisition**. In 2016, 25% of wealth customers and more than 60% of Singapore SME customers were acquired via digital channels. In India, DBS launched digibank, the country's first mobile-only bank, a groundbreaking proposition, to penetrate the retail banking segment. The bank has acquired more than 840,000 digibank customers in just 10 months.

- **Efficiency of the bank**. Our cost-income ratio improved two percentage points to 43%, due in part to improved productivity arising from digitalisation initiatives. In particular, fewer manual processes have enabled the bank to support higher business volumes with the same level of resources. For example, digibank India uses one-fifth of the resources required in a traditional bank set-up.

- **Harnessing the power of analytics**. We have leveraged analytics for various purposes; for example, providing contextual offers and advice to customers, reducing ATM downtime, predicting and preventing trade fraud, and lowering employee attrition. DBS' digital transformation has won us external validation not just in Asia but globally—DBS was named World's Best Digital Bank by *Euromoney* and recognised as being best in the world for digital distribution at the Efma Accenture Innovation Awards.

The cost-income ratio improved from 45% to 43% as we yielded faster productivity gains from digitalisation and strategic cost management. There was strong growth in the digital acquisition of customers at lower unit costs. We also drove more transactions and execution towards digital channels, which had lower cost to serve compared to traditional channels. We had higher straight-through processing, which reduced or eliminated the amount of manual inputs and paperwork for an increasing number of mid- and back-office functions. This enabled us to process higher business volumes with fewer resources, improving operating leverage as additional income earned flowed to the bottom line.

2017

Being truly digital involves a complete transformation of the bank, from front to back end. To be successful, we have to invest in people and skills differently, re-architect our technology infrastructure in the back end to be cloud-native, have systems and ways of working that shorten the release times.

Digitalisation was a major factor for the growth of our customer franchise during the year. There are two principal reasons how digitalisation boosts operating performance. First, it lowers the costs of signing up customers and serving them—the marginal cost of transacting over digital platforms is significantly lower than for traditional methods where relationship managers or sales people are needed. Second, the convenience, ease of use and instant completion of transactions that digital platforms offer improve customer engagement. As a result, customers transact multiple times more than non-digital customers, giving us a higher share of wallet across all products. The higher level of engagement also results in consistently faster income growth for digital customers over time.

In the consumer and SME businesses in Singapore and Hong Kong, where the impact of digitalisation is most visible, digital customers formed 42% of the base in 2017 but accounted for a larger 63% of total income and 72% of profit before allowances. The return on equity (ROE) of digitally engaged customers was 27%, a significant nine percentage points higher than for traditional customers.

We believe we are the only bank to have developed a methodology for measuring the financial value created by digitalisation. And because one can manage only what one measures, we have been able to draw up an effective business plan to drive digital behaviour among customers. The intent is to make it easy for customers to sign up and transact with us online. The proportion of customers that are digital has risen nine percentage points since 2015 to 42% today, contributing to the improvement in the group's cost-income ratio.

Banks often tout operating metrics to demonstrate the progress of their digitalisation efforts. However, the impact on earnings is unclear. We believe we are the first bank to have developed a methodology, which has been tested over three years, to measure the financial impact of digitalisation. We intend to provide updates to the financial data annually.

Our profit and loss measurement is for the consumer and SME businesses in Singapore and Hong Kong, where the impact of digitalisation is most clearly visible. The businesses currently account for 44% of the group and could rise to half in five years.

Customers in these businesses are delineated into two segments—digital and traditional—based on how they interact with us. Digital customers are those who have used digital channels to either purchase a product or upgrade to a higher customer segment; or carry out more than half of their financial transactions; or carry out more than half of non-financial transactions over a 12-month period. Those that do not continue to do so revert to being classified as traditional.

Digital customers made up 42% of the total base in 2017 but contributed 63% of income and 72% of profit before allowances. Since 2015, income from these customers has also grown at a compounded annual growth rate (CAGR) of 27% compared to a 4% decline for traditional ones. Digital customers gave us an ROE(5) of 27% in 2017, nine percentage points ahead of the traditional segment.

There are two reasons for the superior financial metrics of digitalisation. First, the costs of acquiring and serving customers are lower each time digital channels are used. As customers increasingly adopt digital behaviours, we are able to reduce reliance on physical infrastructure such as branches to support customers. This will enable us to optimise enterprise costs over time. All these mean that more of the income earned from customers contributes directly to the bottom line.

Second, digital consumer and SME customers bring twice as much income per head than their traditional peers. This is because digitalisation improves customer engagement, translating into a higher share of wallet. The deeper relationship is broad-based across multiple products and has been consistently so over the years.

We also found that when traditional customers adopted digital behaviours, they would become more engaged and transact more with us. This provided corroborating evidence that digitalisation increases the stickiness of customer relationships.

2018

Being truly digital involves a complete transformation of the bank, from front to back end, to enable us to be nimbler and faster to market. To be successful, we have to re-architect our technology infrastructure in the back end to be cloud-native, enable scalability through ecosystem partnerships, improve business/technology co-working and maximise the use of data. Good progress has been made. In 2017, 66% of our open systems were cloud-ready—as at the end of 2018, this had risen to over 80%. Our cloud-native applications have nearly doubled to more than 60. Through increased automation, our release cadence of new applications in the market has improved by close to 10 times, enabling us to constantly learn, test and iterate in much the same way that large technology companies do.

In 2017, we launched the world's largest API platform for a bank. Over the year, we continued to enhance this platform, and now have over 350 APIs, enabling third-party brands to integrate our technologies to make banking simpler. This has allowed us to accelerate our ecosystems agenda. With the pervasiveness of digital, tech is business and business is tech. Recognising this, we no longer view technology as a support function. Instead, we have organised ourselves such that business and technology teams are now co-drivers in 33 platforms, and work together to deliver on shared goals and key performance indicators. On the data front, we have established an analytics centre of excellence, trained over 10,000 of our people on a data-driven curriculum, and developed a framework on responsible data usage.

DBS has shown the power of being articulate about digital banking and the bank has long since entrenched an entrepreneurial, tech-led culture which pervades every business line and every level of seniority.

We have been named "World's Best Digital Bank" twice in the past three years, so we have done a few things right! Perhaps our most important achievement has been in recognising that a digital transformation requires both hardware and heartware to change technology a well as culture.

Our technology journey actually began in 2009, when we upped our investment in technology to create resilience and standardisation. We upgraded our networks, moved to active-active systems and put in a common application stack across most of our countries and products. By 2014, we were ready for the next great leap by re-architecting our systems to be cloud ready in respect of both hardware and software. Five years on, while we are far from done, I do feel that we have made very significant progress.

The increasing digitalisation of our consumer and SME businesses in Singapore and Hong Kong has progressively improved our cost-income ratio since 2015, when the fruits of our efforts began to be felt in earnest. Digital customers grew from 33% of the base in 2015 to 48% in 2018. Because they have a significantly lower cost-income ratio of 34% than the 54% for traditional customers, the rising proportion of digital customers has lowered the cost-income ratio of these businesses by one percentage point a year when distortions caused by net interest margin changes are neutralised. Since these businesses account for almost half of the group, digitalisation has structurally lowered the group's cost-income ratio by half a percentage point a year.

Our relentless focus on digitalisation is driven by the desire to make banking invisible so that our customers can enjoy a lot more of their lives, with a lot less hassle. We developed multiple ecosystem partnerships to enable customers to seamlessly fulfill their needs. To this end, we have signed strategic partnerships with leading industry players such as Gojek, Carousell, SISTIC and BigBasket.

In Singapore, we have launched marketplaces on our website with listings of cars, properties and electricity retailers. We also introduced an InstaRewards feature within the DBS Lifestyle app so customers can offset purchases with their DBS Rewards points. DBS PayLah! remains Singapore's leading mobile wallet with more than one million accounts and has integrated partners such as Golden Village, Chubb and Chope into its platform. We became one of the first in Singapore to enable seamless online multi-currency settlement. We introduced online fund investment capabilities, so customers can purchase and redeem funds, and be matched to funds and unit trusts suitable for their risk-profile. DBS Remit, which offers same-day free transfers to 47 countries, recorded solid growth in Singapore and was also launched in Hong Kong.

We made a foray into chat banking with Foodster—Southeast Asia's first bank-led retail chatbot. Launched in partnership with startup Every Botty, Foodster allows customers to order and pay for their meals seamlessly via Facebook Messenger and DBS payment channels. In Hong Kong, we launched a ground-breaking card onboarding journey. Customers can get a credit card approved, and start using it from their mobile phone in minutes, as well as get access to DBS Omni, our credit card companion app. In Taiwan, we launched the DBS Card+ app and acquired more than 200,000 users. We enhanced our digital onboarding capabilities, allowing customers to open an account to apply for a credit card online in minutes.

ING

I have known ING well for many years and took particular note of a comment made by ING Direct's then CEO and chairman for the United States, Arkadi Kuhlmann, back in 2008. He stated:

> "We don't hire bankers because bankers come in with their DNA and they have their legacy which won't fit. Instead we hire dancers, musicians and artists. People who can deliver a great and different experience."[66]

I knew this bank was different. The main difference is that ING grew a successful business model globally based on doing banking without branches by being digital first. That model was based on the belief that it could never leverage its domestic banking capabilities overseas if it had to use buildings and humans, and that learning has been key to both its expansion into a global bank brand and its transformation domestically since the global financial crisis in 2008. The management team has realigned and rebuilt the bank, laid off thousands of people and focused on being digital and customer first. The strategy seems to be working.

Figure 7.4 With ING's mascot, logo and emblem ... just lion around

66 Chris Skinner, "ING Direct: Rebels with a Cause," Finanser (blog), 21 November 2008, https://thefinanser.com/2008/11/ing-direct-rebe.html/.

Here are a few highlights from its annual reports to give further background:

2013

Information technology (IT) has vastly transformed the way both the banking and insurance industries interact with their customers. Mobile, particularly in banking, and direct channels in general have become a significant force in distribution. Increasingly, the innovative use of technology will be essential in creating a superior customer experience and will more and more play a leading role in the way ING does business. By continuously investing in innovative technology, developing superior IT skills and putting the customer's interest first in everything we do, ING aims to distinguish itself as a leading financial services company.

At the Bank, ING announced its new IT strategy "Creating value for our customers through six strategic pillars—the power of IT." The strategy is aimed at meeting customer needs such as reliability, security and customer centricity by being agile, efficient and working collaboratively. The new strategy is in line with ING's vision that technology and innovation play a crucial role in the future of ING Bank.

ING aims to further strengthen its ability to replicate applications and reuse solutions across different countries and business units. An example of this was the creation of responsive websites (no matter what device customers use, the content of the site will always fit perfectly on the screen) in several countries, which was developed through sharing knowledge, applications and expertise across countries.

The IT department remains committed to further embedding an agile way of working throughout its whole organisation as a core principle in the way it works, because ING's aim is to respond swiftly and efficiently to changing customer demands. Also, IT will continue to further automate IT processes, where possible. This results in products and services coming to market faster and at lower IT cost.

2014

In the past few years, Retail Banking has been working towards converging its traditional banking model to a digital-first model. Our customers are increasingly self-directed. A digital-first offering allows us to offer transparent products, consistent fair pricing and process excellence at low costs.

Innovations in products and with distribution channels, especially digital, are making banking with ING easier and more accessible. By offering customers easy and transparent products, tools and advice, we aim to empower them to take smarter financial decisions.

The customer—individuals, SMEs and mid-corporations—is at the heart of our retail business. Customers want easy and transparent products, tools and advice to empower them to take smarter financial decisions during their lifetime, such as when buying a house, saving for retirement or for their children's education. We are prominent in innovative distribution via mobile, the internet, call centres and face to face.

'Highlight': Our business transformation programme aims to deliver harmonisation of our client services, standardised products and channels and to improve mobile and online capabilities, substantially enhancing the client experience.

2015

The pace of disruption affecting the banking industry further accelerated in 2015. New business models based on easily accessible, digital services are challenging bank revenue streams. They are focusing not on price leadership but on offering a superior customer experience, confirming that this is the area banks will need to focus on to succeed.

Consumers are rapidly turning to digital services for an increasing number of needs. What they are experiencing with digital leaders is shaping their expectations. In ING's case, nearly 90 percent of retail customers now use digital channels to contact us, and just under 70 percent use them exclusively. This makes it more and more important that digital contact be clear and easy for them, with for example digital onboarding and end-to-end mobile sales processes.

All these developments in the external environment confirm to us that we are on the right track with our strategy to create a differentiating customer experience based on digital leadership.

In 2015 we continued to build on our Think Forward strategy to empower customers and provide them with a differentiating customer experience. That includes a focus on being leaders in the digital customer experience based on easy, 24/7 access, simple products and services and tools to help customers make sound financial decisions.

We also introduced innovative payment services and new functionality to our digital channels that contribute to a differentiating customer experience. In doing so, we build more primary relationships, which allows us to better understand customers and their needs, and provide them with a more-tailored service.

Operating expenses were slightly lower at €6,430 million compared with €6,456 million in 2014, which included €349 million of redundancy provisions, mainly related to the further digitalisation of our banking services in the Netherlands.

2016

In most markets ING offers a full range of retail banking products and services, covering payments, savings, investments, and secured and unsecured lending. ING pursues a digital-first approach, complemented by advice when needed, with omnichannel contact and distribution possibilities.

Retail Banking continued to pursue a digital-first operating model with a clear and easy, anytime- anywhere experience for customers. It also made progress in earning an increased number of primary relationships.

This is our pledge to customers to be Clear and Easy, available Anytime and Anywhere, to Empower and to Keep Getting Better. We do that by striving to be leaders in the digital customer experience based on easy access, simplified products and services, and tools to help customers make smart financial decisions.

We also see that technology is reducing barriers to enter the financial services markets, resulting in a wave of newcomers targeting segments underserved by traditional banks. In addition, new regulations are opening up Europe's payment market to non-banks and we are seeing the development of digital ecosystems that allow users to access social media, online purchases, services and payments all in one app. To keep up with these developments and remain among the leaders in digital banking, we need to offer a customer experience that's instant, personal, frictionless and relevant—one that meets the expectations customers have from their interactions with other leaders in the online digital experience.

We also envisage connecting our customers to solutions offered by third parties. And we will connect our ecosystem to selected digital ecosystems, to be visible and present in the places where customers go when they are online.

In 2016, the bank announced an intention to converge our various banking models into one to create an integrated digital platform that can cater to all our customers' financial needs and provide new and relevant offers to enhance the customer experience. Such a transformation should put our business on a solid footing for the future.

ING is on a path of convergence towards one digital banking platform (and) €787 million related to the intended digital transformation programmes, as announced on ING's Investor Day on 3 October 2016.

2017

Digitalisation is increasing, changing how people interact with service providers and their expectations as customers.

Customers' expectations are being set by the personal, instant, relevant and seamless experience provided by digital platforms like Amazon, Apple, Facebook and Google. These leaders offer access to platforms where customers connect to one another and to businesses and where they spend more and more of their time.

We aim to be the go-to and open platform for all our customers' financial needs, including providing relevant third-party offerings. And a platform that can integrate into other digital ecosystems so we are there for customers and other users wherever they need financial advice and services online.

2018

The future is digital—and mobile-first, with a superior digital experience. Products won't differentiate us—they have become commodities. People, whether consumers or business professionals, are spending more and more time online in the places that provide for a variety of their needs—their digital platforms of choice. For banks, the future is to be present on those platforms or be a platform ourselves. For the latter to be successful, we need a strong brand backed by a solid customer proposition.

To pursue these platform opportunities, we are transforming ING. The goal is to create one global platform providing a uniform, borderless customer experience and one that is easily scalable, so we can grow quickly at low cost. It should be ready for open banking and relevant third-party offerings, capable of interfacing with other digital platforms and support advanced analytics capabilities to turn data insights into benefits for customers.

With digital disruption changing customer expectations we are looking for new ways to be relevant and stand out from the crowd. Looking back on 2018, we continued to empower customers with innovative solutions in many areas, including mobile and digital access, to make banking easier, faster and available anytime and anywhere. With 97 percent of customer contact now digital, and an increasing proportion via mobile devices, we continued to enhance our offerings with innovations like digital advisors and forecasting tools to support a uniform and differentiating experience through customers' channel of choice. We are combining our strengths in our various retail markets and moving towards shared digital banking platforms. We therefore have to find new ways to be relevant to our customers. Open banking offers opportunities here. By partnering with others or developing our own digital platforms, we can offer customers new and complementary services that go beyond banking—and create new revenue streams for ING.

Important milestones were the steps taken towards creating a globally scalable digital platform for customers and further digitalising our offering. We took a majority stake in payments service provider Payvision to expand our offering to business customers in the fast-growing e-commerce segment. And we partnered with insurer AXA to create a digital insurance platform for retail customers in a number of markets that will be accessible via the ING mobile banking app with offerings in the areas of Living, Mobility and Wellness.

JPMORGAN CHASE

JPMorgan Chase came to my attention way back in 2004 when a merger took place with Bank One whose CEO was Jamie Dimon. Dimon became the CEO of the combined group and his first decision was to break a massive outsourcing contract signed with IBM. The reason behind this decision? "We believe managing our own technology infrastructure is best for the long-term growth and success of our company, as well as our shareholders," said Austin Adams, JPMorgan's then CIO,[67] on behalf of Jamie Dimon. Since then, Dimon has consistently cited technology as a competitive differentiator and was one of the key advocates for digital change in the 2010s.

At JPMorgan Chase's Investor Day in 2014, Dimon went on to note: "When I go to Silicon Valley... they all want to eat our lunch. Every single one of them is going to try."[68]

And in his 2015 annual shareholder newsletter, Dimon made a clear mark in the ground that banking was going head-to-head with Silicon Valley. In that newsletter, he talked about "hundreds of startups with a lot of brains and money working on various alternatives to traditional banking" and that "the ones you read about most are in the lending business, whereby the firms can lend to individuals and small businesses very quickly and—these entities believe—effectively by using Big Data to enhance credit underwriting." These are the ones of concern because "they are very good at reducing the 'pain points' in that they can make loans in minutes, which might take banks weeks."[69]

Since then, the bank has hired a lot of developers from Silicon Valley's leading firms, as well as invested billions in innovation. Its 2018

---

67 Dawn Kawamoto, "JPMorgan Chase cancels IBM outsourcing contract," CNET, 15 September 2004, https://www.cnet.com/news/jpmorgan-chase-cancels-ibm-outsourcing-contract/.
68 Mark DeCambre, "JPMorgan is poaching talent from Silicon Valley," Quartz, 8 May 2014, https://qz.com/207163/jpmorgan-is-poaching-talent-from-silicon-valley/.
69 Seth Fiegerman, "The CEO of America's biggest bank is worried about Silicon Valley and Bitcoin stealing his business," Mashable, 10 April 2015, https://mashable.com/2015/04/10/jp-morgan-ceo-letter/.

technology budget amounted to a staggering $11 billion, of which almost a third was directed towards innovation and new projects.[70] As a direct result, I would get news almost every day of how JPMC was reducing time and cost through AI, how it had invested its own digital currency for internal clearing and settlement, how it was using blockchain technologies to create faster global processing, how it was applying cloud and moving to agile services, and so on. Therefore, it would be ridiculous to ignore what this bank is doing, and it made it a mandatory inclusion in *Doing Digital*.

Figure 7.5 Standing outside JPMorgan Chase in New York

Here are a few highlights from its annual reports to give further background:

2013

Gordon Smith, CEO Consumer & Community Banking:

"Technology is changing our business rapidly, and consumer adoption of digital and mobile channels is staggering. In just the past three years, customer deposits made through self-service channels increased from 38% to 53%. The number of active mobile customers has more than tripled from 2010."

Matt Zames, Chief Operating Officer:

"Technology fuels almost every aspect of this company and is a core part of our value proposition to clients and customers. Over the past five years, the firm has invested 8%–9% of its annual revenue to fund our global technology capabilities. This is one of our largest investments as a company. Technology enables our business growth, supports our worldwide operations, helps us build stronger controls and meet regulatory requirements, enhances our productivity and efficiency, and, most important, protects the safety of our clients' assets."

---

70 "This $11 Billion Tech Investment Could Disrupt Banking," JPMorgan Chase press release, September 2018, https://www.jpmorganchase.com/corporate/news/stories/tech-investment-could-disrupt-banking.htm.

"We've nearly doubled our investment in cybersecurity, including deployment of increased monitoring and protection technology, and we've expanded the number of dedicated cybersecurity professionals in the company to focus on protecting our customers and our staff."

"As we look to 2014, our reliance on technology will continue to expand. IT will be at the core of what we need to do to adapt to the new global financial architecture and to meet regulatory requirements."

2014

For the sixth consecutive year, JPMC has invested 8%–9% of the firm's annual revenue in global technology capabilities and digital innovation.

Gordon Smith, CEO Consumer & Community Banking:

"Digital is transforming our industry. We've seen tremendous growth rates in customer adoption of our digital services. The number of customers who are active on Chase mobile went from 8.2 million in 2011 to 19.1 million in 2014. On average, we added about 18,000 new mobile users per day throughout 2014. Quite simply, we plan to be the bank of choice for digitally savvy customers. Digital is core to our commitment to an outstanding customer experience. We're bringing digital service to everything from routine deposits to credit card applications, rewards redemptions and mortgage application tracking … here are some of the indicators of the rapid growth in digital in just one year:

- 19 million mobile app users, up 20%

- 45 million Mobile QuickDepositSM transactions, up 25%

- 30 million Mobile Chase QuickPaySM transactions, up 80%

- 60 million in Mobile Bill Pay, up 30%

- 200 million deposits made in a Chase ATM, up 10%."

Matt Zames, Chief Operating Officer:

"We will continue to innovate in 2015 by improving branch automation and efficiency, extending our electronic trading platforms, launching an advisor workstation platform for Asset Management and implementing a new commercial real estate loan originations system."

2015

Gordon Smith, CEO Consumer & Community Banking:

"Digital is a core part of our customer experience. We know digitally centric customers are happier with Chase and stay with us longer. Since 2012, nearly 100 million transactions that used to be done in branches are increasingly migrating to faster and easier digital channels. Of the 3.7 million new checking accounts we acquired in 2015, almost 60% of these were for millennial customers, who often choose Chase because of our digital capabilities. While millennials clearly are a digital-first generation, research shows that approximately 60% of all consumers rate mobile banking as an important or extremely important factor when switching banks. In fact, for new customers of Consumer Banking, 65% actively use mobile banking after six months, up from 53% in 2014."

Matt Zames, Chief Operating Officer:

"We spent more than $9 billion last year on technology. Importantly, 30% of this total amount was spent on new investments for the future. Today, we have more than 40,000 technologists, from programmers and analysts to systems engineers and application designers. In addition, our resources include 31 data centers, 67,000 physical servers globally, 27,920 databases and a global network that operates smoothly for all our clients.

"One of our growing teams is our digital group, including more than 400 professionals focused on product and platform design and innovation. In addition, the digital technology organization has over 1,200 technologists that deliver digital solutions, including frameworks, development and architecture.

"We are intently focused on delivering differentiated digital experiences across our consumer businesses. For example, we added new functionality to our mobile app with account preview and check viewing, and we redesigned chase.com with simpler navigation and more personalized experiences, making it easier for our customers to bank and interact with us when and how they want – via smartphones, laptops and other mobile devices. We now have nearly 23 million active Chase Mobile customers, a 20% increase over the prior year.

"It is unquestionable that FinTech will force financial institutions to move more quickly, and banks, regulators and government policy will need to keep pace. Services will be rolled out faster, and more of them will be executed on a mobile device. FinTech has been great at making it easier and often less expensive for customers and will likely lead to many more people, including more lower-income people, joining the banking system in the United States and abroad.

"Technology is the lifeblood of our organization, and it drives the delivery of the secure products, platforms and services our customers and clients value and trust. We serve nearly 40 million digital customers and process $1 trillion in merchant transactions annually. Each day, we process $5 trillion of payments, as well as trade and settle $1.5 trillion of securities. We see technology as an essential core competency and a key differentiator to drive future growth in all of our businesses."

2016

Jamie Dimon, Chairman and Chief Executive Officer:

"One of the reasons we're performing well as a company is we never stopped investing in technology—this should never change. In 2016, we spent more than $9.5 billion in technology firmwide, of which approximately $3 billion is dedicated toward new initiatives. Of that amount, approximately $600 million is spent on emerging fintech solutions—which include building and improving digital and mobile services and partnering with fintech companies. The reasons we invest so much in technology (whether it's digital, Big Data or machine learning) are simple: to benefit customers with better, faster and often cheaper products and services, to reduce errors and to make the firm more efficient."

Gordon Smith, CEO Consumer & Community Banking:

"We think we can confidently say that Chase is the digital leader in the industry. We have the #1 rated mobile banking app, #1 ATM network and #1 most visited banking portal in the U.S. This is important because, increasingly, digital is a critical driver in why customers choose to do business with Chase. Banking no longer is a sometimes activity—customers engage with us every day. More than 26 million customers are active on our mobile app today. Digital also drives tremendous loyalty. Households that use our digital channels have credit and debit spend levels over 90% higher than those that don't. Customers who are digitally engaged have higher satisfaction and retention rates, spend more and have far lower transaction costs. Advancing our digital and technology capabilities is job #1, but we are also paying close attention to the emerging technologies in our industry. Many new fintech companies are mastering ways to simplify the customer experience. Those we meet with have huge respect for the Chase brand, and they envy our scale and distribution. In cases where we think their solutions will improve the customer experience quickly, we partner with them."

2017

Jamie Dimon, Chairman and Chief Executive Officer:

"We have thousands of employees who are data scientists or have advanced degrees in science, technology, engineering and math. Of the nearly 50,000 people in technology at the company, more than 31,000 are in development and engineering jobs, and more than 2,500 are in digital technology. Think of these talented individuals as driving change across the company.

"Artificial intelligence, Big Data and machine learning are helping us reduce risk and fraud, upgrade service, improve underwriting and enhance marketing across the firm. And this is just the beginning.

"Our shared technology infrastructure—our networks, data centers, and the public and private cloud—decreases costs, enhances efficiency and makes all our businesses more productive. In addition, this allows us to embrace the fact that every business and merchant has its own software and also wants easy, integrated access to our products and services. We are delivering on that through the creation of a common JPMorgan Chase API (application programming interface) store that allows customers to add simple, secure payments to their software. And we are building everything digital—both for individual customers and large corporations—from onboarding to idea generation."

Gordon Smith, CEO Consumer & Community Banking:

"Our active digital customers grew to 47 million, and 30 million of them are active on mobile, the largest in our industry."

Douglas Petno, CEO Commercial Banking:

"In 2017, we partnered with Consumer & Community Banking to launch a new digital platform, Chase Connect, that is tailored to meet the needs of small and midsized companies. This platform provides our clients with a simple and convenient experience, integrating account information, payables and receivables. Chase Connect allows clients to see all of their accounts in one place, stay organized when paying bills, view payment history, approve transactions quickly and easily from one location, and receive customized account alerts. We are focused on having the best integrated, digital capabilities for clients and will continue to invest in enhancing the functionality of this robust platform."

2018

Jamie Dimon, Chairman and Chief Executive Officer:

"We have acknowledged that companies like Square and PayPal have done things that we could have done but did not. They looked at clients' problems, improved straight through processing, added data and analytics to products, and moved quickly. We recently sent one of our senior teams to China to study what's being achieved there with artificial intelligence (AI) and fintech, and it's hard not to be both impressed and a little worried about the progress China has made—it made our management team even more motivated to move quickly. Suffice it to say, no matter what our current performance is, we cannot rest on our laurels."

"We were a little slow in adopting the cloud, for which I am partially responsible. My early thinking about the cloud was that it was just another term for outsourcing. I held firm to the view, which is somewhat still true, that we can run our own data centers, networks and applications as efficiently as anyone. But here's the critical point: Cloud capabilities are far more extensive, and we are now full speed ahead. Let me cite a couple of examples:

- The cloud gives us the ability to achieve rapid scale and elasticity of computing power exponentially beyond our own capacity. This will be especially relevant as we scale up our artificial intelligence efforts.

- The cloud platform is agile and flexible. It offers access to data sets, advanced analytics and machine learning capabilities beyond our own. It increases developers' effectiveness by multiples—you can almost "click and drop" new elements into existing programs as opposed to writing extensive new code. For instance, adding databases and/or machine learning to an application can be done almost instantaneously. And certain tasks, such as testing code and provisioning compute power, are automated.

- The cloud provides a software development experience that is frictionless and allows our engineers to prototype quickly and learn fast, as well as increase the speed of delivering new capabilities to our customers and clients.

"It is important to note that the cloud has matured to the point where it can meet the high expectations that are set by large enterprises that have fairly intense demands around security, audit procedures, access to systems, cyber security and business resiliency. We will be rapidly 'refactoring' most of our applications to take full advantage of Cloud Computing. We then can decide whether it is more advantageous to run our applications on the external cloud or the internal cloud (the internal cloud will have many of the benefits of the external cloud's scalable and efficient platforms).

"One final but key issue: Agile platforms and cloud capabilities not only allow you to do things much faster but also enable you to organize teams differently. You can create smaller teams of five to 20 people who can be continually reimagining, reinventing and rolling out new products and services in a few days instead of months."

"The power of artificial intelligence and machine learning is real. These technologies already are helping us reduce risk and fraud, upgrade customer service, improve underwriting and enhance marketing across the firm. And this is just the beginning. As our management teams get better at understanding the power of AI and machine learning, these tools are rapidly being deployed across virtually everything we do. We can also use artificial intelligence to try to achieve certain desired outcomes, such as making mortgages even more available to minorities. A few examples will suffice:

- In the Corporate & Investment Bank, DeepX leverages machine learning to assist our equities algorithms globally to execute transactions across 1,300 stocks a day, and this total is rising as we roll out DeepX to new countries.

- Across our company, we will be deploying virtual assistants (robots driven by artificial intelligence) to handle tasks such as maintaining internal help desks, tracking down errors and routing inquiries.

- In Consumer Marketing, we are better able to customize insights and offerings for individual customers, based on, for example, their ability to save or invest, their travel preferences or the availability of discounts on brands they like.

- Technological solutions help us do better underwriting, expediting the mortgage or automobile loan approval process, letting the customer accept the loan in a couple of clicks and then start shopping for a home or car.

- In our Consumer Operations, we are using AI and machine learning techniques for ATM cash management to optimize cash in devices, reduce the cost of reloads and schedule ATM maintenance.

- And our initial results from machine learning fraud applications are expected to drive approximately $150 million of annual benefits and countless efficiencies. For example, machine learning is helping to deliver a better customer experience while also prioritizing safety at the point of sale, where fraud losses have been reduced significantly, with automated decisions on transactions made in milliseconds. We are now able to approve 1 million additional good customers (who would have been declined for potential fraud) and also decline approximately 1 million additional fraudsters (who would have been approved). Machine learning will also curtail check fraud losses by analyzing signatures, payee names and check features in real time.

- Over time, AI will also dramatically improve Anti-Money Laundering/ Bank Secrecy Act protocols and processes as well as other complex compliance requirements."

"We will try to retrain and redeploy our workforce as AI reduces certain types of jobs. We are evaluating all of our jobs to determine which are most susceptible to being lost through AI. We will plan ahead so we can retrain or deploy our employees both for other roles inside the company and, if necessary, outside the company. The combined power of virtually unlimited computing strength, AI applied to almost anything and the ability to use vast sets of data and rapidly change applications is extraordinary—we have only begun to take advantage of the opportunities for the company and for our customers."

"The onboarding experience for new customers is being simplified. Customers can open a new deposit account digitally in three to five minutes, functionality that added approximately 1.5 million new accounts since its February 2018 launch; we're expanding this functionality inside our branches as well. We also recently announced Chase MyHome, our new digitally enabled mortgage fulfillment process that prefills applications for our existing customers. It's 20% faster than our paper-based process, allowing us to close a mortgage within three weeks. Our confidence in our enhanced approach is reflected in our money-back guarantee."

Gordon Smith, CEO Consumer & Community Banking:

"We are always focused on improving the customer experience. Across all of our products, we have made it quicker and easier to become a Chase customer. Increasingly, that experience is digital, online or mobile. More than 1 million customers opened a checking or savings account digitally in 2018. For existing customers who were adding an account, it took less than three minutes. We have plans to reduce that time even further."